LUNCH

The Meals Series
as part of the Rowman & Littlefield Studies in
Food and Gastronomy

General Editor: Ken Albala, Professor of History, University of the Pacific (kalbala@pacific.edu)
Rowman & Littlefield Executive Editor: Suzanne Staszak-Silva (sstaszak-silva @rowman.com)

The Meals series examines our daily meals—breakfast, lunch, dinner, tea—as well as special meals such as the picnic and barbeque, both as historical construct and global phenomena. We take these meals for granted, but the series volumes provide surprising information that will change the way you think about eating. A single meal in each volume is anatomized, its social and cultural meaning brought into sharp focus, and the customs and manners of various peoples are explained in context. Each volume also looks closely at the foods we commonly include and why.

Breakfast: A History, by Heather Arndt Anderson (2013)

The Picnic: A History, by Walter Levy (2013)

Lunch: A History, by Megan Elias (2014)

LUNCH

A HISTORY

Megan Elias

ROWMAN & LITTLEFIELD
Lanham • Boulder • New York • Toronto • Plymouth, UK

Published by Rowman & Littlefield
4501 Forbes Boulevard, Suite 200, Lanham, Maryland 20706
www.rowman.com

10 Thornbury Road, Plymouth PL6 7PP, United Kingdom

British Library Cataloguing in Publication Information Available

Library of Congress Cataloging-in-Publication Data
Elias, Megan J.
  Lunch : a history / Megan Elias.
      pages cm. — (The meals series) (Rowman & Littlefield studies in food and gastronomy)
  Includes bibliographical references and index.
  ISBN 978-1-4422-2746-0 (cloth : alk. paper) — ISBN 978-1-4422-2747-7 (electronic)
1. Luncheons—History. 2. Food habits—History. I. Title.
  GT2960.E45 2014
  394.1'209—dc23

                                                                                      2013037133

∞™ The paper used in this publication meets the minimum requirements of American National Standard for Information Sciences—Permanence of Paper for Printed Library Materials, ANSI/NISO Z39.48-1992.

Printed in the United States of America

CONTENTS

SERIES
FOREWORD

Custom becomes second nature, and this especially true of meals. We expect to eat them at a certain time and place, and we have a set of scripted foods considered appropriate for each. Bacon, eggs, and toast are breakfast; sandwiches are lunch; meat, potatoes, and vegetables are dinner, followed by dessert. Breakfast for dinner is so much fun precisely because it is out of the ordinary and transgressive. But meal patterns were not always this way. In the Middle Ages people ate two meals, the larger in the morning. Today the idea of a heavy meal with meat and wine at 11:00 a.m. strikes us as strange and decidedly unpleasant. Likewise when abroad, the food that people eat, at what seems to us the wrong time of day, can be shocking. Again, our customs have become so ingrained that we assume they are natural, correct, and biologically sound.

The Meals series will demonstrate exactly the opposite. Not only have meal times changed but the menu as well, both through history and around the globe. Only a simple bowl of soup with a crust of bread for supper? That's where the name comes from. Our dinner, coming from *disner* in Old French, *disjejeunare* in Latin, actually means to break fast and was eaten in the morning. Each meal also has its own unique characteristics that evolve over time. We will see the invention of the picnic and barbecue, the gradual adoption of lunch as a new midday meal, and even certain meals practiced as hallowed institutions in some places but scarcely at all elsewhere, such as tea—the meal, not the drink. Often food items suddenly appear in a meal as quintessential, such as cold breakfast cereal, the invention of men like Kellogg and Post. Or they disappear, like oysters for breakfast. Sometimes an entire meal springs from nowhere under unique social conditions, like brunch.

Of course, the decay of the family meal is a topic that deeply concerns us, as people catch a quick bite at their desk or on the go, or eat with their eyes glued to the television set. If eating is one of the greatest pleasures in life, one has to wonder what it says about us when we wolf down a meal in a few minutes flat or when no one talks at the dinner table. Still, meal time traditions persist for special occasions. They are the time we remind ourselves of who we are and where we come from, when grandma's special lasagna comes to the table for a Sunday dinner, or a Passover Seder is set exactly the same way it has been for thousands of years. We treasure these food rituals precisely because they keep us rooted in a rapidly changing world.

The Meals series examines the meal as both a historical construct and a global phenomenon. Each volume anatomizes a single meal, bringing its social and cultural meaning into sharp focus and explaining the customs and manners of various people in context. Each volume also looks closely at the foods we commonly include and why. In the end I hope you will never take your meal time customs for granted again.

Ken Albala
University of the Pacific

ACKNOWLEDGMENTS

I have wanted to write this book for several years, so thanks are first due to Ken Albala for creating the Meals series at Rowman & Littlefield and allowing me to take lunch. Ken is an ideal editor, both supportive and informative. I also thank Suzanne Staszak-Silva and Kathryn Knigge for shepherding the book through production. Farha Ternikar (Brunch) and Heather Arndt Anderson (Breakfast) deserve recognition for sharing ideas with me along the way. The Wertheim Study, at the New York Public Library, brilliantly curated by Jay Barksdale, gave me a beautiful and quiet place to work on this book and I will always be grateful. Warmest thanks are due to my family, Preston Johnson and Petra Diana Johnson, who gave me time to write and shared many meals, midday and otherwise with me.

INTRODUCTION

A traditional Mongolian proverb advises: "Keep breakfast for yourself, share lunch with your friend and give dinner to your enemy." The meal most often eaten in public, lunch has a long history of establishing social status and cementing alliances. From the Ploughman's Lunch in the field to the Power Lunch at the Four Seasons, where, with whom, and upon what we lunch marks our place in the world.

Lunch has never been *just* a meal. The American School Lunch Act of 1946, inspired by the malnutrition discovered by wartime recruiters, demonstrated that lunch could represent the very health of the nation. In the 1960s, the right to eat at one of America's ubiquitous lunch counters came to represent America's moral health. Issues of who cooks lunch, and who eats what and how and even when (before exercise or after?) in public institutions continues to galvanize activists. Extremes of approach range from prepackaged "lunchables" to Alice Waters's edible schoolyards, agriculture and lunchroom linked ideologically as well as materially.

In 1987, the death knell seemed to sound for lunch when *Wall Street*'s Gordon Gekko proclaimed that "Lunch is for wimps" and millions of office workers began to eat over their keyboards. But lunch persists and has even inspired a revivalist movement in "Take Back Your Lunch," a nationwide encouragement to take the time allotted and actually leave our desks.

Lunch emerged first as a necessary pause in the hard labor of agricultural peasants and then as a facet of a new middle-class culture in Europe at the end of the eighteenth century. The word itself derived in the modern era from an old term for a slice of something, which makes the contemporary American expression "let's go for a slice," meaning pizza, a historically accurate invitation to lunch.

For most of human history a matter of necessity for the laborer, it became a fashionable experience by the late nineteenth century and eventually a multi-billion-dollar industry for competitive fast food chains. Known also as dinner, the meal, unlike any other, has its own purpose-built accoutrements as well as international aid organizations dedicated to its provision.

The concept of lunch as a meal between two others is a feature of modern Western culture. Lunch as we know it today exists in relation to these two other meals, but it was not always so. For most of human history, most people only had food and fuel resources for one meal each day. Because it took time to prepare—gathering firewood, allowing bread to rise or steaming rice—the meal could not be eaten right after waking up, but because most people lived physically demanding lives, they could not wait until evening to eat. So eating meant lunching if we take lunch to be the meal eaten in the middle of the day. Those with access to more resources—the rich of any time and place—could afford to have workers up early preparing morning meals and could eat again in company later in the day. When those workers got their own daily meal was purely a matter of luck. Eventually, among English aristocrats, however, this first meal of the day, known as dinner, became so elaborate and took so long to make that some began to eat small meals just after waking up to tide them over for the main event, creating breakfast as they waited for lunch. As a mercantile middle class emerged in Europe, they adopted the three-meal habit, starting the day with breakfast, pausing for lunch, and taking a meal called supper—originally just a bowl of light soup or broth—in the evening. Some also enjoyed such novelties as the French *déjeuner à la fourchette*—breakfast with a fork—and elevenses—the distinctly English post-breakfast-pre-lunch little something. Soon the not-very-strenuous days of elite ladies and gentlemen were crowded with snacks. Those who had least need of midday sustenance got the most of it.

The Industrial Revolution brought important changes to lunch that made it the meal we know today. Once sociable lunch partners, mid-nineteenth-century workers and employers ceased to take their midday breaks together. While the hungry clerk stepped out for a ten-minute sixpence dinner, his employer lounged amid cigars in a private club and the factory worker found noontime nutrition in the nearest saloon.

Lunch changed for those who did not work for wages, too. Away from home attending the nation's first public schools, children began to carry their lunches in a wide variety of receptacles, from old cigar tins to large napkins. And in the late nineteenth century, as the first department stores emerged in American cities, middle-class women found their own kind of lunch club in on-site tea rooms. There they could pause to refresh themselves before continuing the important work of shopping.

Worldwide, lunch has taken particular shapes in different places in the modern urbanizing world. The bento boxes of Japan are full of neatly rolled and often fancifully assembled rice-based treats. In Korea, the contents of bento-type boxes are left intentionally wild so that they can be shaken into a delicious mélange. The amazing tiffin carriers of India are charged with not only not shaking the hundreds of boxes they carry from homes to offices but also with getting each meal to its designated eater, a feat of fantastic organization and transportation. In the West, urban office workers must be their own tiffin dhabas, racing out to grab preboxed sandwiches, or, if employed in office parks, driving through fast food restaurants, shouting their orders into static-prone intercoms.

The custom of eating lunch at home has largely disappeared from the industrialized world. Where it lingers, especially around the Mediterranean and in South America, it is often accompanied by that beloved but endangered phenomenon, the siesta. Most of us now work too far from home and are too busy looking busy to indulge in such delights. Middle-class women of the Western world experienced a golden age of lunch at home from the late nineteenth century through the 1950s. Not expected to work outside the home, and often able to afford household help, ladies were able to entertain each other with whimsical lunch fare such as sandwiches dressed up like cakes, and salad arrangements that looked like flower gardens in bloom. This was also the era during which middle-class women took up their important work as the family's shoppers. While groceries and other humdrum goods were often left to the servants to purchase, department stores offered gorgeous arrays of fashionable clothes and housewares to tempt women from their homes into urban centers. There, they inevitably grew hungry and found they could restore themselves with light sandwiches, pastries, and ice cream dishes without even leaving the building. Marshall Fields's Walnut Room was the archetype of the ladies' lunchroom, a gorgeous space that served elegant treats, making the shopper feel that she was really a guest in a palace, not a pawn of industrial capitalism.

Chapters 3 and 4 divide the act of lunch into a private performance at home and a public pursuit in restaurants, on street corners, and (too often!) at the desk. Chapter 3, "Lunch at Home," looks closely at the phenomenon of the heaving boards provided for agricultural workers in nineteenth-century American farmhouses and contrasts this with the intimate social luncheons in the private home that were a feature of turn-of-the-century women's sociability, completes a unique cuisine. In this chapter lunches for one are compared to meals prepared for guests, making the argument that while lunch can be seen as a preeminently social meal, it can also be a remarkably private pause amid the swirl of family life and group activities.

The elegant lunching ladies of Western department stores were surrounded in their public consumption of midday meals by construction workers perching on I-beams, factory workers lunching on curbs, and clerks bolting down meals at crowded lunch counters. Cities had always provided hot and cold snacking options, but the late nineteenth century saw the rise of the lunch hour, when streets filled with crowds in search of something to eat before work. Private men's clubs and expensive restaurants catered to those who could spend more time and money on the meal, but for most, it remained something of a mad dash.

Perhaps because it brings so many of us out into the open to perform a domestic, even intimate act, artists have been interested in lunch for several hundred years, taking it as their theme in some of the world's most famous works. It has appealed less to writers and filmmakers, lacking the opportunities for display and drama that dinner offers as a meal. From Pieter Brueghel's seasonal lunch painting, *The Harvesters*, to Philip Guston's globular sandwiches, lunch has figured in at least four hundred years of artwork. Sometimes lunch represents a rural idyll as with Winslow Homer's *The Dinner Horn*. In other cases, as when Charlie Chaplin's Little Tramp works through his break to disastrous results, the standardized lunch break is a symptom of complex modernity.

THE HISTORY
OF LUNCH

Did cavemen lunch? Probably not. The notion of the midday meal pre-supposes a particular pattern to life: work-refresh-work. This pattern probably did not emerge until the process that we call civilization, the settling down to a daily routine made possible only by the storing of grain and the domestication of animals. In order to have lunch, you have to know where it is. In the hunter-gatherer communities that were the norm for the great majority of human history, food supply was not so reliable that it would have been wise to abstain until some preordained hour of the day. The bird in the hand went straight into the mouth.

Mealtimes have always been determined both by what was available to cook and by what was available as fuel. A fire kept warm overnight could be rekindled in the morning with material gathered earlier, and the day's cooking could begin. Because the amount of work required to prepare food—even a simple pottage—could be quite time-consuming, mealtimes depended on cooking times, rather than the opposite formulation that is more common to modern cooks.

The archeological record suggests that for Neolithic cooks, limited in tools and materials as well as slowed down by fuels that were not perpetually available, as gas and electricity are, mealtimes were any time after the food had cooked. Thus, the first meal of the day might come nearer to noon than sunrise and it might, given the advantages to conserving fuel and the shortages prevalent in most societies, be the only one of the day. In ancient Palestine, for instance, families had to grind their grain for several hours in the morning before they could make bread. In other words, for most of human history, all cooked meals were lunch—the meal that comes between waking and sleeping. All else was snacking.[1]

With the domestication of both plants and animals for food came also the specialized work patterns of planting and harvest, fattening and butchery, and the arts of preservation—pickling, cheesemaking, smoking and curing, brewing and winemaking—that make this work worth doing. The season of harvest typically invited communal labor, more hands making the heavy work lighter. This resulted in more communally shared meals during this time than at others. In the cold winter months, families might huddle together around a fire to eat, hoarding the precious resource of fuel. During harvest time they ate outside with their friends and neighbors, sharing food so as to bolster the crew for more work. This lunch is the subject of Pieter Breughel's painting *The Harvesters*, discussed in chapter 5.

Communal and informal, harvest season lunches could serve as times for conducting some of a community's most important business—courtship. Agricultural societies typically employ all hands to bring in harvests, so gender segregation of labor often breaks down for a short time, bringing young people into contact in ways that could reveal important aspects of their potential for partnership—romantic and domestic.

The meal prepared for harvesters would have had a few practical requirements—that it be portable, restorative, and easy to eat seated in a field. As anyone who has gone on a picnic knows, bread and cheese work well in this situation. In Mesopotamia, wheat crops would have dictated that the lunch take the form of wheat-flour flatbreads because flatbreads take less time to cook than do risen ones and are also lighter to carry. The same grain mush that might have served as a cold leftover breakfast could be slapped together into small, flattened cakes that would be quickly baked to become lunch.[2]

A tradition of goat and sheep herding suggests a fresh goat- or sheep-milk cheese, something like feta, easy to carry to the fields and refreshing in the midday heat. The third essential element of the lunch would have been beer, brewed at home and carried in jugs. Mesopotamians took beer so seriously that they attributed its invention to a goddess, Ninkasi. Awkward to transport, beer was nonetheless crucial if lunch was to have a restorative effect. Beer refreshed, and nourished, important functions for agricultural laborers' physical needs.

In many ways, this Mesopotamian lunch was the ancient forerunner of the famous English "ploughman's lunch" which over the centuries acquired a bit of pickle on the side, and, with the popularization of tea in England in the nineteenth century, a thermos of tea as an alternative to a pint (or more) of ale. In societies where both bread and cheese are made, they seem to have joined forces early as lunch fare. The ancient Celts, for example, baked wheat flour breads on the sides of ovens like modern-day tandoors and also enjoyed "wild fruit, fresh game, and curdled milk," more politely known as cheese, for lunch. Like the Mesopotamians, Celts also drank a fermented grain drink that no doubt refreshed and gladdened them for afternoon work.[3]

LUNCH IN THE EARLY CITY

As small agricultural settlements grew and cities developed, urban life gave an interesting new shape to mealtimes. Members of agricultural communities worked, ate, and worked again, feeding themselves during pauses in labor. In larger towns, however, street vendors called constantly to passersby, rousing their appetites regardless of any calories already burned or meals already taken. In second-century AD Egyptian villages, for example, "Porridge sellers . . . took their place alongside other vendors of fast-food . . . chickpeas and other cooked dishes sold on the street." Workers in local temples, meanwhile, received at least four loaves of bread per day made from the same mixture as the porridge. For these Egyptians, then, the notion of a midday break had no meaning, their days punctuated with four loaves or—if they had taken on extra responsibilities—as many as six. Unlike the contemporary Western worker, whose day is divided into three parts—after breakfast, after lunch, and after dinner—these ancient Egyptian workers experienced time loaf-to-loaf.[4]

Street food catered to the demands of urban life as the business of the day took men and women out of their homes to multiple locations such as temples, markets, and public meeting places. Cooked food could also nourish the poor who lacked their own fuel, materials, and fireplaces. In ancient Rome, for example, where poor people lived in small, kitchenless apartments stacked high above commercial spaces, meals taken at home were necessarily cold—primarily stale bread. Street vendors selling hot foods catered to the desire for something more, and "the urban poor of ancient Rome seem to have been as dependent on convenience foods as many modern city dwellers," quickly handing over what little money they had for meals bought "from stand-up snack bars and street stalls."[5]

MIDDAY MEALS IN THE MEDIEVAL WORLD

With the decline of Rome in Europe and the rise of Christianity as a dominant element in local cultures came new foodways. It also becomes much easier to locate lunch in the medieval world, because texts on all manner of topics, including food and health, were a central feature of this period in European history. The formation of monastic communities in large numbers also provides us with detailed rules and observations about mealtimes and foodways.

The majority of Europeans, of course, were not living the holy life, subject to quasi-mystical regulations about what to eat when. They toiled as peasants, pausing for communal lunches. Their meal, like their crop, was similar to that of the Mesopotamian grain harvester with a few differences. Where Mesopotamians would have lunched on flatbreads, European peasants and their contemporaries enjoyed leavened bread made with yeast. This preference for risen bread was one inherited from the Romans. Both because it requires less fuel to bake and because it keeps longer, flatbread is more economical, but since Europeans had both a steady supply of fuel and communities that supported professional bakers, it became possible for leavened bread to develop a devoted following even among those who were not wealthy.

Although they grew and harvested the wheat that was used to make the fluffiest of risen loaves, peasants had limited access to this grain for their own breadmaking. The unique height and bubbled crumb of white bread was reserved for the elite because it was labor intensive to process the grains, mill them into fine flour, and pound the dough to the extremes of glutinous stretchability. Laborers consumed something that had risen beyond flatbread but remained dense, more like a big baked porridge than a baguette. Bread was not only physically dense but also rich with the strong flavors of rye and barley flours, and it was somewhat crunchy because it was made with less finely milled flour.

Lunching peasants would also have been able to supplement their bread with cheese. Depending on where a particular peasant lived, his lunch cheese might derive from goat, sheep, or cow milk and might have any one of a wide range of flavors. A tradition of cheesemaking in western Europe provided workers there with harder cheeses, better suited for transport into the field. Beer would have served to wash down the bread and cheese lunch of the European peasant just as it did the Mesopotamians, but cider and wine were both also options, depending on region—cider wherever Celts had settled, in the north of France and northern Spain and southern England, and wine in the southern regions of Europe, including France, Spain, and Italy.

LUNCH AT LEISURE

For peasants, who had few choices, a midday meal was probably the only substantial meal of the day. Physical need and available materials dictated its consumption. For the elite and moderately wealthy, mealtimes were not determined by physical labor's demands. Instead, complex rules based in the latest knowledge of anatomy dictated what was eaten when—not only what and when but also "the order in which one ate what had been prepared, were matters of concern to the physician and to the cook." The capacity to care about such things was a side effect of material wealth.[6]

An English proverb, for example, advised that "Butter is gold in the morning, silver at noon and lead at night," reflecting a theory that metabolism slows down over the course of the day.[7] The elites consulted physicians, and the wealthy aped the customs of the elites, who followed (more or less) contemporary trends in declaring that one should eat only when hungry. Physicians reasoned that one was only truly hungry once whatever had been eaten for the most recent meal was entirely digested. Thus, eating "before a previous meal had made its way completely out of the stomach was declared to be a most dangerous practice." Yet this had to be balanced with the realities of social life in which people ate together, not each person at her own whim.[8]

Applying these rules to normal human patterns of digestion, a historian of this era deduces that if the elite followed these directives, they ate only two full meals each day: "Given that the average 'modern' digestive system seems comfortably able to handle only two *substantial* meals in a day, and given that the professional cook was required to lay on nothing less *than* substantial meals, the two-meal pattern remained the norm for most of medieval Europe." These two meals were "dinner," and "supper," the equivalent in modern America of lunch and dinner.[9]

The midday meal, known as dinner in England, was served sometime close to noon because the substantial meals required by European elites took several hours to prepare. Medieval era writer John of Milan proscribed a schedule that placed lunch much earlier in the day—"Rise at 5, dine at 9, sup at 5, retire at 9, for a long life"—but still allowed four hours between waking and eating, enough time for servants to prepare a large amount of food.[10]

The wealthy classes grew both wealthier and more numerous during the medieval period, creating an expanded market for luxury goods and services. Professional cooks were one group who developed their skills to impress this audience. Demanding ever-greater levels of style as well as substance in their meals, western European elites were forced to wait longer for lunch as the kitchen worked to provide acceptable bounty. As dinner was pushed later, supper had to drift past dusk in order to accommodate physiology. Eventually, by the end of the era, "hunger became unwilling to wait until noon or 1:00 pm to be satisfied." Tormented by "the delicious odours that began wafting from the kitchen at the earliest light of dawn" in preparation for dinner, ravening elites decided that it was "acceptable" if not a matter of true necessity "to *break* one's overnight *fast* with a small bite at some time before dinner." Thus did midday feast beget morning breakfast.[11]

In the Netherlands, the expanding wealth of the region brought about not only breakfast but another meal, something like the teatime that the British would later adopt. For prosperous households, lunch remained the heaviest meal of the day, framed by smaller meals of bread and cheese. Lunch, taken at noon, was "a stew of meat and vegetables, or of fish, with fruit, cooked vegetables, honey cake, or raised pie," a tall, fruit-stuffed confection. One usually ate just the cooked fruit, scooped out, the hard crust serving more as a baking dish than as food. A few hours later, bread and cheese were served again and whatever scraps were left over from lunch returned just before bedtime for an evening snack.[12]

One example of the new fashion for large lunches can be found in the accounts of Count Joachim of Oettingen (d. 1520), who required eight courses for lunch and only six for dinner. Oettingen extended the bounty of his own table to that of his workers, supplying four courses for dinner and three for supper. The work of the laborer had half the value, in food, as the leisure of the lord, an interesting mathematics of the mealtime.[13]

A lunch served in 1486 at the home of the burgher Villach in Austria comprised ten courses, among which were "First course: 3 artificial fish moulded of milk, eggs and almonds, and sprinked [*sic*] in the pan with peeled almonds, raisins and sugared aniseed. Second course: a dish of fowl pate, ground and strained, mixed with cinnamon and ginger. Third course: fattened thrushes and a dish of chicken and other meat." The supper that followed several hours later was only slightly more modest.[14]

While the master used dinners to impress his peers, and supper was merely a matter of not going to bed hungry, variation in the pattern was possible. When vigorous activities were proposed for after lunch, the meal could become lighter, transferring all its postponed glory to the supper table. As fifteenth-century cookbook writer Chiquart advised, "If jousts or tournaments or other recreational activities should be held on that day . . . the cooks would be well advised to prepare all the lighter a dinner [lunch] and to make the supper that much more worthy and generous." As yesterday's jousts become today's sales reports and conference calls, many find that this kind of balance remains common sense.[15]

The practice of using food to impress one's social cohort was certainly not limited to Europe at this time. In fourteenth-century China, elites participated in an elaborate theater of banqueting at which "verses were sung, flowers were scattered, dancers performed, food was served and the guests kowtowed each of the nine times the emperor proffered wine to them." Formal banqueting began at midday both to allow enough time in the morning for food to be prepared and to leave time after the banquet for official business later in the day. Thus while contemporary readers may think of a banquet as an evening meal, the many banquets that punctuate historical texts from China were actually protracted lunches.[16] Just how protracted one can begin to imagine by reflecting that a typical banquet could include over two hundred dishes, from a wide variety of rice preparations to sweet dishes made from fruits. Soup, pies, dumplings, and noodles were all featured at banquets. In the streets, meanwhile, those not socially important enough to attend banquets could buy a wide range of single items, such as sweetened congee, blood soup, and *shao-ping* and *man-t'ou*, just two among the many kinds of buns available.[17]

A pattern of mealtimes based in social class was also found in Japan during the medieval period, and a similar transformation from two to three meals also oc-curred. In the tenth century, the expected meals for the elite class were a breakfast eaten around ten in the morning and a dinner taken in the early evening, around five o'clock. For ordinary people, however, different rules applied. Those who per-formed especially hard work had one meal in the morning and one in the evening but also supplemented those two meals with two more snack breaks during the day.

In the late tenth century, a Japanese noblewoman who happened to observe a group of carpenters having lunch found, "The way in which carpenters eat is really odd." Not only were they eating in the middle of the day—which her class would never have done—but they also first drank their soup, then ate their veg-etables, then finished with rice, rather than alternating among the three dishes as was the elite custom. She was also amazed at the speed with which they dis-patched their meal in contrast to her own class cohort's custom of lingering, an indulgence that the carpenters probably could not afford.[18]

By the thirteenth century, the practice of eating a midday meal that had shocked the young noblewoman had become common in Japanese court circles, where the emperor himself ate three meals. This practice may have spread from Zen monasteries, where there was a tradition of "eating snacks (called *tenshin*) or tea cakes between the two main meals." As other Buddhist monasteries adopted this wise practice, the "snack had been elevated to the position of a substantial noontime meal," and by the end of the seventeenth century "virtu-ally the entire country was eating three meals."[19]

According to Buddhist tradition, Buddha himself decreed midday the ideal time to eat. Believing that all people constantly think about ambition, sex, and food, and given that simply telling them not do so would not be effective, Buddha devised a way to deal with the distraction of food, which he considered "the worst slavery of all." Rather than letting thoughts of food intensify through the day, Buddha decreed that the monks' usual evening meal be moved to just before midday. By filling their bellies earlier in the day, the holy men could free their minds from at least one distraction for the rest of their waking hours. We might argue, then, that lunch is the holiest meal because it liberates us from the mundane for contemplation of the divine.[20] By the medieval era, however, the snacking monks had clearly modified their founder's teachings somewhat to include the occasional small cake.

The Japanese Zen monks who introduced both between-meal snacking and lunch to their countrymen had themselves learned the joys of small cakes and buns during periods of religious training in China. Returning home as committed to the custom of *tenshin* as they were to Zen Buddhism, they enjoyed the same kinds of snacks common in Chinese monasteries, which included "wheat buns with fillings of sweet bean paste or salty vegetable paste." Traditional Japanese mochi—filled rice flour cakes—were also incorporated into this small meal, as was tea, "another custom that spread in Japan" from origins in monasteries where monks were influenced by Chinese Zen culture.[21]

A technological innovation made possible the normalization of three meals a day for laypeople in Japan. The use of vegetable oil lamps in homes, which became popular in the sixteenth century, allowed for more evening activities, which in turn called for more sustenance. Technological innovations in manufacturing, though well before the Industrial Revolution, also increased the amount of labor Japanese workers performed, leading to longer hours, which brought people home later and hungrier, in need of an evening meal. In the context of longer hours, lunch also acquired special significance as a moment of pause and refreshment halfway through the day's labor.[22]

CLOISTERED LUNCHES

The new monastic class that developed in Europe during this period, after the fall of Rome, created its own traditions of food, drink, and mealtimes. Setting themselves apart from all that was worldly, monks and nuns still had to consume food regularly lest they arrive in heaven too soon. Monastic lives were strictly ordered to help religious men and women resist sin; as in Buddhism, mealtimes were an important part of this regimentation.

Monks in Constantinople in the 1300s daily consumed their main meal together in their refectory. This experience, representing "the essence of communal life in a monastery," took place midway through the day's activities, conforming to modern definitions of lunch, but its precise timing varied day to day as it fit into a changing schedule of ritual observances. Liturgy was celebrated at different times on different days and lunch was supposed to follow liturgy, so lunchtime wandered from late morning to midday. During Lent, because of special additions to the liturgy during this season, lunch was postponed until the late afternoon.[23]

A set of guidelines for a Constantinople monastery celebrated the refectory as a place of equality in which "only one table, one sort of food, one sort of drink" was available. This uniformity was representative of "the bond of love and unity in Christ." Other procedural manuals, however, indicate that lunch seating, if not also eating, was arranged hierarchically, with the monastery's highest-ranking official taking the most honored spot and himself determining the placement of inferiors.

Refectories were large rooms designed as important features in the monastic complex, "spatially related" to spaces of worship so that at a sign—in some cases the ringing of a dinner bell—hungry monks could walk directly from the church narthex into the dining hall, making a beeline from the divine to the consumable. In these semi-sacred spaces, monks and nuns typically ate bread, "wine, legumes, such as beans, lentils, or chickpeas, served boiled, or a soup and green vegetables, boiled with olive oil, vinegar, or water." On special occasions, when they were feasting, these meals could include "extra dishes of eggs, cheese, fish and shellfish," but other kinds of meat were generally not allowed.[24]

Feast days were often the posthumous treat of a local benefactor who left not only money but also sometimes menu instructions for the lunch that would feed the monks or nuns who prayed for his recently departed soul. Prayers for the dead appear to have taken place before lunch, however, perhaps so that a cook's incompetence or a benefactor's unpopular menu choice would not turn the blessings to curses.[25]

So much attention was given in refectory guidelines to the ideal of equality in consumption that one begins to wonder if favoritism was a serious problem in service. One fourteenth-century guide to nuns warned, "When you are at table, do not look around at the portions your sisters got, nor allow your mind to be divided by nasty suspicions." As lunch was the only substantive meal of the day, and indeed, the only time in which material goods were regularly dispensed, it may well have served as an ideal time for biased superiors to reward some and punish others. In the confines of the godly, the lunch portion could perform the work of silent rebuke or tacit reward.[26]

EATING IN THE STREETS

Outside the monastery gates in Byzantium, the less pious also consumed two meals a day, although in their case, the early meal, or *ariston*, served around noon was not the "richer meal." This was the *deipnon*, enjoyed in the early evening. Sometimes, the *deipnon* migrated to the afternoon, drifting into lunch territory and redesignated the *aristodeipnon*—a blending of words for the two daily meals not unlike the contemporary term *brunch*. While monks and nuns enjoyed their one cooked meal in the middle of the day, laity during the middle Byzantine period (from the sixth to twelfth centuries) had to wait until evening for a hot meal. Because fuel was precious and cooking labor intensive, neither group enjoyed two hot meals in one day. Thus if lunch were cold, dinner could be hot, and if lunch were hot, dinner would be cold.[27]

In western Europe, emerging in the medieval period from the "de-urbanized world of the early middle ages," when street food vendors would have had few customers, professional cooks and street hawkers once again supplied a market of the poor and busy with hot food that could be eaten standing up. Just as the forerunners of the modern restaurants emerged first in monasteries catering to religious pilgrims, food stalls also began to appear in important church towns, suggesting that demand drove supply. In the English pilgrimage city of Winchester, for example, there were three commercial cooks registered in 1110 and nine thirty-eight years later. Commercial cooks were those who sold ready-made food out of their own stores rather than cooking for wages in an employer's kitchen.[28] They could depend on a steady stream of travelers without kitchens to keep business steady as well as the local urban poor who also had no place to cook.

The kind of food commercial cooks offered had to be of the sort that was easy to carry away and to eat in the street—the medieval equivalent of the hot dog. The food hawkers of fifteenth-century London recorded in the poem "London Lyckpenny" offered hot peascods [peas in the pod] and fresh strawberries and cherries as well as hot sheeps' feet, beef ribs, and meat pies, with different items appearing in different neighborhoods.[29]

Convenience food lunches were common throughout Europe. In Paris there was a wide variety of fast foods available by the thirteenth century, including waffles, stuffed pastries, roasted meats and fowl, hot mashed peas, flans, rissoles, and pancakes. In Turkey, where only two meals—one in the morning and one in the evening—were usually taken, there were, nonetheless, a rich array of street vendors who supplied the need for light lunch with meat patties, grilled eggplant, and grilled summer squash. Confectioners also offered sweets made from wheat flour, almonds, sugar, and rosewater. Among the Seldjoukides, the ruling elite, "Those who became hungry at noontime would drink sherbet, *ayran* or eat a piece of fruit," consuming an informal snack rather than full-fledged lunch. The heavier snacks supplied by the street vendors were more likely to be eaten by the working class or busy urban merchants.[30]

Medieval Cairo also supplied its hungry citizens with street food at lunchtime. One historian of Cairo's Jewish neighborhood noted that a master mason who was given a daily allowance for his lunch "could buy for himself a varied nourishing meal" from his city's street kitchens, while his less well-to-do co-workers, who got no allowance, "probably had to be content with bread and onions and the like." That the elite may also have patronized street kitchens is suggested by the existence of ornate metal food carriers from this era that historians think may have served as carry-out boxes. Rather than bringing a packed lunch from home, the wealthy may have sent servants to local restaurants to buy portions of food that were then loaded into these bento box–like containers.[31]

In London, pasties of all sorts, the British version of the globally popular stuffed triangle or semicircle of pastry, were the most common fare of the many

Figure 1.1. Food box made of engraved brass. Source: © The Trustees of the British Museum.

food shops that lined streets with names such as Cockrow, a shortened version of "Cook Row." The makers of these cheap lunches had such a bad reputation for using low-quality materials that "wealthy residents and travelers routinely shun[ned] the cookshops," preferring to buy materials and hire cooks even when away from home. Local laws were designed to regulate the unsanitary (even by the standards of the time) practices of pasty makers. In 1380, for example, "a set of ordinances was imposed on the pastelers of London, because they had been illegally making pasties of unwholesome rabbits, geese . . . sometimes stinking." Not content just to poison patrons, the commercial cooks also apparently set out to cheat them too, selling as venison pasties that were really made of beef.[32]

LUNCHING IN THE AMERICAS

When Europeans began exploring and settling in North America, they brought these lunching patterns with them. Before their arrival in the Americas in the last years of the fifteenth century, however, agriculture, hunting, and gathering were all used to feed local populations. Lunch probably followed two distinct patterns, depending on what kinds of work one did to supply the community with food. Using clay, skins, baskets, or stone for cooking, native North American cooks began preparing food early in the morning and left it to cook slowly over embers for most of the day. Watched by elderly members of the village community, the food, ready by late morning, was available to anyone who was hungry. Cakes of ground corn meal could be made on heated stones in the hearth to accompany stews; this practice was common in Central America, too, as well as in some parts of the Caribbean, where manioc meal might be used instead of corn. Stews of beans, corn, and squash, with small pieces of dried meat for flavor, served as typical nourishment.[33]

One of the first Europeans to write about Native American foodways, Amerigo Vespucci recounted that "they have no regular time for their meals, but they eat at any time that they have the wish, as often at night as in the day—indeed, they eat at all hours. They take their food on the ground, without napkin or any other cloth, eating out of earthen pots, which they make, or out of half calabashes." Vespucci failed to notice just how the native people he observed were taking their food out of cooking vessels—surely they were not dipping hands into bubbling stews—but more likely they were using something like a tortilla to scoop out stew and then eating the tortilla, too.

During growing months, women typically worked in communal fields, managing crops. We do not know whether they returned to their fire pits for food in the middle of the day, or whether, more likely, they carried dried foods such as corn cakes and salted meat or fish with them into the fields. Because farming was communal work it is reasonable to assume that midday picnics in the field were also collective moments to pause and converse in the Americas as they were in Europe.

When men were present in villages, between hunting trips, they helped themselves from communal cooking pots as hunger struck. These pots also provided evening meals for women returning from the fields. When men were away on hunting trips we can assume that they supplied themselves with dried foods brought from home and supplemented their diet through foraging. One Dutch visitor to Mohawk and Seneca country in the early seventeenth century wrote about buying some cornbread from local Native Americans and finding that "some of the loaves were baked with nuts and cherries and dry blueberries and the grains of the sunflower," making them sound rather like proto-granola bars. This kind of food would have made an excellent midday snack for people either traveling or working in fields.[34]

In Central and South America similar patterns were likely in rural areas, while in urban centers like Mexico City, locals enjoyed street foods available during the day as did their counterparts around the world. Vendors would have sold tortillas and stews, each region offering its own specialties. Europeans who followed Columbus to Central America and the Caribbean remarked that native people seemed to have had smaller appetites than did Europeans. A sixteenth-century traveler, for example, noted that when a native person left home for a voyage, he took only "a little maize, an herb with salt, maybe a lizard or worm, and some chili." That flavorings featured so importantly in what seemed to Mendez a meager package suggests that lunch, whether on the road or at home, was considered worthy of seasoning, and thus attention.[35]

When the Spanish government established political control of parts of Central and South America, foodways for peoples who came in contact with them changed markedly. The most profound changes were for those the Spanish enslaved to work in precious metal mines. Although the Spanish professed a responsibility to feed all workers adequately, reality apparently fell short. One observer in the 1550s noted that enslaved laborers "are made to toil from dawn to dusk, in the raw cold of morning and afternoon, in wind and storm, without other food than those rotten or dried out tortillas, and even of this they have not enough." While we do not know when in the day the tortillas were distributed or consumed, we can assume that some were eaten in the middle of the day, serving as a minor, if monotonous, lunch.[36]

In contrast, historian John Super has also found that although "Indians incorporated into Spanish labor systems . . . probably had less access to hunting and gathering" because of forced labor, they did not actually "lack adequate quantities of food, at least in comparison to what is known about European diets in the sixteenth century." Abundant pasturelands for the newly introduced European livestock meant that even "mine workers in the Caribbean expected [to be given] one pound of meat per day, even on fast days." If we assume that this ration was distributed at the end of the day to be taken home, lunches probably included some portion of cooked meat, probably tucked into a tortilla for convenience. Historian Jeffrey Pilcher notes that tacos serve simultaneously as utensil—carrying fillings to the mouth—carrying case, and warming device for fillings.[37]

For Native Americans surviving the onslaught of European diseases and land seizures, mealtimes changed significantly. One of the first trading goods that Europeans offered Native Americans was the "kettle," or cooking pot made of metal, a commodity that was worth much more to the American than to the trader.

Meals that had traditionally simmered for long hours in clay pots or roasted on hot stones could now be cooked with greater speed, although this also required more fuel than older methods. What this meant practically was that native people could vary their hot meals rather than eating the same stew for all meals at home. Now yeast breads and flatbreads could be quickly fried rather than baked on the fire, and meals could be allowed to grow cold and later reheated.

ANGLO-AMERICAN LUNCH

When northern Europeans left home to settle in North America, they brought with them their mealtime traditions, including use of the term "dinner" for the midday meal and supper for the last meal of the day. As agriculture of both the subsistence and cash crop variety dominated the lives of most settlers, ploughman's lunches were commonly taken in the fields after the style of Mesopotamia's first grain harvesters. Bread, cheese, and beer, all produced according to British traditions, fed men in the field while women busy at home with the myriad responsibilities of colonial housewifery would have snatched bites and gulps of the same material between chores. A colonial era visitor to Albany, a predominantly Dutch area, noted that housewives there paused for a just a few moments in housework to prepare a dinner (lunch) of buttermilk and bread and a large salad "prepared with an abundance of vinegar and very little or no oil." The common drinks were "very weak beer or pure water." When water was drawn from a family well and drunk immediately, it could be trusted to be healthy, but the weak beer, which had been through the purifying process of alcoholization, was generally a safer bet.[38]

Revolutionary leader and third president Thomas Jefferson, according to family legend, took no lunch at all, eating only breakfast and a dinner served at 3:30, and working alone in the hours between. Perhaps as a consequence of the master's indifference, the midday meal at his Monticello estate was "quite informal & handed round to guests" rather than a stately seated affair. This was consistent with Jefferson's general love of informality.[39]

In the colonies and then states of Maryland, Virginia, Georgia, and the Carolinas, large plantations emerged alongside the institution of slavery that made them possible. The job of bringing food to fieldworkers often fell to young children, who carried buckets of food and water to restore energy for long days of planting, weeding, and harvesting. Carrying lunches into the field allowed young people to witness the kind of labor they would soon perform themselves. While lunch breaks provided enslaved workers with moments not only to rest but also to commune with each other, they were also strictly monitored by overseers anxious to wring every ounce of effort out of workers. This custom of a watched lunch for enslaved workers persisted through the end of slavery in 1865.

In the era of the American Revolution, northern towns and cities began to support craftsmen who made finished goods for local luxury markets. Like the maritime stores that had been an important part of the New England economy since the late seventeenth century, luxury goods like Paul Revere's silverware were produced with the use of apprenticed labor. The English traditional relationship between apprentice and master was one that blended contemporary ideas of the workplace, school, and family, all of which were reflected in the foodways of the workshop. Masters and apprentices set their work pace together and took their midday break together, sharing beer, food cooked for them by the master craftsman's wife, and literature or news read aloud by one of the group.[40] One machine maker who invited his nephew to apprentice in his shop wrote that the boy "shall share as just we do. Eat at the same table, that is crackers and cheese eaten on the vice bench." The offer reveals both the simple lunch fare of the workshop and that meals were taken at the workbench rather than in a separate room set aside for dining.[41]

The young Samuel Clemens, who would later become famous as Mark Twain, apprenticed as a printer in a newspaper office in the early nineteenth century. At first he and another apprentice "in traditional fashion slept in the printing office and took their meals in the kitchen." When his coworker was found to be harassing the kitchen maid, however, the two boys were moved into the dining room. There they ate with the family and "discovered that the food in the dining room was no more plentiful than that in the kitchen."[42]

FARM LUNCHES

In the American Midwest, during the second half of the nineteenth century, a new lunch-in-the-fields tradition emerged. Government grants and homesteading policies made it possible for Americans to create some of the largest farms ever known in agricultural history. The size and potential of these farms rivaled the great estates of Russia, but the United States had no tradition of serfdom, so labor had to be hired seasonally. The "hired hands" who traveled from farm to farm during the growing and harvesting seasons were multiethnic crews of men who, since they were itinerant, had no way to feed themselves. Farm wives took on the job of feeding the crews, turning family kitchens into mass-feeding centers.

Because a farmer wanted to get the most work possible out of his hired hands, it was in his interest to serve the workers hearty meals. For farm wives, too, this responsibility also may have supplied an opportunity to demonstrate culinary prowess to a larger than usual audience. One Minnesota farm woman recalled a typical lunch served for a work crew at threshing time, on a long, makeshift table placed outside the house. The table held "trays of bread and dishes of butter, jam, and cabbage slaw . . . platters of pork roast, mashed potatoes, baked beans, and tomatoes," as well as one dish of her locally famous piccalilli relish.[43] Much heartier than just a sandwich, lunches for hired hands often also included freshly baked pies of several flavors. Farm lunches were an expected part of the hired hand's compensation for his work, and a good cook could attract good workers, season to season.

Early in the twentieth century, a Canadian farm journal included suggestions from farm women about how to feed threshing parties. While "so many women view the threshers with the idea that they are bottomless pits or receptacles for all the pies and cakes and rich food that can be concocted," one woman thought differently: "I never fuss with airy nothings when threshers are concerned and do not believe in wasting time and strength icing cakes." Far from scrimping on threshers' food, as this might suggest, she merely had a distinct culinary aesthetic, explaining that, "Good substantial, well-cooked, nicely served food is what hard-working men want."[44] Why spend time frosting one cake if you could use the time to bake another ham?

THE DAWN OF LUNCHEON

By the end of the eighteenth century, a meal actually called "luncheon" began to appear in accounts of fashionable life in England. Luncheon was something eaten after breakfast but before dinner, presumably filling the gap between the day's first, typically frugal meal, and dinner, served later and later among the social elite. In one English play, written in 1788, the practice came in for mocking. Inquiring the whereabouts of a character, another character is told by the man's servant, "I left him, Sir, very busy over his luncheon." When the seeker exclaims, "His luncheon?" he is answered, "Yes, Sir: a small morsel he takes before dinner, just to stay his stomach, consisting of about a pound of beef steaks and a tankard of porter." Although first conceived as something to tide a body over, it quickly became something to knock a person out.[45]

In France, the Revolution of 1789 brought a new fashion in lunching, known as the *déjeuner à la fourchette* or the lunch with a fork. The rationale for this meal seems to have had something to do with the culture of the Revolution; as the Irish Lady Morgan noted in her travel journals, the déjeuner à la fourchette was established as more conformable to the laws of republican ethics and more favorable to the preservation of health and morals, perhaps because it was a simple meal but hearty enough to feed a working man—thus the fork. A later writer claims that since "the dinner hour in France had been moved to accommodate the lengthy National Assembly sessions . . . the usual European time of three o'clock was moved to five or even later," causing Parisians to insert this new meal, the déjeuner à la fourchette, between their morning coffee and their lunch. Among the suggested dishes were "oysters, melons, anchovies and cold chicken."[46]

Lady Morgan agreed that while the déjeuner à la fourchette might have a reputation for modesty and virtue, it was "far from being composed of black broth and bread" and actually combined "every species of luxury and extravagance" available to the new bourgeoisie.[47]

In 1862, a Scottish cookbook defined it as "a fork breakfast, a breakfast at which the use of forks is required from solid dishes being served." Although the author called the meal a breakfast in this text, she explained that in France it was usually served after an earlier meal of coffee and pastry, taken in private. In England, the déjeuner à la fourchette was frequently an "entertainment for company" at which guests could expect "articles provided . . . for a fashionable supper."[48]

In British India, as the dinner hour drifted later in the day, too, breakfast grew larger, supper—the meal after dinner—grew smaller, and lunch, known as tiffin, appeared. In 1799, for example, in one wealthy home, dinner was taken at 4:00 p.m. A generation later, in 1830, it was at 6:30. Sixteen years later it had drifted to 7:00 p.m., and one hundred years later a typical dinnertime among the English in India was 8:30.[49]

One historian of the British in India argues that meals taken earlier in the day reflected Indian traditions while those later in the day "took on a more British cast." Thus, Anglo-Indians ate *chota haziri*, which was an Indian breakfast "designed to accommodate the early rising which the climate encouraged." This was followed by "the large breakfast, called 'brunch' or 'tiffin,'" that usually consisted of a spiced meat or vegetable stew styled a "curry," and which was eaten "earlier than the British luncheon."[50]

Although the addition of a third meal in the day was the result of increased wealth and leisure time, the terms *lunch* and *luncheon* were actually borrowed from working-class life. For farmers and laborers, lunch and luncheon both had the meaning of a small something taken between more substantial meals. Lunch derived from a common word for a slice of something. Robert Burns, in his 1785 poem, "The Holy Fair," for example, related how at noon, fairgoers sat down, "An' cheese an' bread, frae women's laps, Was dealt about in lunches."

Luncheon was etymologically related to the Anglo Saxon "nuncheon," or a drink and snack taken at noon, the drink usually being beer and the snack a piece of bread. When King's Hall at Cambridge University was under construction in 1342, "bread and ale were issued for the 'nonsenchis'"of the laborers.[51] Although probably not in need of the kind of sustenance that fuelled medieval construction workers, well-to-do English men and women adopted these terms for their own use in the eighteenth century.

Jane Austen seems to have had a private family term for the midday meal, referring twice in her diaries to a meal between breakfast and dinner as "noon-shine." Austen did not carry this neologism into her prose, however, allowing two traveling sisters in *Pride and Prejudice* to describe as "the nicest cold luncheon in the world" a meal they had assembled at an inn.[52]

For English women in India, lunch presented a management problem. In England, lunches were typically made from the previous dinner's remains. Indian cooks, however, according to the customs of their culture, expected to have dinner's leftovers for their own use. Charged with management of family finances, the English woman had to fight to have last night's scraps turned into today's lunch for her own family rather than supper for the cook's family. The more fritters of chipped beef were served on Anglo-Indian tables, the more scarce the food of the kitchen staff.[53]

Tiffins could also take the form of a light traveling lunch when English husbands brought the work culture of late-nineteenth-century Europe and America to India. Some of these men began to take sandwiches assembled from leftovers as well as pieces of cake to the office in place of the old habit of returning home in the middle of the day.

On weekends, when men were home from the office, tiffins took on more heft. As one Anglo-Indian woman wrote in 1890, "When guests are invited to tiffin, there is no reason why they should not be tempted to over-eat themselves, as they too often are, by the ludicrously heavy style of the ordinary luncheon party in India." She scoffed at supplying this bounty when "one light entrée and a dressed vegetable would be ample." A self-identified "child and grandchild of the British Raj in India" remembered more fondly "the relaxed Sunday curry *tiffins*; jovial occasions with much gin, beer and merriment, where the 'done thing' was to eat until you were uncomfortably full, then fall asleep on the nearest bed or couch for a nap if you didn't make it home."[54] In tropical climates, the British adopted not only some local foodstuffs but also the local custom of an after-lunch nap, a reminder of how often lunch serves as a point for cultural transformation and also how dependent it is upon context.

SCHOLAR'S LUNCH

The English writer William Howitt, who traveled in Germany in the 1840s, relates a tale of a dangerous lunch spot in one of the university towns. A "terrible swordsman" who was connected to the university had a mother who ran an "eating house" for students. Such businesses were known as a *frass philister*, or "eating philistine," to suggest a low quality of food that was served to students between classes. In this one fabled establishment, the food "could promise very little satisfaction, even to the least delicate and artistical stomachs." Students exercised vigorously to work up their appetite for it and then again vigorously to "conquer the dyspeptic symptoms that rapidly" followed the meal. Yet the place was always busy, and the swordsman's mother thrived because the poor students "had much rather try their teeth on the culinary productions of the mother, than fall under the pitiless sword of the son." An aggressive advertising campaign—eat here or die!—kept this *Philister* in business.[55]

Howitt's dramatic lunch table is a reminder that eating places spring up to serve hungry populations. Just as monasteries had opened their doors when hungry pilgrims began to wander into cathedral towns, frass philisters set the table for hungry students rushing to get back to classes as universities began to proliferate and thrive in Europe.

At Oxford and Cambridge Universities, dinnertime began to shift later in the day during the eighteenth century. For several hundred years, scholars had dined just before noon, but important changes in British society pushed lunch later into the day. The shift came as both universities' emphasis on religious training weakened and an Oxbridge education began to be an attribute of a gentleman as much as of a serious scholar. Sons of the rising middle class enjoyed their college years as an interlude of leisure between childhood and adulthood and were thus loath to rise any earlier in the day than their hangovers accommodated.

At one Oxford college, Brasenose, dinnertime was eleven o'clock in 1730, but it had moved back to one o'clock by 1753 and by the end of the century could be as late as four o'clock in the afternoon. Despite the lazy attitude suggested by this gradual drift of the meal, personal appearance at dinner required rigorous attention to detail. Before dinner "the whole college was occupied with the near-frenzied ritual of dressing" for the meal, which included "the donning of the required white waistcoat, white stockings and low shoes" as well as a powdered wig or hair dressed and powdered like a wig.[56]

Once properly dressed, fellows, bachelors, and gentlemen commoners—the three castes of college life—paraded into their grand dining rooms in order of status. A visitor described the table settings that were provided for the well-dressed crowd as "coarse and dirty and loathsome table cloths, square wooden plates and the wooden bowls into which the bones are thrown." The food was simple fare of a joint of meat, passed down the table to be carved by each diner, potatoes, and beer in a stoneware mug. Once these dainties had been dispatched, one student recalled, "If you choose a pudden or a tart you must vociferate for it with the voice of a fishwoman, and often not get it neither." Despite the pomp of entrance, the meal was clearly not elegant and ended in a free-for-all: "When done, you rise when convenient, waiting for nobody."[57]

In 1836, Alexander Gooden, just beginning his studies at Trinity College, Cambridge, wrote to his mother:

> The dinner is laid out in the Great Hall, in which all the resident members of the College (about 400 in number) sit down at long tables. Meat and bread, beer or water, are the only things provided for you. Plates of pudding, cheese, and glasses of ale are brought to those who call for them, and set down to the account of the respective consumers. The meat consists of joints of mutton, veal, beef (fresh and salt) served up in immense round pewter chargers, and interspersed with greens and potatoes. The dinner occupies about twenty minutes or half an hour.

Writing to his brother, Gooden was somewhat less neutral about the experience, describing dinner, which he said took place at 4:00, as "a savage piece of business" at which "every man mangles the joints for himself and if he would have ale, pudding etc. must pay for it extra. As soon as he has gobbled his fill he goes away, so that this primitive meal takes not more than twenty minutes."[58]

During the eighteenth century, Oxford colleges repeatedly issued injunctions against the practice of students buying dinner from shops instead of dining in the hall. The colleges threatened to punish the "vituallers and cooks" who supplied students either at their own establishments or by catering meals in college rooms. That the prohibitions were repeated is good evidence that they were roundly ignored by those who could afford to buy dinners.

Presumably no one dressed up for these private lunches, which must have made them immediately more appealing. More variety and perhaps a more equitable distribution of foodstuffs could also be had. Treating friends to lunches enabled students to establish their own networks of loyalty and obligation, giving to the "commoners, a measure of social power perhaps at odds with the traditional hierarchy of the university." Indeed, one insider's guide to college life published in 1783 explicitly advised the university student to avoid the dining hall "for he ought to take every opportunity of appearing to disregard the order of the college." Lunch outside the hall was one way to destabilize the traditional order, and perhaps more subtly to establish the primacy of wealth over wisdom.[59]

At catered affairs in their own rooms, defiant diners could enjoy "cooked meats, sausages, tongues, eels, broths and soups and pickles" provided by local victuallers as well as "bottles replete with the juice of the vine" "sweet damson cheese," cakes, and "a sumptuous dessert" of oranges, peaches, grapes, and apples. It is no surprise to find supper described as "the lesser meal . . . which undergraduate memoirs seldom mention."[60]

While Oxbridge undergraduates avoided the dining hall, academic fellows flocked to it, no doubt because they were better fed. In the late eighteenth century, one fellow at Brasenose recorded this dinner: "First course Cod and oyster sauce, Rost Beef, Tongue and boiled Chicken, Peas, Soups, and roots . . . a boiled Turkey . . . a brace of Partridges rosted, 4 Snipes and some Larkes rosted, also an orange pudding, syllabubs and jellies, Madeira and Port Wines to drink and a dish of Fruit." Certainly, a plate of meat and potatoes and a mug of beer paled in comparison with such rich variety.[61]

INDUSTRIAL ERA LUNCH

During the nineteenth century, public lunch was established as an urban phenomenon in both Europe and America. Where agricultural workers had long taken a midday break for food, the emergence of the industrial economy in North America and Europe produced both the working-class lunch—brief, frugal, and not eaten at a table—and the businessman's lunch—prolonged, copious, and taken in great comfort. Mass production and the early factory system first came to America in Lowell, Massachusetts. There the Lowell family established water-powered textile mills that almost exclusively employed young women raised on the surrounding New England farms. These young women were housed in company dormitories and subject to company rules as to their behavior, which included when and where they could eat. Like the master craftsmen of old, the Lowell family felt responsible for the moral well-being of its employees, but they practiced their patronage on a much larger and entirely impersonal scale. As factory timetables show, for example, a lunch bell typically rang at noon, allowing the mill "girls" to leave their stations for a midday meal. Workers were given thirty to forty-five minutes for lunch, which could be taken at factory-owned boarding houses, where three meals per day were included in the $1.00 to $2.00 per week rent. Because most of the young workers sent most of their wages home to their families, there was little left over to seek lunch outside the boarding house.[62]

The era of the Market Revolution was also a time of increased interest in public education, as the new factories demanded literate clerical staff. The gradual establishment of public schools, first in the Northeast and then in the Midwest, brought children to school carrying lunches of all sorts in pails to be warmed by the schoolhouse stove. The history of elementary school lunches follows in chapter 4.

Changing cityscapes dictated when and what working men ate in the United States. Because the rising cost of land in cities forced the working class into neighborhoods farther from their workplaces, one laborer recalled, the man who put in

> ten hours per day in the shop, is forced to eat his breakfast at half past five in the morning, that he may reach his work at seven. He is compelled also to take with him a cold lunch for the mid-day meal, or buy his dinner at a convenient restaurant,—the former course being the most prevalent; he returns from his work, arriving at home at seven, or half-past, in the evening, exhausted physically by his work and the lack of a hearty warm mid-day meal.[63]

Changing real estate values had direct consequences for working men's lunches.

The lunch bell was one among the many innovations used by the Lowells and copied by other entrepreneurs of this era. Lunch bells rang out all over the Northeast in new mill towns and cities, setting workers briefly free and calling them back, always too soon. In the early days of mass production, factories had their own bells, but as more factories congregated in favorable neighborhoods, the utility of having one bell rather than ten ring out led to the use of public bells to serve private owners and their workers. In 1836, the ship carpenters of Boston, seeking to transform their twelve-hour day into a ten-hour day through the introduction of a two-hour lunch break, resolved to petition the city government to ring the lunch bells at noon instead of the usual time—one o'clock. Since the second bell would continue to ring at two o'clock, the workers would have achieved extra lunch time.

To serve this population that had appetite but no time (the movement for two-hour lunch breaks did not succeed) and little money, enterprising food sellers set up their rolling carts at factory gates. Saloonkeepers made a particular

Figure 1.2. Lunch time, Kesler Manufacturing Company. The little one carries the lunch. Usually the hands all go home to dinner. Location: Salisbury, North Carolina.

effort to lure in male lunchgoers by offering "free lunch" with the purchase of a beer—lunches that tended to be very salty, producing great thirst. One temperance advocate complained that at the Hotel Vendome bar in New York City, the "free lunch counter," which was opulently "built of African marble and Mexican onyx," supported a display of "the most tempting food cooked by master hands." Free lunch had to be paid for by *someone* of course, and a *New York Daily Tribune* writer reported that "millions of money are annually expended on this seeming gratuity." As saloons were never in the charitable feeding busi-

Figure 1.3.   The worker's lunch, April 1891. Gianni Dagliu Orti/The Art Archive at Art Resource, New York.

ness, we can assume that "millions of money" more were also recouped on the gambit.[64]

Women factory workers were not encouraged to enter these saloons, leaving them, for most of the nineteenth century, nowhere to eat but the workroom, assuming this was permitted. In fine weather, they could eat outside, perching on street curbs and stoops to eat food bought from nearby shops or brought in a pail or folded napkin from home.

The first lunch wagons appeared on the streets of the industrialized Northeast at the end of the nineteenth century. Known as "owls," they provided food for workers on the night shift when all other restaurants were closed. The term "lunch" has typically been used for meals taken in the middle of the workday, even when that workday began at sundown and ended with the dawn. Hospital staff who work overnight, for example, use the term "midnight lunch" to refer to the meal they eat on the longest break of the shift. As early as 1904, a professional journal for nurses and hospital workers addressed the question of what was "The best method of providing the nurses' 'Midnight Lunch,'" showing that the term was already in use before the emergence of the modern hospital.[65]

The small dining spaces provided in the earliest versions of the dinner wagons were best maximized by counter seating. As some wagons prospered, they took root, establishing permanent positions but largely preserving their cost-effective seating plans.

Long before the open kitchen became a late-twentieth-century dining craze, lunch counter patrons seemed to appreciate their view of the grill as reassurance that all was sanitary. Like the automat, lunch counters also eliminated the pretensions of haute cuisine service while still maintaining the human presence that the automat mostly concealed. Like a bar—a venue that more and more Americans had come to know during Prohibition—the lunch counter established an informal relationship between the diner and the server/cook, eliminating the middle level of waitstaff and thus appearing to offer a bargain in dining.

As railroad dining began to be seen as an elegant experience, some entrepreneurs bought train cars and refurnished them as restaurants, blending the efficiency of the counter with the glamour of the diner car, and in the process picking up the name "diner." This architectural gimmick was so successful that others began to build their lunch counters in shapes to mimic the train car even though no part of the construction had ever rolled down a track.

Burger stands opened along roadsides in the 1920s to serve the increasing numbers of Americans who drove cars as part of their work life, whether as traveling salesmen, truckers, or corporate managers going from branch to branch. Burger stands also catered to the simultaneously growing number of Americans

Figure 1.4. Day and Night Diner, Hamden, Massachusetts. Source: Prints & Photographs Division, Library of Congress, HABS MASS.7-PALM.2—1.

Figure 1.5.   Lunchroom window, New York. Source: Walker Evans, 1929. Art Resource, New York. © The Metropolitan Museum of Art.

who used their cars for leisure activities, driving to sporting events or short trips into the countryside. In their simplicity and efficiency, burger stands seemed to mirror the modern experience of "automobiling," fitting neatly into the new roving lifestyles. Counter-style seating and limited menus also gave these establishments the glow of modernity for a new generation of patrons. Through the 1940s and 1950s, burger stands grew in popularity, producing the famous chains of today that have expanded beyond lunch to open early and close late— if at all—serving lunch-style food at all times of day.

When Prohibition forced the closure of the saloons that had provided free lunches, the burger stands and lunch counters gained customers. Cafeterias, which were primarily a feature in Midwestern and Southern urban life, also provided business district lunch seekers with a quick meal. All food was prepared in the morning and kept warm in steam trays, so lunch eaters were able to choose their own meals from a small range of options and serve themselves, eliminating interactions with waitstaff that might make the meal slower and more expensive. One of the best loved and longest lived of the cafeterias is Cleburne Cafeteria in Houston, Texas. Among the standard vegetable dishes are macaroni and cheese, squash casserole, black-eyed peas, and baked corn. Main dishes, as in most cafeterias, include fried chicken, fried fish, chicken-fried steak, and roast beef. Cafeterias all offer several kinds of pies among dessert options. At Cleburne, the pies are apple (two kinds), pecan, lemon chess, pumpkin, cherry, coconut meringue, and chocolate icebox.[66]

MIDDLE-CLASS LUNCH

Among the bourgeois families of the factory-owning class in Europe and America, the introduction of gaslight enabled the extension of the day, which was then "punctuated and shaped by food and eating." The longer the waking hours, the more little meals could be devised to fill them. An English guide to polite behavior noted the ways in which mealtimes determined sociability, cautioning that "visits are usually paid between the hours of two and four p.m. in winter, and two and five p.m. in summer" in order "to avoid intruding before the luncheon is removed, and leave sufficient time to allow the lady of the house leisure for her dinner toilette." As this dinner was not the final meal of the day— that was supper—and as breakfast was also a regular meal, this guide reveals the existence of two midday meals in the Victorian period.[67]

Even with meals coming so frequently during the day, some social arbiters prescribed a change of costume for each meal, allowing for something simple during breakfast and something more formal for visiting hours, with "jewelry and ornaments not to be worn until the full dress for dinner is assumed." Although this advice was offered specifically to Englishwomen, a Frenchwoman also noted that in the mornings "I work until 10:30. Then I arrange my hair and we have lunch." Lunch was apparently not something one could eat uncoiffed, probably because guests might join the family for this meal, which they would never do for breakfast.[68]

Adults in Victorian England and France ate their main meal of the day—dinner—either early or late in the evening depending on their class. The wealthier crowd usually ate later, around eight, and sometimes they took a light supper even later, especially if they were at social events such as balls, which could stretch far into the night. It was, for urban elites, "a matter of elegance and luxury, rather than a satisfying of appetites." Middle-class children also knew dinner as the main meal of the day, but they had it much earlier than most adults did, sitting down to eat as soon as they got home from school, around 2:00 in the afternoon. The Victorian era, thus, was a time of not only two midday meals but also wide variation in the time and size of these meals. What you ate and when you ate it depended on both age and class as well as whether one lived in a rural or urban setting.[69]

In urban England and France, lunch was conceived of as a light meal, one for which the whole family did not necessarily gather. It had a catch-as-catch-can character. One dispenser of household guidance suggested keeping a sideboard stocked with food so that a family member or guest could help himself "without feeling he is troublesome to either master or servant." The basic items she recommended were "a pat of butter, some bread, a jug of milk, a stilton cheese, a bottle of beer, and a small dish of cold meat." In fact, a ploughman's lunch.[70]

LUNCH AT WAR

The First World War brought new lunch routines to all of the nations involved, especially because women, who had most frequently lunched at home, joined the industrial workforce and took part in agricultural production. While factories typically lacked designated lunchrooms in this era, space could be found to sit at tables or on the floor. Perched in this way, workers consumed whatever they had brought from home wrapped in napkins or lunch pails made from repurposed cigar boxes or coffee cans. Because factories would have lacked facilities to reheat food, war workers began to rely on sandwiches rather than leftover meals that might be less appealing when cold. In both England and America sandwiches could be a way to make the most of foods like roast meats that cost more and were harder to come by during wartime. Scraps were stretched with dressings and turned into "salads," like the ham salad—chopped meat held together with mayonnaise and seasoned with diced pickles—that appears in many war-era books.

The beginning of the war coincided with the emergence of a female clerical workforce in America and northern Europe, a cohort that created a new market for cheap but respectable lunch restaurants, which endured after the war's end. Restaurants that advertised themselves as tearooms were understood to be appropriate for women, but the dainty table service they offered might stretch beyond the budget of the average pink-collar worker. Drugstores often provided the perfect venue in that they were cheap and offered counter service that gave the diner a certain anonymity but also placed behavior under the surveillance of the crowd. The multipurpose nature of the drugstore meant that women had a presence as shoppers as well as lunchers, so a woman need not fear that she would end up surrounded by men, as might have been the case in a chophouse.

Luncheonettes, which mimicked the layout of the drugstore without the mercantile extras, seemed to promise the same combination of cheap food and safe space. The term became common in the 1920s, when the postwar wave of women's entry into urban workforces continued apace. One of the most popular meals at the luncheonette was the grilled cheese sandwich, a variation on the

Figure 1.6. Lunch wagon, Washington, DC, 1918–1920. Source: Prints & Photographs Division, Library of Congress, LC-DIG-npcc-00729.

toasted cheese sandwich, which had usually been served open-faced. In Canadian cookbooks, these sandwiches were sometimes known as "cheese dreams." There were in fact two kinds of cheese dreams, one sweet and the other savory. The sweet version, made with cheese-flavored shortbread and tart jelly, had no analogue in the United States, but the savory version—white bread spread with cheese and a slice of bacon, then broiled, was very familiar across the southern border. Cheese dreams, or what the Americans called "toasties," could also be made by buttering the outside of a cheese sandwich and toasting it in the oven or by using a griddle.[71]

Taking advantage of industrial-scale equipment, lunch-counter cooks were able to use their large, flat grills to brown both sides of the sandwich while melting the inner cheese and thus providing the customer with something that could be eaten without cutlery, unlike its toasted cheese predecessor. Grilled cheese sandwiches were popular because they were warm, and thus satisfying, but also cheap. Sometimes to make up for what seemed like too light a lunch, they were served with bowls of soup, often cream of tomato, one the most popular soups in American public life from the early twentieth century until today. According to the company itself, Campbell's sells two billion cans of soup each year in the United States, with tomato one of the three most popular flavors. The company appears to be anxious about declining sales of these favorites—tomato, chicken noodle, and cream of mushroom—so anxious that it has launched a new line of more multicultural flavors (chorizo, golden lentil with curry) sold not in the iconic soup can but now—for more than twice the price of Andy Warhol's beloved can—in brightly colored foil pouches.[72]

The popularity of the grilled cheese sandwich was assisted by two technological innovations—the advent of presliced bread and the introduction of a square cheese by the Kraft company. Kraft's "American" cheese was processed into a loaf such that each slice could perfectly fit between two slices of standard-sized white bread. For the cold sandwich, too, this alignment offered a boost, but it was especially important for the closed-face grilled sandwich because overlap potentially meant burnt cheese.

The automat also offered women workers and workers of limited means a gender-neutral and affordable place to eat. First opened at the turn of the century, in Germany and then in the United States, the automat format seemed to borrow from the design genius of the industrial age. Customers bought tokens, which they then slid into slots, opening small glass doors behind which sat plates of food. Despite the gleaming modernity of the automat, its fare was traditional New England stuff—baked beans being one of the most beloved dishes. By cutting out the waitstaff, automats were able to appear cheaper than a restaurant, and the novelty of the experience attracted both young women and young men.

During the Second World War, women in England, Canada, and America once again took up work in the industrial sector and in agriculture to fill in for men who were serving in the armed forces and to meet increased production demands. Lunchboxes and their contents became important topics, as reflected in a number of cookbooks that addressed the working person's lunch specifically. This was a new topic for cookbooks, which had always been aimed at a middle-class audience. Prewar cookbooks might offer recipes for social lunches, but the basic assumption was that men would buy lunches close to their workplaces and children would either be fed at school or return home to eat with their mothers. The working woman's lunchbox became an entirely new culinary genre. One of the most famous images of the American home front during the war is Norman Rockwell's painting identified as *Rosie the Riveter*, which shows a strong woman pausing in the midst of heavy industrial labor to eat a hearty sandwich. Rosie's sandwich looks like it might have come from the column labeled "male sand-wiches" in Marion Gregg's *American Women's Voluntary Services Cookbook* of 1942, which suggests how much women's work in the war industries changed popular perceptions of their role in society.[73]

Margaret Wagstaff, who was a "land girl," or agricultural worker in England during the Second World War, recalled that "we were given a packed lunch to take to work with us each day, mostly cheese or corned beef sandwiches with not much filling. Some farmers' wives would kindly give us meals or refresh-ments." When nothing extra could be found to supplement these rations, the women would often go to a local cafe together for steak pie and chips, a lunch to fuel heavy labor.[74]

Mary Stokes remembered the land girl's lunch as even worse than insubstan-tial, recalling that the women were roused at 5:30 a.m. to get ready for the day and "prepare our lunch-boxes (heavy aluminium things)." Lunch "was, more often than not, Spam or grated cheese (sometimes mouldy)." Although many people congratulated her on her position, thinking that because land girls worked on

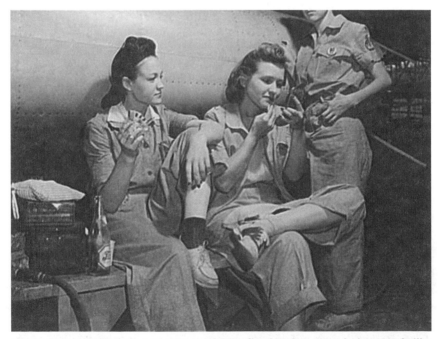

Figure 1.7.   Production. A-31 ("Vengeance") dive bombers. Lunch time, Nashville, Tennessee. Source: Alfred Palmer, 1943. Prints & Photographs Division, Library of Congress, LC-USE6-D.

farms they were well-fed, "living off the fat of the land, getting loads of 'goodies' denied to the general public," Stokes noted bitterly that "nothing could be further [from] the truth! We were on strict rations, like everybody else, with no luxuries on the side. We did not get chicken, meat or eggs."[75] Producing food for the military and public market, the land girls were not rewarded in kind.

Wartime sacrifice was a common theme for lunches during the war. In Japan beginning in 1939, on the first day of each month "restaurants and pubs were forced to take the day off because the sale of alcoholic beverages was banned" so that "everyone could endure the same hardships as soldiers at the front." Most famously, civilians were encouraged to blend patriotism and thrift, though definitely not sensible nutrition, by packing a "rising-sun box lunch," which consisted of a square of rice topped with umeboshi, a pickled apricot. Symbolic aesthetics trumped nourishment.[76]

Entries in the personal diary of well-known Japanese comic Fukukawa Roppa reveal, however, that restaurants continued to serve hearty meals even in the last year of the war. In a black market restaurant in 1944 Roppa ordered a lavish, multicultural lunch of cream soup, beef stew, cauliflower in cream sauce, beefsteak, breaded cutlet, and a rice curry. At a navy officer's club later the same year he was served onion au gratin, shrimps dressed in mayonnaise, breaded beef cutlet with mashed potatoes, melon, sweet adzuki bean soup, and iced tea. These meals indicate both that the well-to-do had access to foods many ordinary people could not find, let alone afford, and that they favored a style of dining that mixed Euro-American and Japanese flavors and preparations. In contrast, the menu for the lunchroom of a local department store offered Japanese lunchboxes of many varieties—eel, sashimi, tempura, stew—but all with a rice substitute such as millet or barley because that essential food had been rationed.[77]

MODERN LUNCHWAYS

The suburbanization of U.S. society that followed the Second World War re-established Victorian era food cultures for the middle class (a growing cohort). Men were now even further distant from home at midday, and children mostly ate at school, so middle-class "housewives," women who did not work for wages or salaries, found themselves alone at lunchtime. For many of those who had worked in the war industries or grown up in crowded urban households, this shift created an isolation that seemed to demand a solution. In order to re-create the camaraderie of war-era lunchtimes, suburban women began to invite one another over for lunch parties that were markedly the opposite of Rosie the Riveter's utilitarian meat sandwich, offering instead whimsical creations in the form of salads that glimmered and wiggled, making lunch itself an entertainment.

Lunch also began to be fun for some urban office workers. The postwar boom in consumer goods production led to a complementary boom in marketing and advertising, which in turn created a class of white-collar workers known as "creatives." These creatives, who included workers in the publishing, advertising, marketing, and research fields, emerged from mornings of deep thought hungry for lunch that could include mental relaxation in liquid form. The three-martini lunch came to stand for a new economy, one in which certain classes of workers had more freedom over their own time than had been true for earlier generations. The nineteenth-century clerk who got drunk at lunch would blur his copy and be fired; the 1960s editor who got tipsy at the Old Town bar could snooze it off at his desk because allowances must be made for genius.

CIVIL RIGHTS AND LUNCH

While for the "creatives" a certain kind of louche lunch came to represent high cultural status in the postwar era, for civil rights activists, lunch at a simple utilitarian lunch counter symbolized citizenship itself. Lunch counters were an essential part of modern life in twentieth-century America, providing cheap, simple food for workers in America's small and large cities. The starkly democratic nature of their architecture—no special tables, each diner shoulder to shoulder with another, attention focused on the grill or on the plate—seemed to reinforce American ideals of equality.

Because of deeply entrenched racial discrimination, however, African Americans could never be certain of admittance, let alone welcome in these establishments, even beyond the officially segregated South. Not eager to risk refusal, traveling African American families brought their lunches with them, usually in shoeboxes—a convenient construction for the purpose. Stopping by the roadside, African American families shared picnics rather than chance being insulted at unfamiliar lunch counters and burger stands.

When the civil rights movement emerged after the Second World War to force America to live up to its own ideals of social equality, lunch counters were a natural choice for integration. They were ubiquitous, innocuous, and symbolic of public life. The first lunch counter sit-in occurred in Greensboro, North Carolina, in February 1960. Four African American students sat at the whites-only counter of a Woolworth's drugstore—the most well known of American lunch-counter chains—and refused to leave when they were denied service. Their protest sparked a wave of sit-ins and resulted by July of 1961 in the desegregation of that particular Woolworth's lunch counter, with many others across the South to follow before the decade ended.

Cookbook author Ruth Gaskins also noted that African Americans had weathered the era of Jim Crow laws by proffering a standing welcome to each other for meals in private homes. Writing in the period immediately following the desegregation of Southern lunch counters, she observed, "I guess it's because of the Welcome that our kitchen table gives us, that we don't make so much use of restaurants." Although she was "glad that we can go to them now, because I eat all my lunches out," she found their quality uninspiring in comparison to her friends' homemade fare: "I admit I'm kind of spoiled." Civil rights were important to Gaskins, but so was taste.[78]

Postwar modernity altered the relationship between lunch and labor in Mexico, too, where until the 1940s there had been few restaurants because workers—both middle and working class—returned home for lunch and a rest in the middle of the day. Through the 1950s and 1960s, however, the number of restaurants almost doubled. White-collar workers in Mexico City now ate close to their offices

Figure 1.8. Civil rights activists occupying a lunchroom counter during a sit-in. Source: Danny Lyon, Magnum Photos.

because "the growth of commuter traffic" made it too difficult to go home and come back in the middle of the day. Although they "refused to move their meals forward to the twelve noon lunchtime favored north of the border, they did take shorter breaks at nearby cafeterias and *fondas*" in exchange for leaving the office at 5:00 p.m. rather than the traditional 7:00.[79]

In America, the postwar boom lasted until the 1970s, when a recession hit that markedly changed work life and lunch. Nervous about their jobs, workers were now less likely to be seen lingering over long lunches and instead began to emulate the do-it-yourself ethos of the counterculture and "brown bag it" to work. Even with the economic recovery of the 1980s, the sense that lunch was a luxury persisted in the popular imagination. As Gordon Gekko, the antihero of the film *Wall Street*, declared, "Lunch is for wimps." The character, played by Michael Douglas, uttered this statement on the phone with a potential business partner who had presumably asked him to meet for lunch. Gekko's rejection signaled his nonstop energy in pursuit of wealth and suggested that anyone who needed to stop for lunch would miss all the action.

In this mood, the lunch of the boss began more closely to resemble that of the factory worker—a brief pause in unremarkable surroundings to eat something from a container. While construction workers picnicked on I-beams or sidewalks, chief financial officers and their secretaries scarfed something down at their desks or while walking between appointments.

When lunch did occur, for businessmen of the Gekko generation it was best combined with deal making. It was during this era that the Four Seasons restaurant in New York City became a showplace for the so-called power lunch. Important figures from the worlds of business, politics, and entertainment lunched with each other while conducting a kind of midday diplomacy. The politics of who sat where and with whom actually earned the sustained attention of social reporters in the city's major newspapers.

Publisher Michael Korda, a representative of the creative class, wrote in the *New York Times* in 1977 that he belonged to a cohort for whom "the expense account lunch is an essential tool of the trade, like a carpenter's adze." He explained, "not for us a quick bacon cheeseburger at the counter or a pleasant lunch" at a modestly priced French café. No, "powerlunchers would rather be seen eating yogurt at their desks than be eating an unpowerful meal in a restaurant full of nobodies." At that moment, Korda declared, the Grill Room at the Four Seasons was the "most powerful place to eat lunch in town." Korda noted that dining habits of the powerlunchers had taken a turn for the lean. The Four Seasons' *bundnerfleish*, "a plate of thinly sliced, air-cured beef," was not just popular but "*important*." Its importance was as a symbol for the new fashion for abstemious dining. Korda noted that Perrier water had replaced the martini as the favorite drink because it signaled both that you were in control of your faculties—ready to wheel and deal—and that you knew you would be lunching out every day of the week and should pace yourself. Korda identified salads and simple grilled seafood as the most powerful foods and reminded readers that "the more you eat, the less powerful you are."[80]

The increasing prevalence of desktop computers also made it more possible for white-collar workers who were not power brokers to keep up productivity even in the act of breaking for lunch. While it is not advisable, for instance, to dictate a memo while eating a sandwich, the new technology enabled managers to do their own secretarial work—lunch in hand, crumbs in keyboard. Installation of microwaves in many offices simultaneously gave workers a chance to have a hot meal for lunch and less incentive to leave the building. This was an attractive outcome for managers, who were less likely to lose worker's time to the charms of the corporate kitchen than to the fascinations of the street.

This trend away from the sociable and unhurried lunch strikes some as unhealthy both physically and psychologically. In 2010, Tony Schwartz started the "Take Back Your Lunch" movement to reclaim the lost lunch hour. Participants take a pledge to take their time and commit to encouraging coworkers to do the same. As one devotee declared, "I don't think there are a lot of people on their deathbeds who wish they would have eaten more lunches at their desk."[81]

In another twist on changing meal patterns, the vast consumer market for snacks may once again erase lunch as a distinct meal, leaving us more like our hunter-gatherer ancestors than we might like to think.

CLASSIC LUNCH
FARE AND CULTURAL
IMPORTANCE IN THE
UNITED STATES AND
AROUND THE WORLD

City dwellers all over the world would recognize the dilemma, described by one Nigerian blogger as "what to do about lunch." Like many others of his generation, this writer ponders multiple options: "Should I send Richard [his assistant] to Tetrazzini to buy their jollof rice, Moi Moi and chicken, or should I brave the lunch time Lagos island traffic for a short journey either to Jevnik or Yellow Chilli?" At Yellow Chilli he might eat the staple meal of mashed cassava, mashed yam, or mashed millet and vegetable soup. At Jevnik, he could order the coconut rice, ofe owerri (a soup made with smoked fish, greens, and cocoyam, a tuber), or "mama's delight," a weekly special soup.[1]

Global urbanization and industrialization bring ever-increasing variety to the question of what to do about lunch. Refrigerators and microwaves in workplaces make it more possible to bring something from home, but local establishments and multinational chains sing their siren songs in more and more business districts worldwide. In addition, as noted in chapter 1, what kind of impression we make by either eating at our desks or disappearing for the midday meal is bound to factor into our decision.

Because it offers such rich opportunities for the performance of culture, lunch is a meal in perpetual transition, so that any account of what is commonly eaten in any one place or time is likely to change within a generation. It is a distinctly provisional pastime to generalize about what lunch is likely to be around the world.

The following wide-ranging tour of global lunches reveals variety within regions and also suggests that rural and urban lunches continue to vary significantly in character. Agricultural communities are less likely to break for lunch than are highly urbanized and industrialized societies, a difference that may seem counterintuitive. It would seem to make sense for those performing heavy farm labor to stop for refreshment while office workers expending few calories ought just to "power through" from breakfast to dinner. This does not seem to be the case, however, particularly in the developing world, in which resources are allocated for meals at the beginnings and ends of days and nothing more than a snack—if that—intervenes in the middle of the workday.

For those who take it, the two main categories of lunch globally appear to be hot and cold. In some places, such as the United States, lunch can be either hot or cold, but in others, lunch is always a hot or always a cold meal. To some extent, hot lunches are associated with more traditional societies, where lunch is ideally a meal eaten at home or in a convivial setting. Hot lunches also seem more popular in societies that allow for siestas, since they may have a soporific effect. Cold lunches are frequently small lunches, taken in parts of the world where the afternoon is seen as a time for work rather than relaxation. Lunch temperature, interestingly, does not seem to depend much on climate; Scandinavians favor cold sandwiches while Sub-Saharan Africans like soups and stews served with warm mush.

COLD LUNCH

The "Closed-Face" Sandwich

In the contemporary United States, cold lunch is slightly more common than hot lunch, usually taking the form of a sandwich or salad. The designation of these particular foodstuffs as lunch fare, as chapter 1 explains, is relatively recent. Sandwiches are always "closed face" and either assembled at home and toted in brown bags or purchased at deli-style shops. Some of these shops are locally owned while others belong to national chains such as Subway, Potbelly, and Quizno's. American sandwiches are prepared on large, square slices of bread or on long or round rolls, almost always made with white flour and of the fluffy variety. Sandwich fillings usually include more than one element, sometimes chosen by the customer, sometimes suggested by the shop owner or chain's menu. The Carnegie Deli in New York City, for example, offers the "Woody Allen" sandwich with "lotsa corned beef plus lotsa pastrami." According to the Quizno's website, the classic Italian sandwich—capicola, genoa salami, ham, pepperoni, mozzarella, black olives, iceberg lettuce, tomatoes, onions, red wine vinaigrette—was recently dethroned as the most popular sandwich in favor of the mesquite chicken sandwich—chicken, bacon, cheddar, lettuce, tomatoes, onions, and ranch dressing. This echoes both the growing popularity of Chipotle's Tex-Mex flavors and Taco Bell's recent success with its own version of Chipotle's recipes.

Typical meats in American sandwiches reflect the nation's English, Italian, and Jewish heritages, including (potentially in the same sandwich) roast beef, salami, pastrami, roast turkey, bologna, and corned beef. Cheeses are limited to a few, including swiss, provolone, muenster, and American. A twenty-first-century trend in paninis (a peculiar American neologism, since "panini" is the Italian plural of panino), has made mozzarella a more common cheese in American sandwiches, but it is not usually served cold. Lettuce and tomato are the ubiquitous accompaniments to the typical sandwich, which may also be spread with mayonnaise or mustard. The lettuce is often shredded and mounded on the salad. Commonly used mustard is most often of the mild, yellow variety, but perhaps thanks to an aggressive advertising campaign by Grey Poupon, customers are now often offered the option of dijon, too. Ketchup is virtually never used on cold sandwiches, and relish is also exclusively used on hot foods, particularly hot dogs and hamburgers. One notable exception to this is New Orleans's famous muffaletta sandwich, which includes a much-loved olive and pickled vegetable relish under layers of Italian-style meats and cheese. Perhaps to make up for the lack of relish, many sandwich shops serve pickles on the side, completing the lunch with a sour dill spear—never bread-and-butter.

Most sandwiches are of the composite kind—ham and swiss on rye, for example—but a few salads also remain popular with the sandwich-eating public. Tuna fish salad prepared with a mild mixture of chopped celery and mayonnaise is the most frequently found, although customers' fear of fat has led some sandwich shops to begin offering tuna salads without mayonnaise, variously designated "Italian" or "Spanish," suggesting a Mediterranean inspiration. Chicken salad is most often identical to mayonnaise-based tuna salad—so much so that on platters of mixed sandwiches one often has to look embarrassingly close to tell them apart.

Salads for Lunch

In the early 1980s, the lunch salad arose as a rival to the sandwich, which itself had only been ubiquitous for adults since the 1950s. Lunch salads rose in popularity as part of the diet and health craze of the 1970s. Salads appealed (at least theoretically) to those interested in losing weight and in getting more vitamin-rich vegetables in their diets. Salad bars had begun appearing in dinner restaurants in the late 1960s and easily made the transition into lunch-focused delis. Space was cleared and salad bars set up, often incorporating steam table elements, too, so that customers could add interesting materials such as chunks of warm sesame chicken to their salads. The concept of the salad bar as a place to get a healthy and nonfattening lunch was a little garbled in translation, as salad bars offered not only cooked foods but also bacon bits, rich cubes of cheese, and mayonnaise-laden tuna salads as "toppings" for their chopped lettuces. Lettuce in salad bars is almost always a mixture of iceberg and romaine because both are sturdy. Salads are also frequently topped with rich dressings, thousand island, ranch, and blue cheese being three of the creamiest favorites. Lunch thus offers the opportunity to seem to perform virtuously while actually enjoying the "sins" of the high-calorie lunch. As long as there was no bread, the consensus seemed to be, the meal was a "healthy" salad and not actually more material than one would consume in a normal sandwich.

The popularity of lunch salads is also likely the result of the increase in numbers of women in the workforce. Because American women have historically been socialized to worry more about their weight than men have, lunch venues strive to offer female customers something they will not see as fattening. Being seen in public by one's coworkers eating a bright green salad daintily with a fork still fits better into our national ideal for proper female behavior than does chowing down on a mile-high pastrami sandwich. The good (or perhaps bad) news for the self-conscious lady luncher, however, is that she is likely to be consuming just as many calories either way.

While the lunch salad of the composite, salad bar type seems to be uniquely American, the sandwich lunch is not. The most famous consumers of sandwiches in the world are Scandinavians, who remain devoted to the open-faced sandwich, a more architecturally interesting and visually appealing variation on the theme.

Open-Faced Sandwiches

The use of the term "lunch" is complicated in Norway by the presence of another meal before supper. "Dinner" is the most substantial meal of the day, occurring at noon in rural areas and in the early evening, around 5:00 p.m., in urban centers. While breakfast is a hearty affair featuring fish, meat, or cheese, lunch is more simple, consisting of just a few open-faced sandwiches. Dinner is a little heartier than breakfast: potatoes and either meat or fish, vegetables, and gravy made from the meat juices, or a white sauce made from milk, fat, and flour. Another small meal, usually of bread and cheese, is taken later in the evening to tide one over until breakfast.[2]

Most of the lunches that both rural and urban Norwegians eat are brought from home. Typical open-faced sandwiches are sliced ham, cheese, radishes, tomatoes, and dill, providing a mixture of textures, proteins, and colors. Schoolchildren and chief executives alike march off in the morning with bags of open-faced sandwiches separated by layers of waxed paper. One cookbook writer finds similarities between Norwegian sandwiches and Japanese bento boxes, arguing that both inspire creativity. She advises lunch makers, "Your sandwiches should not only taste good, but they should look good, too."[3] There is such uniformity of taste, however, that it is a common saying that lunches always include "one with yellow cheese, one with brown cheese.[4] Brown cheese is the caramelized goat's milk cheese that is a special favorite among Norwegians. Yellow cheese is jarlsberg, a type of cheese that enjoys a bit more popularity worldwide.

A Norwegian cookbook writer confesses that the famous array of open-faced sandwiches that is so much associated with her native culture is both "confusing and delicious." Without proper strategy, the novice is likely to come away unsatisfied. The first rule is not to take everything at once, but to manage the bounty thematically, in courses. Beginning with "salty fish sandwiches, one should return again and yet again to the table, taking [next] meat and cheese sandwiches, and then sweets."[5] The idea of the midday meal as a kind of dance to and from the table is very unlike both the French and southern European traditions of leisurely lingering at the lunch table or of the Anglo-American custom of gobble-and-go.

Far from the uniformity of Norwegian lunches, a British cookbook from 1993 suggested a multicultural array of sandwiches loosely defined, from rotis filled with South African "bunny chow," to "spicy chicken tacos," Greek pita bread filled with chickpeas and feta cheese, and corned beef sandwiches. The same book advised that sandwiches should be frozen because "a frozen sandwich packed in the lunch box will thaw by lunch time and be fresh and cool."[6] Sandwiches have been a part of English culture since the mid-nineteenth century, although they were until recently mostly associated with teatime. The custom of providing a variety of light sandwiches as a pick-me-up between the "dinner" of cold roast meat or cold meat pie and the supper of hot roast meat transformed in the late twentieth century into a culture of the cold sandwich lunch.

When British clothing and household goods retailer Marks and Spencers began offering fresh sandwiches in distinctive triangular packages, lunch culture in England underwent a major change. Having lacked a take-out culture beyond fish and chip shops, British office workers had largely had to rely on food brought from home or pub lunches, delicious but on the heavy side. Pub menus, incidentally, always include that ur-lunch, the ploughman's bread, cheese, and beer that once satisfied Mesopotamian harvesters and all other cultures that have ever grown wheat, made cheese, and practiced the arts of brewing. Other hearty offerings were pork pies, and "bangers and mash."

Marks and Spencers first introduced its now very popular ready-made sandwiches in 1980. According to corporate legend, the lunch-altering event happened by accident when an employee packaged some leftovers from the shop's café and put them out for sale. When they were immediately snapped up, the company experimented with offering ready-made sandwiches at several branches and discovered that there was a very lucrative market. The pioneer sandwiches mimicked the tea sandwiches universally associated with British culture. Bread was thin; fillings were scant and did not require much chewing. One of the first combinations was salmon and tomato, a pairing that a contemporary representative of the company remarked "doesn't sound that appetizing" by 2010. Changing tastes caused salmon and tomato to be dropped from the menu, but prawn mayonnaise, which debuted in 1981, seemingly eons ago in the world of lunch fashions, remains a favorite.[7]

Marks and Spencers was soon followed into the light, premade sandwich market by the drugstore chain, Boots. In 1986, Pret a Manger launched a business solely dedicated to this new English style of lunch, minus the school uniforms and face creams that M&S and Boots also offered. In short order, the staff of Buckingham Palace, as well as the queen herself, became fans, validating the store's essential Britishness.

In 2012, the company's chief executive discussed tailoring menus for local markets in the four regions where the chain operates—Britain, the United States, France, and Hong Kong. According to the company's research, lunchers in Hong Kong expect hot food and regular bargain packages, whereas in France there is much greater demand for desserts as part of lunch than there is in England or the United States. Thus, little pots of chocolate mousse fly off the shelves in Paris alongside triangular packages of *les sandwiches*.[8]

Pret a Manger includes preboxed sushi rolls among its offerings, reflecting the mainstreaming of this East Asian food in Western culture. Sushi is perhaps particularly welcome as lunch fare in the United States and England because it fits neatly into the tradition of cold lunch. Sushi also mirrors the Anglo-American devotion to a protein wrapped in starch.

East Asia provides the other main tradition of cold lunch, including sushi and anything else that can be packed in the many variations of the bento box. The bento box serves as a carrier for meals based on cold rice and assorted proteins and condiments. It is traditionally carried from home, setting it apart from the sandwich and salad culture; these lunches are usually purchased during the workday. The bento box, then, ties the luncher to home while the Western-style deli offers a moment of edible freedom. It can also reinforce gender stereotypes, as one cookbook writer notes that "boys' and men's lunches are packed with more calories than girls' and women's and it is not uncommon to find two carbohydrates, like a sandwich and rice, in one box for a teenage or adult son." Lunch bentos are still primarily prepared by mothers at home, presumably working from models set by their own mothers.[9]

One notable exception to the homemade bento is found in Taiwan. In Taiwan, the *biandang*, a term adapted from the Japanese bento to describe a premade lunch box, has been very popular since before the Second World War. Biandangs are closely associated with rail travel because they are sold in train stations as a whole meal that can be purchased quickly and eaten neatly on board. A Japanese equivalent is the *eki-ben*, or "station bento," which is also sold from railroad station kiosks and often features regional specialties, which connect the meal with the idea of travel between unique places.[10]

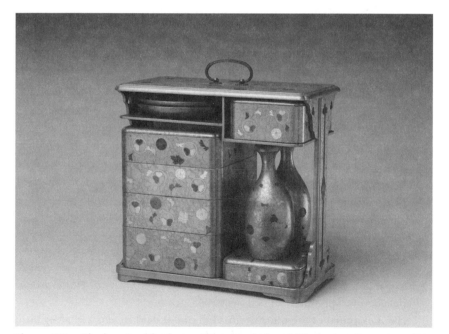

Figure 2.1. Picnic set with chrysanthemum design. Mid-nineteenth century. Edo period. Gold and silver maki-e on "pear-skin" lacquered ground. Source: Art Resource, NYImage Reference: ART377726. © The Metropolitan Museum of Art.

Taiwanese biandangs are not limited to the train station and are also found in business neighborhoods in Taiwan. The meal typically includes rice and either meat, tofu, or fish and pickled vegetables. The biandang as a cheap, convenient meal has also served as a symbol for the economic health of the nation. In May 2012, for example, a student at a public event informed the nation's president, Ma Ying-jeou, that because of price increases in food, "he does not feel full now after eating one biandang." The president seemed to channel Marie Antoinette as he responded, "You don't feel full? So now you need to eat one more biandang?" There was a significant difference when a voter asked Ma's political opponent, "What happens when a biandang can't keep me full?" Ma's opponent, Tsai Ing-wen, responded that the voter needed to "speak out if you don't feel full. That way, the people in power would hear not only the voices of the rich."[11] That the biandang could serve as measure both of national prosperity and as a gauge of sensitivity to the needs of voters reflects the importance of this boxed lunch to Taiwanese society.

Another observer of Taiwanese culture noted that lunch offerings reflect economic well-being in more formal settings, too. When the stock market "is up," meaning that the well off can feel confident of their wealth, "fancy restaurants offering expensive gourmet dishes are crowded with hardly a table unoccupied" in the middle of the day. When the stock market stagnates and slumps, on the other hand, restaurants "may start serving low-priced business lunch or 'all you can eat' meals."[12]

Dosirak is the Korean version of the bento, with some important differences. Japanese bento box lunches are often celebrated as pieces of design, each morsel placed carefully in a thoughtful composition of foodstuffs, sometimes mimicking an animal or cartoon character. Dosiraks, in contrast, contain rice that is not tightly molded, vegetables, kimchi, and a fried egg. As the box travels to school on a child's back, these ingredients are shaken together to create what turns out to be a very palatable mixture. The phenomenon is so fondly recalled that waiters in restaurants will actually shake dosiraks for customers to indulge their nostalgia. As one non-Korean who tried a shaken dosirak in Los Angeles rhapsodized, "All of those elements break apart and fuse together into a glorious whole, not unlike fried rice but minus all that frying business. You have the richness of the egg yolk, the heat of the kimchi, the ocean-flavor of the seaweed and the heartiness of the tofu. It's a fantastic lunch."[13]

In Japan, where bento culture originated, lunch choices are shaped by local ideals of what makes a meal. As one historian of Japanese food culture found in an interview, "Any food with bread is not considered 'filling,' and so for lunch [the interviewee] and his university friends look for *donburi tei shoku*—a large bowl of rice topped with various ingredients." Thus for some, though not all, McDonald's and presumably other American sandwich or burger chains had little appeal as lunchtime venues. Indeed, this particular informant disdained hamburgers in favor of a riceburger, described as "a slice of meat, fish, or vegetable sandwiched between bun-shaped rice patties." When rice took the place of bread, the meal became real, rather than a snack.[14]

In an effort to stir up locavorism in the Miyagi prefecture of Japan, a "specialist cook of traditional cuisine" has begun selling a "classic cuisine lunch box" that one scholar describes as "a way to connect to the culinary heritage of prefectural cooking" through lunch. Although only a lunchbox, this meal "enables visitors to experience the taste of the sophisticated banquet cuisine of the Edo period." Using historical cookbooks, the chef assembles lunches of sashimi, grilled foods, dry boiled foods—usually vegetables—and snacks.[15]

Both northern and southern Russia also have traditions of cold lunching. A cookbook compiled in the last days of the Soviet Union offered lunch menus distinct to the different regions governed by the USSR. A Baltic lunch included flavors from Lithuania, Latvia, and Estonia, such as cold veal meatloaf with horseradish sauce, cucumbers in sour cream, and Riga rye bread, as well as Estonian herring and potato salad. This last dish reflects culinary similarities between the Baltic region and Scandinavia. The meal was to be accompanied by Aquavit, another Scandinavian specialty, and Alexandertort, a kind of cookie sandwich made with lingonberry jam.[16]

An entirely different set of foodways inspires the suggested "Backyard luncheon from the Caucasus," featuring flavors of Georgian cooking that show kinship with Turkish cuisine, hinting more at the warm Mediterranean than the icy Baltic. Cold cucumber and yogurt soup seems very Slavic but also uses ingredients common in Middle Eastern kitchens. The cold tuna in walnut sauce is reminiscent of Persian fesenjan. Cold bulgur and vegetable pilaf and pepper and eggplant salad also suggest Southern influences, while the apricot mousse recommended as dessert and the Vouvray demi sec suggested as accompaniment reflect the major influence of France on Russian elite lifestyles before the Revolution.

In post-soviet Russia, the introduction of private industry has enabled the establishment of fast-food chains such as the American lunch standards, McDonald's and Subway. Beginning in 1999, Teremok, a Russian chain specializing in blinis, has opened restaurants in major cities, with plans to expand into western Europe. Teremok blinis can be stuffed with savory fillings such as red caviar or mushrooms or with sweets such as chocolate or jam. The chain also serves traditional eastern European soups—borscht, mushroom broth—and porridges. Along with beer and cider, Teremok also offers kvass, a particularly Russian beverage made by fermenting rye bread.

The Coldest Lunch

Perhaps the world's strangest venue for a cold lunch is Antarctica, where researchers at McMurdoo Station eat food provided in cafeterias, paid for as part of the researcher's salary. The usual protocol is all-you-can-eat, in direct contradiction to the barren environment beyond the cafeteria's insulated walls. Following the foodways of the West, lunch is served between 11:00 and 1:00 and is distinctly American, consisting of "deli style cold cuts."[17] At the other end of the planet, in the Arctic Circle, where there exist more permanent communities with long-standing traditions, a visitor observed of a nighttime Inuit fishing party that "one night of collaborative fishing will feed the families for weeks to come." One Arctic char, caught, gutted, and dried by the community, will provide "our lunch and dinner for three days."[18] Other Arctic cultures also rely on the ocean's bounty for midday and all other meals. In Greenland, for example, a common lunch is dried cod with whale blubber, typically served cold.[19]

HOT LUNCH

The choice between hot and cold lunch seems to be one most common in urban and industrial areas of the world, where there is constant access to both refrigeration and fuel. The contemporary consciousness of globalization, too, leads to trends in lunching that reflect that reality. Whereas the choices that the Nigerian blogger mentioned above were all based on local foodways, the typical office worker in Los Angeles can dither over whether to "go" Thai, Mexican, Japanese, American Jewish, or Vietnamese, among other possibilities for lunch.

While sandwiches and salads tend to reflect a somewhat homogeneous American cuisine, the world of the hot lunch is much more culturally diverse. Among the most common hot lunches in the United States today is a slice of pizza, an Italian American creation. In some ways a kind of warmed-up, open-faced sandwich, the slice has many advantages to recommend it as lunch. Not least of these is that it tends to be cheap and quickly obtained. It is cheap because its ingredients are purchased in bulk and do not include anything hard to procure or prepare. The labor required to make a pizza can produce roughly eight lunches, or something like $20, whereas a sandwich or salad, with its custom-ordered components, which must be layered and (in the case of the sandwich) wrapped, only feeds one. The usual toppings for pizza—pepperoni, sliced onions, green peppers, black olives, chopped vegetables—can offer the customer variety with very little extra labor on the part of the pizza maker, who only has to toss them on.

Pizza's warmth also enables the luncher to feel satisfied while not actually eating very much food—just a bit of bread, some tomato sauce, and a little less cheese than might go into a sandwich. Because they are cheap and tend to make people happy, pizzas appear frequently for group lunches.

In North America, the lunchtime slice is rivaled by the takeout hamburger, more typical in areas with office parks than in dense urban centers. Where there are no sidewalks to stroll in pursuit of lunch, drive-through hamburger chains offer a quick way to get lunch and return to work. Although the major fast food hamburger chains—McDonald's, Burger King, and Wendy's—serve meals all day, about one-third of business is typically lunch fare.[20] The burger has a unique history in the United States as a food that is considered legitimate for both lunch and dinner. While it is unusual to hear of families dining on turkey sandwiches in the evening, for instance, a sack of hamburgers may be consumed at any time after noon, though it has not yet breached the breakfast barrier. In Canada, the famous donut-and-coffee chain, Tim Hortons, is angling to challenge McDonald's for control of the lunch market. By introducing hot sandwiches—paninis—Tim Hortons hopes to keep its breakfast crowd coming back for lunch.[21]

In 2013, Subway had the largest share of the lunch market for business travelers in the United States, a group that, though not perfectly representative of the larger working population, is also not radically different. Until this year, McDonald's had had the largest share of the market. Subway and McDonald's are followed by Starbucks, which, although it only has a limited line of lunch items, probably gains market share through ubiquity.[22]

Other major players in the lunch market are Taco Bell and its newer rival, Chipotle, which both specialize in Tex-Mex food. Chipotle has earned the praise of "real food" advocates for its sourcing policies, but Taco Bell has recently made a blatant and so far successful attempt to challenge Chipotle's appeal to health-conscious eaters by creating a menu that neatly mimics Chipotle's but costs less. The older chain's leaders seem confident that money will trump agricultural ethics for the lunch crowd.

Once a mainstay of the lunch hour, the simple melted cheese sandwich, often served with cream of tomato soup, perhaps seems old-fashioned in the new world of multicultural fast food. Perhaps a clear sign that grilled cheese sandwiches are outmoded is that the Milk Truck, a trendy New York food truck, has taken up their cause, identifying the regional origins of each cheese (Wisconsin gruyere, Vermont aged cheddar) and using only bread from star bakers such as Balthazar and Blue Ribbon. In a nod to tradition, the Milk Truck also serves tomato soup. Famous Indian-born actress and cookbook author Madhur Jaffrey offers her own take on the classic, using sharp cheddar, cilantro, and either fresh green chilies or "the pickled Greek ones." Some in her family like to add a mixture of hardboiled eggs and mustard to the cheese before toasting the sandwich in a buttered frying pan.[23]

The cheese present at the dawn of the American grilled cheese sandwich obsession, Kraft, has ironically been suffering from sluggish sales, largely because people do not want grilled American cheese sandwiches anymore. There are now so many options for lunch, including paninis, which provide some of the pleasures but less of the griddle grease of the classic grilled cheese, that the humble melted-American-on-white is battling for its life. Kraft has been trying to revive flagging sales of its plastic-wrapped single slices by encouraging nostalgia for grilled cheese and tomato soup lunches.

As one marketing executive for the company explained in 2007, "If we can grow grilled cheese, and get grilled cheese back on the list of quick menu options, we can grow our Kraft singles business." To the end of "growing" grilled cheese sandwiches, the company launched its "Have a Happy Sandwich" campaign, complete with the requisite social media campaign and contest to produce the most appealing variation on the theme.[24]

It is interesting to reflect that two of the biggest trends in American lunches—pizza and tacos—are foods that represent the hybridization of other cuisines with American foodways. It may be that when they lunch Americans are more likely to take an adventurous approach than when they dine, perhaps reasoning that it is "just lunch," a smaller meal, and that since they are away from home physically, they might as well leave home culinarily, too.

This pattern of transcultural eating holds true also in Kenya, where samosas are a popular lunch food, delicious vestiges of the British Empire's importation of Indian indentured workers to Kenya. East Africans tend to eat only two meals per day, one around noon and the other in the evening. One cookbook writer suggests this as a typical East African meal, appropriate for either lunch or dinner: chapattis, samusas [samosas], avocado and papaya salad, groundnut sauce with rice, and kashata, a coconut candy for dessert.[25]

A typical African meal is the common lunch of a starch such as rice or ugali (made from corn flour) accompanied by an assortment of stews. In some cultures of Africa, it is expected that the stew and starch will be mixed, but in others combination is not considered proper. Thus, one researcher noted that when employers feed their employees, "it is far preferable for the employer to serve the two dishes separately as many workers are likely to complain bitterly when they receive food mixed on one plate." The separation of the two dishes can be understood when one considers that the traditional method of eating the meal was to roll the starch into small balls which are then dipped into the stew. While people who eat this way consume starch and stew simultaneously, others prefer to eat first one, then the other. In Xhosa communities, for example, "the meat is eaten first, then the porridge, then the gravy."[26] The impact of Indian cuisines in Kenya reappears when the stews are served, as they commonly are, with Indian-style chapattis instead of rice or corn mush.[27]

Despite many cultural differences, the hot lunch of a stew served with a kind of porridge is typical throughout Sub-Saharan Africa. Stews made of vegetables, sometimes with small pieces of meat included, go by many names but can be found in most places. What varies region to region are the kinds of vegetables, the kinds of flavoring, and perhaps most significant, the starch base with which the stew is served. In some places, such as Nigeria, the starch is millet, an ancient African grain; in others it is corn, a more recent introduction. South Africans prefer corn and "throughout the region may start the day with a bowl of sugar-sweetened cornmeal porridge, enjoy a bowl of savory porridge and vegetables for lunch, snack on roasted corn on the cob in the afternoon, and eat samp—another cornmeal dish—and beans with grilled steak or roast chicken for dinner."[28]

In Senegal, the staple grain is rice. A typical, bountiful Senegalese luncheon can include *thiebou dienn*, senegalese tea, and mangoes. Thiebou dienn, also known internationally as jolof rice, is a well-loved dish of rice flavored with onions, tomato, chilies, and a variety of vegetables, usually including okra and squash. The rice is typically served with fish stew. Food historian Jessica Harris suggests that this meal is best enjoyed thusly: "Spread a beautiful European tablecloth on the clean floor or carpet and arrange large enamel serving bowls on the floor. Present each guest with a 2½-yard piece of bright African fabric called a *pagne* to use as a wrap or large napkin. Eat with your hands. Music should be Senegalese classics like Youssou N'Dour and the Star band."[29]

This appetizing lunch appears in a much less leisurely manner in the United States, where many Senegalese women "make ends meet by running small, homey eateries tucked into apartments in the tenements where they live." These underground restaurants cater to a lunch crowd of Senegalese taxi drivers and businessmen. Active in the bustle of U.S. urban life, expatriates can have a warm taste of home at midday.[30]

For Thai city dwellers, hot lunch food often comes from street carts—just as informal as the Senegalese kitchens of the United States but more public. In

Thailand, lunch is usually the biggest meal of the day, but Thais may eat much more often than three times a day, as the omnipresence of food vendors cleverly able to cook something with the sparsest equipment suggests. Believing that a night's sleep will be better following a smaller meal than a larger one, Thais prefer to snack lightly throughout the day with one somewhat bigger snack in the middle of the day, long before bedtime. Noodle soups, quick-fried meats and vegetables, and dumplings of many kinds are some of the foods dispensed from carts that can add up to a midday meal in Thailand, where there are no strict rules about what time of day one eats any particular food.[31]

Hot lunches are also the norm in the Caribbean, where lunch can take many forms and is, according to one regional cookbook, the best way to taste local cuisines. Virginie and George A. Elbert advise visitors to the Caribbean that "the easiest places to sample the local cookery are the public beaches. There are normal gathering places for local island people and for tourists who break away from the resorts looking for . . . better lunches." In Puerto Rico, one might find deep-fried empanadas sold from a hut by the road, or grilled fish or skewered meat. Food trucks serving crepes filled with "bewildering variety" can be found at the beaches in Guadeloupe. Lobsters are for sale for lunch on Tortola, as are "fabulous rotis," reflecting both the ocean bounty that surrounds the island and the South Asian influence on its cuisine. Grilled meats are cooked up in mobile kitchens at many of the other beaches in the region.[32]

HOT AND COLD LUNCHES

While in North America, lunch eaters usually choose to have a hot or a cold lunch, in other parts of the world, the two types are regularly combined in one meal. North African lunches, for example, include elements of both cold and hot, starting with a variety of salads, including the transnationally popular *ful mudammas*, a cold salad of fava beans that goes by many names. In Egypt, an old saying designates ful mudammas "the rich man's breakfast, the shopkeeper's lunch, the poor man's supper." In other words, everyone eats it but some have more elaborate meals waiting for them, while to others *ful* is a feast.[33] A typical recipe for ful mudammas includes cooked fava beans, olive oil, chopped herbs, and finely diced tomato.

In North African cooking more generally, other dishes besides ful may recur through the day. The midday meal known as *al ghada* includes small plates of salads that may turn up again as appetizers for the evening meal. These dishes, such as cucumber with mint, oranges, and radishes, and a grilled pepper salad, *slata fel fel,* are frequently followed by couscous and tajine.[34] Where Anglo-American culture dictates that lunch and dinner should be entirely different meals, North African culture allows for repetition of themes.

The couscous that follows salads in North African cultures takes the lunch from cold to hot and also echoes the stew-and-mush pattern found in Sub-Saharan Africa. Tajines, made just with vegetables such as eggplant, tomato, and squash, or also with chicken, lamb, or fish, may reappear at dinnertime, too, freshly cooked under the ceramic towers that bear their name. With lunch, one drinks hot mint tea or a yogurt-based drink that is similar to the south Asian lassi.

In the Middle East, lunches continue the tradition of mixing cold and hot, including close cousins of North African salads. Instead of stews, however, the peoples of this region are more likely to eat grilled meats, served with hot flatbreads rather than couscous. Throughout the Middle East, patties—both meat and made from chickpeas or beans—also appear, ready to be tucked warm into bread pockets filled with cold salads. As in North Africa, all of the dishes one eats at lunch can also be considered dinner fare.

Depending on one's social class, lunch in the Middle East may be a private or a very public meal. Cookbook writer Maideh Mazda notes, "If you walk down the avenue in Tehran during lunch hour, you will find the mason, the cobbler, the storekeeper—everybody—eating *nan va panir,* or bread and cheese. . . . Very often Persians eat *nan va panir* with either fresh mint or fresh tarragon. In summer, when grapes are abundant, they eat *nan va panir* with grapes."[35] This roving lunch fits well with the assessment of one Baghdad native who had lived in Tehran that "in both Iraq and Iran the eating tradition is not oriented toward the three square meals a day as it is in America. There is frequent snacking and nibbling."[36]

The bread consumed in the open would most likely be *nan-e sangak,* or stone-baked bread, the type of bread most associated with lunchtime. Other meals have other breads. Nan-e sangak is a whole wheat bread, reckoned especially good for holding cubes of kebab, served with fresh herbs. So complementary are the flavors of the bread and charred meat that the baker and kebab seller usually set up shop very close to each other.[37] Another common hot meal for workers out in public is lamb soup, *abgoosht,* which is ladled from large cooking vats on the street into the *deeze,* small ceramic pots that Iranians carry with them for just this purpose.[38]

For the economic elite, soup from the street and strolling kebabs are not a proper lunch. Wealthy families dine indoors as a family, partaking of a variety of warm dishes in which both rice and bread play important roles. Remembering her childhood in Iran, Maideh Mazda fondly recalled lunchtime rituals: "After the hand washing ceremony, two servants, similarly attired, entered, bowed before us, and offered us tea. Shortly afterward, these servants spread a white tablecloth over a blue Persian rug and set the 'table' for lunch. In those days it was customary to eat lunch on the floor. . . . On a large copper platter the servants brought in various types of *khoreshes* (sauces), *chelo* (cooked rice), *polos* (pilafs), Nane Lavash (thin Persian bread), *mast* (yogurt), Mahi Dudi (smoked fish) and many other delicacies." The family ate together, unhurried, taking a little from each dish.[39]

A contemporary Iranian cookbook suggests a lunch menu in the street food tradition, perhaps more in tune with the less formal lunching style of Western societies: "Ground meat or chicken kabab and grilled tomato with sumac, lavash bread, fresh herbs and yogurt drink."[40] In fact, this meal is not too far off from a hamburger and milkshake.

LUNCH AND SIESTA

Where tradition sends workers of all kinds home for an afternoon nap, this kind of street-fare lunch is unheard of. In societies of the northern Mediterranean, and in former colonies of Spain and Portugal, the long lunch and postprandial nap remain common, although Western 24/7 business practices may be encroaching. A good example of the difference between the lunch-is-a-brief-pause philosophy and the siesta tradition can be seen in the account of one American man adjusting to life in Greece.

The expatriate, a professional with a position in an office, began at his new job in Greece by bringing sandwiches from home and eating them at noon. However, "no one else seemed interested in eating then." By the time he had finished lunch, colleagues had begun tidying up their desks, "turning off their computers, and leaving the office." The office became a quiet and lonely place for him between 1:00 and 4:00 p.m. Then, just as his "energy was fading and he searched for coffee or better yet chocolate," his coworkers returned, "refreshed, as if it were another morning." They had gone home for a substantial lunch and a nap, after which they would work until late evening and go home again to enjoy a light meal before bed. Experimenting with the ways of his new home, the expat was soon enjoying lunches of "caramelized oven-braised vegetable dishes, stuffed vegetables, crusty breads, and a glass or two of wine" with his wife, followed by a blissful nap in a darkened room. Far from a solitary meal grabbed on the go, lunch became "a weekday retreat" for this man and his wife. Her daily routine was clearly also altered, as she now became responsible for lunch as a substantial meal for which she should also be home.[41]

There is some difference in Greece between urban and rural habits in contemporary society. Urban Greeks prefer a lunch that is lighter than the evening meal, while in rural areas, lunch remains the main meal of the day. Both businesses and schools close after lunch, a habit that is only possible in the kinds of small communities where no one ever gets too far from home during the day. Even when resting at home after lunch, many Greeks indulge in small sweets and return to the world of activity only after drinking coffee at home.[42]

Many of the countries of South America inherited similar Mediterranean meal habits from the Spanish empire. In Buenos Aires, according to one travel guide, lunch begins at 1:00 p.m. and may last for two hours. Perhaps because breakfast is just a small meal consisting of a roll and *café con leche*, lunches for the middle class have several courses, including appetizers in the antipasto style—thin slices of meats and cheeses, soup, a main dish, salad, dessert, and coffee. As of 1998, one writer found that "business lunches are still a relatively uncommon phenomenon," perhaps indicating that the enjoyment of the long lunch in an intimate setting has high value for Argentines.[43] More recently, reviews of popular restaurants mention "the 45-minutes and gone business lunch crowd," suggesting that priorities have changed for some in Buenos Aires at least.[44]

The soporific effects of some dishes can determine when they are eaten. In Brazil, for example, the dish *feijoada* is a specialty only enjoyed for lunch on Saturdays. This is a rich black bean and shredded meat stew considered one of Brazil's national specialties. One cultural interpreter explains, "*feijoada* is such a heavy dish, it should be eaten for lunch, after which people can go to the beach to sleep it off."[45]

Far from retreating to their private homes for a hot meal, laborers in Uruguay, whether in the countryside or in cities, routinely set up portable grills to prepare roast leg of lamb for a shared lunch.[46] For others in South America, soups make an easier lunch. In Paraguay, for example, a common lunch is stew made with beef, beans, corn, and yucca. Less filling and also popular are soups such as *pucheros*, *locros*, and *caldos*, which have different ingredients in different parts of the Spanish-speaking world.[47] In Venezuela and Colombia, however, *arepas* suffice, not just for dinner but for breakfast and lunch, too. These flat, round corn meal cakes are filled with cheese, spinach, chicken, avocado, pork, scrambled eggs, beef, black beans, or any combination of the above.[48]

In La Paz, Bolivia, "a common urban meal pattern consists of a light breakfast of coffee and bread, a midmorning *saltena* (meat pie snack), a heavy multicourse lunch, teatime pastries in the afternoon, and a light dinner." The multicourse lunch includes appetizer, soup, main dish, and dessert. Thalia Rios, a foreigner who lived in the city, noted that Sunday lunches usually featured a "spicy dish" like *picante de lengua*, which was "more extravagant than daily fare" and perhaps, like *feijoada* in Brazil, induced napping.[49]

Sometimes a hot lunch is a special event in itself. Remembering a childhood in Puerto Rico, chef Yvonne Ortiz recalled, "As a curious teenager," in Humacao, where her grandmother lived,

> I wandered the streets around the town looking for something interesting to do. One possibility was to eat lunch in the *fonda*, a kind of casual restaurant like the French *bistro* or Italian *trattoria*. The menu usually had typical peasant fare: tripe soup, boiled root vegetables, and rice and beans. These occasions became a ritual for me every summer, something I looked forward to all year.

During the school year, she did not fare too badly either, for "I had a nanny, Delfa, who used to make this delicious [white bean] soup. At lunchtime I would run home from school and find her waiting for me with a steaming bowl of bright red soup filled with white beans and chunks of salami." In contemporary Puerto Rico, the same writer notes that these traditional lunch items are in competition with the mainland staples of fast food cuisine—pizza, burgers, and sandwiches, as well as salad bars, a typically North American mixture of hot and cold options. These changes reflect a transition from the older Spanish-influenced siesta-taking culture of the island to a more restless American model.[50]

FRENCH LUNCH

While contemporary French people do not typically take a siesta, they do enjoy long lunch hours, and it is considered perfectly appropriate for workers of all kinds and salary levels to drink wine, beer, or cider at lunch. This tolerance reflects the nation's importance as a wine-producing region, but also the reality that France never experienced the powerful temperance movements that altered social expectations in both England and America.

One of the most popular kinds of lunch restaurants in contemporary Paris is the *couscouserie*, a vestige of France's imperial history in North Africa. The introduction of couscous as urban French lunch fare created a taboo-busting hybrid because North African Islam does not typically allow for the drinking of wine, a common accompaniment to the Parisian couscous lunch.

The French traditionally do not consider eggs breakfast food and are more likely to serve them for dinner, but several egg dishes are considered acceptable for lunch fare. One contemporary Parisian noted that "sometimes I'll order an omelette for lunch, but only in very expensive restaurants where they know how to prepare them" because "there's nothing more horrifying than a poorly cooked egg, don't you agree?" Another Parisian favorite lunchtime egg dish, both at home and in cafes, is a *frisee* salad served with bacon vinaigrette with a lightly poached egg on top.[51]

The French are, of course, also famous for their lunchtime soups, particularly *soupe* à *l'oignon*, typically served in an earthenware crock and topped with a slice of toast drowned in melting cheese. This soup brings together in one bowl the soup-and-sandwich combination that has been popular in American diners and luncheonettes since the 1920s. Another lunchtime soup popular in French cities is *pho*, the anise-flavored broth and noodle soup adopted from Vietnam, a former colony of France.

While living temporarily in Switzerland, an American family discovered a profound difference between the two cultures' treatments of the midday meal. When the family returned to the United States, the family's mother asked her son what was "the most difficult aspect of his transition" from his life in Geneva. Without a moment's hesitation, he said "lunch." In Geneva, schools provide two-hour lunch breaks so that students can return home to eat with their families. The boy's mother recalled this interlude as "a relaxed lunch period that left time for a game of soccer with friends, review of a French lesson, or just a rest." By contrast, the American lunch period, scheduled for half an hour, was in reality made even shorter because kids encouraged each other to finish quickly so that all could be dismissed for outdoor play.[52] This seemingly idyllic version of lunch, of course, relies on having one parent at home to prepare the food and on short distances between schools and homes, features that are not common to all communities.

CHANGING LUNCH PATTERNS IN CHINA

A long tradition of soup making in China places the nation in the hot lunch tradition. Soups are often served with noodles to make the meal more filling. The Chinese techniques of wok cooking and deep frying also make it possible to serve hot lunches quickly that are similar in style to typical dinner dishes. In Chinese American restaurants, lunch menus offer dishes that are also found on the dinner menu, only in slightly smaller servings and thus at lower prices. As in North Africa, there is generally not a distinct difference between lunch and dinner dishes.

In rural southern China, one anthropologist notes, "It can be seen from the way it is arranged that lunch is the main meal of the day" for Chaoshan people. Families eat together, enjoying rice and "plenty of meat and vegetable dishes and soup." The leisure and community given to the meal are similar to that found in elite Iranian homes, as is the profusion of dishes.[53]

In southwest China, among the Lahu people, lunchboxes play an important role in local wedding ceremonies. To symbolize their unification through marriage, bride and groom jointly close a lunchbox made in the traditional style out of bamboo sticks. In this ceremony, "The bride holds the container with her left hand and the groom holds the cover with his right hand. Standing side-by-side they cross their arms in an interlocked position to unify the box into one." Reopening the box, they then eat its traditional contents of sticky rice together.[54]

Typical lunches in urban China today are less ritualistic. From the 1950s through the end of the twentieth century, state-owned eating places dominated the public dining scene, but their high prices kept many workers away. Since the loosening of the economic control of the central government, a greater variety of restaurants can be found in Chinese cities, and it has become more common to go out to eat, especially for lunch. Unlike their Western counterparts, each with an individually wrapped sandwich, burrito, or salad, Chinese office workers are more likely to share dishes at casual restaurants. This practice, however, may be on the wane for two reasons. The introduction of American fast food chains to Chinese cities brings with it the individual serving as norm. Local events have served to reinforce the attractiveness of this idea. In 2003, an outbreak of SARS brought to public attention the health risks of shared meals, helping to support the trend toward individual servings, which can now even be found at some banquets.[55]

Building on the success of Western fast food restaurants Kentucky Fried Chicken, McDonald's, Pizza Hut, and Taco Bell, Chinese entrepreneurs have opened their own chains such as Yonghe Dawang, which specializes in noodle dishes, or Sun Ya Da Bao, famous for steamed buns. Noodle carts, ubiquitous on city streets, also provide quick lunches for China's urban population. In China, as in other countries where American fast food chains have set up shop, offerings cater to local tastes but also reflect an outsider's view of American culture, resulting in such interesting offerings as the abalone bacon mushroom pizza. Pizza Hut in China also serves red wine, perhaps hewing closer to the diffusely Italian origins of the food than the chain does at home in America.

Figure 2.2.   Tiffin wallahs near Churchgate Railway Station. Source: Corbis 42-29214919.

Perhaps the most important change in Chinese lunching came in the 1980s, when the national government put an end to what had been a long and respected tradition of napping after lunch. Seeking to increase productivity nationwide, officials banned *xiuxi*, the Chinese version of the siesta. One American had an opportunity to witness this tradition before its demise when he visited an offshore oil rig staffed by Chinese workers and featuring the latest technologies. At noon, all of the Chinese workers turned off their machines and went first for lunch and then for a nap. The workers had merely taken with them mainland Chinese traditions. At home, through the 1970s, "Typically, from Monday to Saturday, a bell would ring at 11:30 a.m., signaling the beginning of the lunch break. The street would soon be packed with people on their bicycles rushing home from work. With kids coming home for lunch, parents usually prepared a meal more formal than noodle soup." Once the meal was finished and the dishes washed, everyone lay down to nap. Around 2:00 p.m. naps ended and crowds of people poured back into the streets for the second rush hour of the day as they returned to work.[56]

Although most Chinese were quite dedicated to this pattern, by the 1970s, critics of tradition worried that it was keeping the nation from developing its full economic potential because it had to compete against countries like the United States, where business did not come to a halt each day for three hours. Others worried that getting rid of the daily nap would make the lunch hour chaotic for workers, who would now have to wait in lines at cafeterias and food carts for their meals instead of eating at home. One Western traveler in China encountered the problem of the strictly timed state-run restaurant in the town of Yangshuo. There, the People's Restaurant, run by the government and the only restaurant in town, only provided a ninety-minute window of time for each meal. If you missed the deadline "by one minute, you wouldn't be served." Food could only be purchased by first buying coupons from an unfriendly clerk. The particular visitor found the food of the People's Restaurant "simple, but good," eating a bowl of rice with greens and a bowl of rice with spicy tofu as well as beer served in soup bowls.[57]

By the mid-1980s, the nation's government had reorganized the workday to eliminate the after-lunch naps and, for the most part, to keep workers from going home for lunch at all.[58]

Lunch in twenty-first-century Russia is also undergoing a change in the emergence from communist culture. The Russian Revolution profoundly changed lunch in what became the Soviet Union. Government-subsidized cafeterias were the most common lunch providers for urban Russians, made especially necessary by the regime's encouragement of female employment. With women in the workplace, men and children had no lunch to return home to, so each member of the family was provided lunch at school or his or her workplace. With the decline of the Soviet Union in the 1990s, state subsidization has disappeared, making workplace cafeterias more expensive and thus less appealing. Corporate cafeterias provide a traditional Russian lunch of soup, a meat dish, a starch dish of potatoes or pasta, and a salad, usually of the pickled vegetable variety. The drink which usually accompanies this meal is *kompot*—an infusion of dried fruits in hot water. Tea and a dessert, typically a pastry, often follow this meal. As cafeterias become less of a bargain financially, urban Russians alternately patronize street stalls or a new generation of restaurants offering *biznes lanch* (business lunch), a hot meal that is prepared and eaten quickly in a restaurant.[59] Business lunches are popular for their good economic value, too, especially in Moscow, where food is very expensive. A writer in the *Moscow News* recommends the Club Petrovich, where business lunch offerings are "often heavy on offal—liver stroganoff with buckwheat being a favourite." The availability of a buffet serving soup and salad as well as small cakes makes up for what may not be everyone's favorite main dishes.[60]

TIFFINS: NOT QUITE HOT, NOT QUITE COLD

A legacy of the British Empire, the use of the term "tiffin" to describe a small, midday meal has survived and become uniquely Indian. One writer recalled asking a group of workers what they were doing as they paused in their labor, only to be told, "we're doing tiffin," designating the meal as an action, not merely a consumable. These workmen's tiffins depend on the season, in cooler weather consisting of "puffed rice, toasted chickpeas [and] samosas," but in very hot weather being nothing more than rice flakes soaked in water, served with sugar and coconut flakes.[61]

Office workers lunch on tiffins delivered by special delivery services and containing an assortment of dishes in small quantities such as rice, dal, and vegetable stew. Tiffin carriers are also known as *dabbawalas*; there are several thousand of them at work in Mumbai, the city where this tradition predominates. Recruited by family members from villages outside the city, the dabbawalas must quickly learn their way around the city but also need to memorize the diverse set of markings on the tiffin boxes they will be both delivering and collecting. Markings may be numbers, letters, symbols, or geographic shapes and are painted on the boxes in a variety of colors.

So important are these lunch carriers to the functioning of Mumbai that in 2003 the British prince Charles asked to meet some dabbawalas and also fretted

Figure 2.3. Chinese construction workers lunching on site. Source: Corbis 42-29214919.

that his conversation would keep them from their work. By one commentator's account, the dabbawalas are able to "deliver *dabbas* [tiffins] from one point to another several km away, through a pretty complex system of picking up the *dabba*, loading and unloading at numerous points in handcarts, buses and trains resulting in only one mistake in millions of cases."[62]

To serve the expatriate community in the United States, tiffin services have sprung up in major urban areas such as New York City and Chicago. American tiffins, however, are not transported from individual homes but rather filled in central kitchens, making the service more like a subscription to takeout than a taste of home cooking. Patrons pay for a week's worth of lunches and may be offered choices, another variation on the traditional process in which the woman making the tiffin decided on its contents.

For those Indians who do not lunch from a tiffin, there are other notable lunch customs. In Karnataka, in southern India, even in elegant restaurants, lunch is served on a banana leaf and might include fillets of fish "aflame with the redness of the local bedige," chilies with a variety of vegetable dishes and rice. Rather than a sweet dessert, the meal typically concludes with "curd rice," made of "small-grained rice cooked with plain yogurt" and seasoned with mustard seeds, salt, and curry leaves. This savory pudding is consumed with fiery yogurt-cured chilies.[63]

At the Golden Temple of the Sikh faith, Amritsar's holiest site, all are welcome for lunch in the *langar*, or dining hall. Visitors sit cross-legged on the floor and raise their arms to standing servers to receive the freshly made bread. This bread is then eaten with scoops of cooked lentils and rice prepared as a simple pilaf "glistening with ghee." Once lunch is complete, diners receive a portion of semolina halva that is then consecrated by being carried into the temple and divided so that half can be returned to the holy site and half eaten by the devotee.[64]

Parathas are essential for weekend lunching in Delhi. There the Paranthewali Gali, or "alley of paratha makers," serves "a mixture of working-class and middle-class families out for their Sunday lunch" with as many as eighteen different varieties of paratha, a stuffed, savory bread cooked in a tandoor. Among the possibilities for paratha filling are potato, cauliflower, carrots, peas, or cashews. Sweet parathas are stuffed with "solidified milk" (*mewa*) or sometimes just sugar. At one paratha restaurant, the proprietor urged a foreign visitor to eat more and more, remarking, "You'll never eat a meal like this in America. Who will feed you with so much love in that cold, rich country?" The paratha lunch served as a tempting symbol of hospitality.[65]

In a Gujarati home, where cookbook author Chitrita Banerji had lunch, "the first thing I noticed was the rolled up khandavi," which are chickpea flour and buttermilk pancakes rolled up and sprinkled with coconut and mustard seeds. There were vegetable stews and

> fried whole wheat breads called theplas. Frequent dips into the pickle containers were irresistible. In between, we sampled ladoos—spherical sweets, made with wheat flour, brown sugar and ghee. Portions of rice and khichdi (rice cooked together with green . . . moong dal) were served with hot, melted ghee poured on top.

The meal was accompanied by small bowls of *khadi*, a buttermilk and chickpea flour soup and concluded with *oondhiu*, "that classic of Gujarati cuisine." Banerji describes this dish as "a perfect blend of seasonal vegetables, exquisitely spiced and dotted with tiny dumplings flavored with fenugreek seeds." As it was served, she "noticed that my own excitement was matched by the anticipatory exhalations of everyone around me." As common as such a lunch might be to her hosts, Banerji noticed, they still appreciated it fully.[66]

A Parsi cookbook writer offers an interesting study in contrasts with her "traditional" and "modern" versions of lunch. The traditional Sunday lunch is a pottage of lentils and vegetables made with chicken or lamb; caramelized fried rice; shrimp, squid, or fish balls; simple onion *kachumbar*; mangoes, or tangerines. For the modern "light summer lunch" she recommends a meal more reflective of Western health food trends: eggs on anything, served over sweet-sour tomatoes, toasted *papads*, sunflower sprouts with a dressing of rice bran oil and lemon juice, and fruit.[67]

As noted above, lunch seems especially suited to experimentation and blending of foodways, even as it may also serve as a daily reaffirmation of tradition. The newest trend in urban lunching is the glamorized food truck, which became popular in American cities in the second decade of the twenty-first century. Food trucks had a long history of serving workers on construction sites, usually offering basic cold sandwiches and often items cooked on a grill, depending on the size of the truck. The larger box trucks were able to offer grilled dishes such as hot dogs, hamburgers, egg dishes, and hot sandwiches. Food trucks fitted out in the backs of pickups tended to supply prewrapped sandwiches and packaged snacks. Larger food trucks offered food made to order and primarily stuck to diner cuisine.

In Los Angeles, however, where many construction workers were Mexican American, food trucks, or *loncheras*, provided dishes to appeal to this particular clientele. Taco trucks became popular with late-night partygoers and others, expanding their audience beyond the working person's lunch. The now-famous

Figure 2.4.   Portland, Oregon's famous food trucks. Source: Heather Arendt Anderson.

Kogi truck then expanded the offerings beyond the traditional by introducing the Korean taco, a blending of local LA foodways.

The city of Portland, Oregon, institutionalized its food trucks in 1987 by offering four permanent parking spots in a busy area of town. The space and the numbers of trucks have since grown to include a full city block, with multinational flavors so diverse one can eat one's way across the world from truck to truck.

Despite the popularity of the food truck lunch, which brings lobster rolls, falafel, souvlaki, grilled cheese, barbecue, and of course tacos to New York

Figure 2.5. Lunchtime in New York City, 2013. Source: Craig Holden.

City's business districts, however, arcane city laws make it hard for trucks to operate and thrive. The existing system favors the "dirty water dog" carts that have long been a mainstay of the city's streets. Another challenge to the hotdog cart is emerging as recent waves of immigration from Muslim countries create a market and supply for halal food lunch carts. Filling city air with the perfume of spices and grilling meat, halal carts offer meals such as lamb and rice or chicken and rice to customers of many cultural backgrounds.

Never "just lunch," this midday meal globally is a nexus of municipal politics, cultural adventure, and assimilation both into and out of dominant national foodways.

LUNCH AT HOME

Much to the delight of fast food chains, almost no one in America eats lunch at home anymore. Worldwide, a little less than half of all women and about three-quarters of all men are in the paid workforce Monday to Friday. The majority of school-age children spend their weekdays in classrooms from morning to late afternoon. This leaves only the weekend for families to lunch at home. While the tradition of the lavish after-church Sunday lunch may survive in some communities, Saturday lunches are more likely a free-for-all in families with children. Others living less hectically replace weekend lunch with brunch, enjoyed outside the home (and the subject of another book in this series).

In the United States, the last golden era of lunch at home ended in the 1960s, but up to that point, and beginning in the early twentieth century, lunch was a popular topic for cookbooks. Titles such as *365 Luncheon Dishes*, *What to Have for Luncheon*, and *100 Luncheon Dishes*, all published around the turn of the century, provided interested readers with a plethora of ideas for the meal. Before the advent of the at-home lunch party, lovingly treated by these many volumes, family lunch was a simple affair.

Writing in 1881, cookbook author Catherine Owen lamented of the United States that "luncheon is usually in this country, either a forlorn meal of cold meat or hash, or else a sort of early dinner, both of which are a mistake."[1] The great mistress of British culinary arts, Isabella Beeton, described just such an approach to lunch in her famous book *Household Management*. Beeton admitted that lunch was "a very necessary meal between an early breakfast and a late dinner," and suggested that, with regular exercise, a healthy person ought to have a meal every four hours. Nonetheless, lunch required little thought: "The remains of cold joints, nicely garnished, a few sweets, or a little hashed meat, poultry, or game are the usual items placed on the table for luncheon along with bread and cheese, biscuits and butter, etc." Beeton's description of this meal as "set out on the table" suggests something taken casually, perhaps by different family members at different times, more like a buffet than a formal meal. If something heartier were desired, a rump steak, veal chops, or kidneys could be served—Owen's "early dinner." In homes with children, Beeton noted, mothers often took lunch in the nursery with their children, relegating the meal to even lower status in terms of formality.[2]

For lunch to be *luncheon*, and not this kind of afterthought of a meal, Catherine Owen advised later in the century that it must be "as unlike [dinner] as possible for variety's sake." To make lunch a minor dinner was to ignore the truth that there were many dishes more perfectly suited to a midday meal than to an evening repast. Owen acknowledged food prejudices, but she hoped that Americans might overcome them to enjoy "many of the cold dishes which are popular on the other side of the Atlantic," by which she seems to have meant England and France, in particular.[3]

Cold dishes would set lunch apart from the hot breakfast and dinner that were very much the norm for middle-class Americans at the end of the nineteenth century. In warm weather, Owen explained, a cold lunch was refreshing. In winter, warm soup could be added to the beginning of the meal to balance out the chill. For a large family's lunch she recommended a menu that relied on British favorites—a galantine (meat, usually chicken, stuffed with chopped meat and seasonings and served in aspic); a "collared fish," by which she presumably meant a fish collar, or the area where a fish's shoulders would be and a delicacy in her era; and a meat pie, of the "raised" kind popular in England. Raised pies are tall pastry cases in which can be enclosed jellied chopped meats or stews. These delicacies would be followed by a steak, cutlets, or "warmed over meats" remaining from an earlier meal.[4] For a smaller family, Owen's contemporary, Alice James, recommended simple but still hearty dishes such as eggs au gratin, oyster patties, or salmon with hollandaise sauce.[5]

Cookbook author Mary Lincoln, who dedicated a whole book to luncheons, suggested that the terminology of lunch was revealing in this transitional era. When it was just the family, she noted, "Usually we say in daily parlance, 'What shall we have for lunch today?' but when we invite our friends to share the meal, we use instinctively the more formal and elegant word 'luncheon.'" The extra syllable, Lincoln remarked, added up to "one of the most elaborate functions of modern society life."[6]

By the time Ruth Langland Holberg wrote her *Luncheon Cookbook* in 1961, three generations of women had become accustomed to the sorts of *luncheons* that Catherine Owen approved, luncheons in which elaborate and inventive salads were showcased and real attention paid to presentation. Holberg might be said to be the guiding spirit of this chapter, in that, though she wrote in an era when lunch at home was about to wane, she dedicated much thought not just to luncheon menus but also to imaginative scenarios of problems for which each menu was a solution. When, for example, "only the weekend [is] free, a working woman must find time to give a garden party for her godchild who is about to be married," and, because it is August, and "the guests will arrive hot and thirsty," Holberg had a menu ready.[7] She advised serving punch, seafood au gratin, pecan rice, jellied ham loaf, vegetable salad, rolls, Hawaiian cake, Florentine cookies, and iced coffee. The Hawaiian cake, featuring pineapple, was a reflection of increased interest in those islands when they officially became a state in 1959.

Especially attuned to the challenges of the working woman's life, Holberg's *The Luncheon Cookbook* is a classic artifact of a moment in American history when middle-class women's lives were becoming less leisured but expectations for entertaining remained high.[8] Less interested in the "career girl," *Betty Crocker's New Picture Cook Book* presented everyday lunches as three-course affairs with one hot, one cold, and one sweet dish. An illustration to accompany the book's seven sample menus shows a table set with steaming food, a woman seated, and a child running toward a door that is just opening to admit a man in a suit and coat, who is removing his hat. The suggestion that both businessmen and schoolchildren were still coming home for lunch perhaps expressed aspirations more than realities by 1961. The lunches this anachronistic family might enjoy included a lettuce wedge with French dressing followed by "Texas hash," a ground beef, tomato, and rice casserole seasoned with onions, pepper, and chili powder. For dessert a molded fruit gelatin was deemed appropriate. That both the "hash" and the gelatin would take at least an hour to prepare indicated that Betty Crocker's creators addressed themselves to women who did not work outside the home.[9]

Among the other menus suggested by Betty Crocker was a lunch of spicy tomato soup and toasted cheese sandwiches, by now a classic of lunch-counter fare brought home and, in the private kitchen, supplemented with shoestring potatoes. To complete the meal, the Betty Crocker authors suggested "walnut bonnie butter cake with browned butter icing," more toothsome fare than the average drugstore counter could offer the lunch crowd.

Food writer and editor Barbara Kafka admitted that "I almost never entertain at lunch," but she nonetheless included in her most personal book, *Food for*

Friends, a recipe for chicken, avocado, and bacon salad with blue cheese dressing that is "neither a first course nor a dinner main course," so it must be lunch. It was, indeed, a "knock-off of a fabulous salad that the Plaza Hotel in New York used to make for lunch." As many savvy diners know, it is a thrifty trick to eat at expensive restaurants for lunch when the food will be just as good but the prices a little lower. Kafka took the trick one step farther by recreating a favorite restaurant lunch dish at home. For those who would entertain at lunch, Kafka suggested a few recipes "light as dandelion silk and still evidencing culinary care," that could serve for "an elegant lunch on a hot summer's day." Dishes for such an occasion are nicoise salad, lobster and chicken liver salad, and "pot cheese and vegetable salad," which leaves to the lunch guests the fun of mixing diced fresh vegetables with either pot cheese—cream cheese—sour cream, or both.[10]

A fashion in America for what was termed "comfort food" in the 1990s reintroduced the idea of lunch at home. Comfort food's nature was determined by nostalgia for the 1950s, when many women and children at least still lunched at home, but it also harked back to the golden age of the diner; thus much of comfort food is really lunch-counter food. Martha Stewart's *Favorite Comfort Food* cookbook, which promises *A Satisfying Collection of Home Cooking Classics*, includes a section of recipes titled "Home for Lunch." In 1999, when the book was published, it was unlikely that many of her readers were home for lunch, as she herself probably seldom was. The recipes featured in this section include french onion soup, an open-faced turkey sandwich with gravy, "the best BLT," matzoh ball soup, egg salad, and a tuna melt, as well as both "creamy tomato soup" and a grilled cheese sandwich that is featured on the book's cover. These American diner classics are joined by a few more contemporary dishes: home-baked focaccia, roast pork loin with fruit chutney, and ginger squash soup with parmesan croutons.[11]

SUNDAY LUNCHES

Perhaps because they seem an endangered species, Sunday lunches have earned special attention from cookbook writers. The most common theme in these books is the notion of return, both that family return to the home that is presumed to be the source of their strength and that merely by having Sunday lunches in a group, families can return to an older, more valuable way of living. The titles of two recent books, *Return to Sunday Dinner* and *Whatever Happened to Sunday Dinner?* typify this sense of longing for something lost. Writers argue for the restorative effects of lunching together with extended family and friends.

Food writers Jane and Michael Stern comment that "there was a time when 'come for Sunday dinner' was a gilt-edged guarantee of a square meal." According to the legend of this meal, the whole family came together in multiple generations to feast on Anglo-American staples such as pot roast and roast chicken. The Sterns designate as the archetypal "Mother's Sunday Dinner" a menu of pot roast with gravy, mashed potatoes, minted carrots and peas, anadama bread (a dense, rich yeast bread made with several kinds of flour), and deep-dish apple pie.[12]

Sunday dinners usually occurred in the late afternoons, after the hour of a typical workday lunch but well before suppertime. The great amount of work they required tacitly broke any pretensions to women's keeping the Sabbath, while their rich bulk enforced post meal leisure on all who dined. In England, a Sunday lunch, sometimes still called Sunday dinner, has traditionally been a large joint of either mutton, lamb, or beef, roasted with potatoes and served with a green vegetable on the side. Yorkshire pudding is also often served with Sunday lunch, adding another comforting blanket of starch to the meal's weight. A favorite dessert for Sunday lunch is summer pudding, made with thin slices of white bread, berries, and whipped cream.[13]

Despite the association of large Sunday lunches with churchgoing, the two activities were actually at odds in early-twentieth-century Britain. When Protestant churches decided to offer one time for Sunday services in contrast to the multiple masses offered by Catholic churches, women's attendance dropped dramatically. Because they had to prepare the large, after-church meal, women could no longer actually go to church with their families on Sunday mornings. Middle- and upper-class families could, of course, rely on servants to do their cooking. Working-class families shared the deep commitment to Sunday lunch as a ritual meal, even as working-class women had no help in preparing the feast. As one woman recalled of her childhood in England between the world wars, "My mother wouldn't have thought Sunday was a Sunday without a joint of meat." Those who could not afford a whole joint served whatever scraps of meat they could come up with for the sacred meal.[14]

Reflecting British influences on culture in the commonwealth, one Australian recalled his family's Sunday lunches fondly as a time for community and good eating: "When we were little, we would usually have guests: cousins, uncles and aunts around to Sunday lunch. We were all dressed in our Sunday best. . . . The lunch was always something grand: no cheap meat like rabbit or stew—no, we had roast lamb or beef and gobs of gravy and mashed potatoes, and in the later years champagne." That last, bubbly element set the Australian family apart from British tradition slightly.[15]

For British author Nigel Slater, Sunday lunch was not an unmixed blessing because his mother "finds Sunday lunch a meal too many. Her hatred of it is pure and unhidden. She starts to twitch about it Saturday afternoon. The beef, the potatoes, the beans, the carrots, the gravy, oh God, the gravy. Horseradish sauce may or may not appear." Surprisingly, or perhaps not, Slater grew up to be a well-known cookbook author.[16]

Across the English Channel, French tradition dictates a similar meal of "lamb, pot roast, or *cote de boeuf* or whatever the butcher has recommended," roasted with potatoes and served with a green vegetable—perhaps asparagus if it is spring—on the side. Where the French meal differs from the English is in the serving of wine and the intervention of a cheese plate before the dessert. Dessert would typically be something bought from a patisserie, rather than something made at home in the English style. One cookbook author emphasizes that this should be a meal that is both elegant and relaxing, one used to reinforce the importance of family in French culture. The best tableware is used, but "in no way is this a time for stuffiness or formality." Most importantly, "We do not use *le déjeuner* as a time to work out the family's inevitable little arguments or any disagreements we might have over politics." Civility is just as important to the scene as are the roast potatoes.[17]

A cookbook writer from North Carolina recalled that her family's Sunday lunches were so much dedicated to hospitality that they were served in three seatings, with the children eating last. The entire week seemed to lead to this event: "A week from Monday morning to Sunday noon, worked up to a mighty crescendo, the culmination being Sunday dinner, a culinary event that was like a party. Not only was the food superb and more plentiful than usual, but also the meal included an element of surprise in that it was never certain who was coming." An archetypal menu for southern Sunday lunch, according to this writer, was fried chicken with cream gravy, country ham with city redeye gravy, crispy fatback, candied sweet potatoes, black-eyed peas, butter beans, green beans, collard greens, cucumbers and tomatoes, buttermilk biscuits, and cornbread. Dessert was banana pudding and sweet potato pie; sweetened iced tea accompanied the meal.[18]

American southern food historian John Egerton attended a Sunday dinner prepared by one woman, Maggie Dunlap, for her entire church community. Dunlap prepared the feast once a year, as "a way of saying 'thanks' to people I love." One hundred members of the Mount Pisgah United Methodist Church in Davidson County, Tennessee, were the lucky beneficiaries of Dunlap's love. With the help of a few assistants, she set out baked ham, fried chicken, meatloaf, cornbread dressing, gravy, Jell-O salads, deviled eggs, potato salad, sliced tomatoes, marinated onions

OTHER SALADS

IMPERIAL SALAD

Drain juice from half a can of pineapple, add one tablespoonful of vinegar and enough water to make a pint. Heat to boiling point and add one package of Lemon Jell-O. Just as Jell-O begins to set, add three slices of canned pineapple, cubed, one-half can Spanish pimentos, shredded, and one medium size cucumber, salted and cut fine. Mould in individual moulds or in one large mould and slice. Serve with cream salad dressing.

GINGER ALE SALAD

Pour one-half cup of boiling water over one package of Lemon Jell-O, set in hot water till thoroughly dissolved, stirring all the time. Cool and add one and one-half cups ginger ale. Set in a cold place until it begins to thicken, then stir in one-fourth cup finely cut nutmeats, one-fourth cup finely cut celery, one cup finely cut assorted fruits (pineapple, orange, apple, cherries or grapes), one tablespoonful finely cut crystallized ginger.

TOMATO JELL-O SALAD

Cook half a can tomatoes with half a cup celery, half a bay leaf and a small onion cut fine, for five minutes. Strain through a coarse sieve, add two tablespoonfuls vinegar and enough water to make a pint. Heat to boiling point and pour it over a package of Lemon Jell-O. Add a dash of red pepper and salt to taste. Pour in individual moulds and when firm serve on lettuce leaves with salad dressing, or jell in border mould, turn on a platter and fill center with chicken or celery salad.

MINT JELLO

To one and three-fourths cups of water add one-fourth cup of vinegar and two tablespoonfuls of sugar. Let come to boiling point; add one-fourth cup of finely chopped fresh mint leaves, and boil one minute. Strain through fine cloth and dissolve one package of Lemon Jell-O in the liquid while it is still at boiling point.

14

ON THE PRAIRIES

In the Wheat Belt a thing has to prove its worth before it finds a place on a table like this. As a dessert or as a salad, Jell-O has no stauncher friends than those of the sort pictured here.

IMPERIAL SALAD

13

Figure 3.1. Jell-O Salads. Source: Duke University, http://library.duke.edu/digitalcollections/eaa_CK0051_CK0051-08.

and cucumbers, chowchow, turnip greens, pinto beans, corn, sweet potatoes, broccoli casserole, cornbread, rolls, coffee, mint tea, chess pies and pecan pies, brownies, and four kinds of cakes, which Egerton fails to name, perhaps stupefied at that point by all he has consumed in the afternoon.[19]

LUNCH PARTIES

Lunch parties are something of a relic in contemporary American society. If friends gather for a meal on weekends, it is usually for a meal designated "brunch," although it may happen at lunchtime and involve lunch-appropriate foods, and weekdays are typically given over to busyness of one sort or another. As the authors of the Emily Post etiquette guide note, although "the lunch hour can be the perfect time to join friends and colleagues and conduct a little business," most such lunches take place in restaurants. Despite trends, however, "at-home lunch is a very nice way to host a club, or committee meeting," two events that are largely relics of mid-century American women's lives. In contemporary life, the authors note that bridge and wedding lunches, where they still occur, tend to happen on weekends.[20]

The lunch party in a private home is not a timeless tradition, but rather a distinct genre of performance unique to a period of approximately one hundred years, between the last quarter of the nineteenth century and the end of the 1960s. Semiformal luncheons held in private homes were made possible by the emergence of a middle-class family culture in which women performed managerial but not productive work in their households. Men spent weekdays at a distance from home that precluded returning for lunch. Children were increasingly provided for at school, whether through a program of institutional feeding or from home-packed lunch pails.

A custom of weekday lunch parties for women emerged at the end of the nineteenth century. The suburbanization that began in this era and picked up force after the Second World War supported this trend and another simultaneous fashion for weekend lunch parties that mixed genders. Writing in 1904, famous cookbook author Mary Lincoln declared that at luncheon parties, held any time between twelve and two o'clock, "the guests are generally limited to women." Because lunch was so much associated with femininity, Lincoln wrote, "It is a brave man indeed who can go through the trying ordeal of the one man at a ladies' luncheon." Of course, we can imagine that the one man who might be invited to serve this role might be the kind of gender-indifferent person who would enjoy the occasion.[21]

Lincoln suggested that if her reader wanted to be the kind of charming person who could invite a friend over for lunch on the spur of the moment she would need to order her domestic life so that such a thing would actually be possible. Supplies must always be on hand, and the domestic help, here designated "Katy," should not be overworked to make one more person welcome for lunch. A true sense of bravado was required for such spontaneity, it seemed, as Lincoln emphasized that the lady of the house serve what she had *"without a word of apology."* What was good enough for the family should be good enough for the friend.[22] When more advance warning was given, invitations sent and a grander menu planned, Lincoln advised that hats would remain on throughout the meal, signaling its true formality, even among friends.[23]

Lunch parties—both single-sex and mixed—often included card games, which gave the gatherings at least a nominal rationale and organizing principle. Instead of standing around forcing small talk, friends and neighbors could be seated four to a table and given something to do.

A self-identified "Member of the Aristocracy" in England who published a guide to entertaining on the eve of the First World War argued, "the institution of luncheon is invaluable to people who have many friends, acquaintances and relatives to entertain," because invitations could be offered for any day of the week, at short notice, and without formality. Lunch offered an experience distinct from dinner, this anonymous expert believed, because "ladies enjoy the society of their hostess at luncheon far more than at a dinner party." Lunch allowed for free conversation around the table rather than the very formal tradition of only speaking to those who sat on one's right and left at dinners. Shouting across the dinner table was apparently not encouraged by this arbiter of aristocratic style.[24]

A slightly earlier guide to upper-class luncheons, published in 1891 in London, offered more specific details about the dishes that ought to be served as well as the arrangement of the table. Decorations should be kept at a minimum to differentiate the midday meal from the grandeur of the evening dinner party. Drawing on a family recipe collection that stretched back to the late seventeenth century, Macaire and Mary Allen recommended a spring luncheon menu that began with a few smaller dishes—plovers' eggs on thin bread and reindeer tongue ramekins with olives, then went on to slightly larger dishes including oyster cutlets, rice timbales, truffled sweetbreads, bobotages, which were a kind of steamed curried meat pudding, and chicken and ham cutlets in aspic. These lighter dishes were followed by more substantial fare—stewed, pressed beef, ham, a galantine of veal, a guinea hen and asparagus salad, and potato balls. Four kinds of sweets—prune jelly with cream, venoise pudding, pineapple whips, and chantry sponge cake—were offered. Venoise pudding was made with breadcrumbs, candied fruit, and sherry. A chantry sponge cake was a simple, unflavored sponge. These sweets were then followed by a final savory course of shrimp aspic, parmesan aigrettes—a kind of deep fried cheese fritter—and cream cheese. This was a far cry from the ploughman's chunk of cheese and slice of bread.[25]

Lunch Parties for Women

Alone at home for most of the day, middle-class women sought the company of their peers by giving lunch parties. These events brought together people who were engaged in parallel work in different spaces. The hostess could showcase her cooking and presentation skills, and her visitors could enjoy being treated as guests, relieved of housework and catered to. Lunch parties in private homes allowed for news to be shared confidentially and for wives and mothers to commiserate or congratulate over issues unique to their social positions.

Soul food cookbook author Ruth Gaskins wrote comically of her own mother's attempt to participate in a lunch club. For Gaskins, this was not something a working-class African American woman should aspire to. Admitting that "my Mama is not going to like this," Gaskins nonetheless felt

> I have to say something about her Luncheon Club. . . . Mama and about a dozen of her friends would get all dressed up in hats and good dresses and gloves in the middle of the day and go to a member's house for lunch. The hostess would really get away from the traditional foods. The menus always sounded like something out of the Thursday food page in the newspaper . . . creamed chicken in patty shells or crab salad with all the little decorations around it. They'd sit at the dining room table which was set with the best linen and every piece of silver that the hostess owned.

Gaskins and the other club members' daughters "knew all along they wouldn't last, because all these women were doing was playing White, and that's just not their style." The club disbanded after almost two years.[26]

The Emily Post etiquette guide recommends menus for the early twenty-first-century at-home lunch that would have been perfectly normal in the mid-twentieth century: dishes that are lighter than dinner food, particularly salads, soups, and sandwiches. While the guide's authors think most guests would turn down a cocktail at lunchtime, they suggest that a glass of champagne or wine might be welcome. In general, hot or iced tea and coffee are "the mainstays of luncheon beverages."

The bridge luncheon, popular from the 1920s through the 1960s, was a favorite topic for cookbook writers. In 1951, the *Better Homes and Gardens New Cookbook* suggested bridge luncheons for both cold and hot weather. In cold weather, guests could be served baked crabmeat and shrimp, tiny green beans, assorted relishes, cheese toasted rolls, plum pudding with fluffy hard sauce, french almonds, and coffee. In the warmer months, perhaps seated outside on a patio, bridge-playing friends could be given tomato jelly rings, tuna fish and celery salad, thin nut-bread sandwiches, watermelon pickles, angel cake topped with pineapple-marshmallow filling, and iced tea or iced coffee.[27]

The pièce de résistance of many a lunch party was the "sandwich loaf," a brilliant work of trompe l'oeil assembly that made guests think they were going to eat a sweet cake for lunch, when really the offering was savory. To make this tricky treat, one sliced a loaf of white bread lengthwise into four layers and filled each layer with a different spread—salmon salad, ham salad, and egg salad were three popular possibilities. Once the layers were all assembled, the loaf was "frosted" with a mixture of cream cheese and cream and garnished with the usual parsley sprigs, radish slices, and pimentos. The sandwich loaf impressed and amused guests, striking a festive atmosphere while also providing an excellent variety of sandwiches all in one loaf.

Another classic for the at-home lunch was a plate of "pinwheel sandwiches," which Lila Perl included in the "Something for the Girls" chapter of her 1961 *What Cooks in Suburbia*. Pinwheel sandwiches were made by cutting a loaf of bread horizontally into about five quarter-inch slices. Some cookbooks recommended using a rolling pin to flatten the slices. Slices were buttered well, covered in a variety of fillings, and rolled up. The rolls were then refrigerated, preferably overnight, and then sliced just before they were to be eaten and arranged tastefully on a platter. The sandwich maker should aim for colorful as well as tasteful combinations and could achieve "bright and flavorful centers" by placing pimento-stuffed olives in a row down the center of the bread slice to be rolled.[28]

Some of Perl's suggested fillings were egg salad, sardine spread, flavored cream cheeses, deviled ham, and mayonnaise mixed with pickles or cheese. Although Perl had included pinwheel sandwiches in her section for ladies' lunches, she assured readers that really, all of her recipes "for the girls" had "at one time or another, been offered to male guests with highly gratifying results!" Pinwheel sandwiches, blueberry blintzes, and Danish party sandwiches were not dangerous to a person's masculinity.[29]

Just in case the suburban housewife who was the audience for Perl's book worried about lunch fare leading to gender confusion, Perl helpfully included

"Something for the Boys," a chapter that perhaps condescendingly offered male lunchers a dish called "little heroes" based on the larger sandwiches of deli fame. Hamburger pizzas were also an option, as were a hearty casserole of lima beans and sausage and "grinders," which were "really do-it-yourselfers" for the man who wanted to make his own sandwich. One final touch—a shake of hot, dried pepper—would "separate the men from the boys," and presumably it was not a move for women to attempt.[30]

Perl seems to have considered mixed-gender lunches more elegant occasions, designing multicourse menus, although allowing that "for the hostess without a maid or with limited help, the two-course luncheon consisting of a main-dish course and a dessert course is surely the happiest, and indeed a most adequate choice."[31] The ideal menu, only possible where hired help was on hand, was creamed chicken on rice with crisp Chinese noodles, buttered baby sprouts, broiled honey peaches, and a mixed Chinese fruit sundae served with tea or coffee. In case the reader missed it, Perl pointed out that this menu "is also subtly infused with the flavor of the East." A cold luncheon menu with a Euro-American flavor began with shrimp ravigote with a sauce "reminiscent of the famous shrimps-in-dressing offered . . . at a well-known New York restaurant." This cosmopolitan dish was followed by avocado and cucumber mousse, marinated artichoke hearts, hot sesame rolls, and lemon pudding tarts. The artichoke hearts were "very simple to do and really have an air about them," while the lemon pudding tarts were "queenly." It is to be hoped that neither cook nor guests would find the pedigree of the lunch intimidating. It might help to know that the sesame rolls were merely any old bread roll dipped in hot butter and sesame seeds.[32]

Recording the specific traditions of ladies' bridge clubs in the American South, the authors of *The Blue Willow Inn Cookbook* write, "The ladies have a glass of wine during the last round before lunch. Some of the ladies like more than one glass and some like quite a few." The unwritten rule, however, is that the bottle must be put away before lunch starts so that no one becomes too tipsy to play well. After this preparatory glass, a typical luncheon "served in the dining room with good silver, crystal, fine china and linens" would include frozen fruit salad, asparagus and ham, and a brownie for dessert. Players could drink iced tea and coffee (but no more wine!) with the meal.[33]

The vogue for garden clubs, which emerged in the first half of the twentieth century, offered yet another way for middle-class women without careers to socialize with each other. Garden clubs also went naturally with festive luncheons, sometimes held out of doors. For a garden party luncheon that "features the delicious foods one associates with women in sheer fluttery dresses," Ruth Holberg recommended fruit salad with pineapple dressing, Roquefort mousse, assorted breads, and a Hungarian walnut torte with butter frosting, served not just with coffee, but with *coffee a la mode* to make all elements appropriately frothy.[34]

Another "delicious luncheon for the girls" was to be made "pretty as a picture, with your best china and silverware and table linen, and flowers galore," despite the lack of any special occasion. Amidst these elegant settings, Ruth Holberg recommended melon halves, chicken à la king in noodle nests, stuffed tomatoes, and a toffee icebox dessert. This kind of treatment would surely make a hostess popular in her neighborhood.[35]

Lunch Parties with Men

According to stereotypes of the mid-twentieth century in the United States, not only did men prefer "hearty" fare, but they would actually reject meals that did not suit their expectations for proper food. Cookbooks constantly warned readers, assumed to be female, that men could not be enticed to the table by the kinds of foods that many women liked. This insistence on the gendered enjoyment of food injected a note of tension and anxiety into meal making and privileged men's supposed preferences over women's. The female palate—itself an invention of writers—became something indulged in secret, only among peers. Paradoxically, this may have served to give extra relish to the lunches that women made for other women, a sense of naughtiness that would not otherwise seem to adhere in a chicken salad.

Ruth Langland Holberg advised readers that one particular menu "is a hearty luncheon, so plan it for a group with men present." The man-worthy luncheon menu that Holberg suggested was comprised of sherry, veal rolls, rice with croutons, viennese green beans, hot buttered french bread, charlotte russe, and coffee—in the end not exactly Rabelaisian.[36] For the bachelor entertaining "a man known for his epicurean tastes, perhaps one who lectures on food and wine," Holberg recommended lobster supreme, rice, a salad printaniere with French dressing, French bread, and crepes with strawberries. Recognizing that the epicure might like wine with lunch, but admitting that she was herself "no authority on wines," she recommended that the lunchmaking bachelor "consult someone who knows what to serve with what" so that the wines complemented the lunch fare.[37] For a summer version of the gender-integrated luncheon "hearty enough to please the men and pretty enough to delight the women," Holberg recommended lemon wine cooler, chicken letitia, cucumber mousse, poppy seed toast, a cottage cheese ring, and coffee and tea.[38]

At an "outdoor luncheon or dinner for eight" proposed by famous chef and cookbook writer James Beard, the male presence was central. Contributing to a book of celebrity menus and recipes, Beard wrote, "We have with us an outdoor party where Papa can show off." Papa impressed the guests with "Oversize Rum Collins for the onlookers; marinated hip steaks, Genoese inspiration; garden provender in ice with an herbed sour cream dunking bowl; garlicked French and Italian bread; griddle shortcakes with heavy cream," and some coffee to sober up and go home. Beard concluded that this luncheon was "pretty exciting food—for the affinity of flavors is one of those happy things that might be called a natural."[39]

For the woman who lunched at home but prepared a meal for her husband to take to work, Jinx Morgan had lots of advice: "If your husband works in an office, whether he is the purveyor of paper clips or president of the corporation, he may well have fallen into the loathsome habit of ordering a chopped egg on white and a waxy carton of milk for lunch. Of course there are long martini-prefaced business lunches occasionally, but he can't indulge in those too often if he hopes to keep two steps ahead of your Saks bill."

Morgan offered "Brown-bagging it" as the solution. And if a husband felt embarrassed to be seen economizing, and "refuses to carry a Mickey Mouse lunch pail," he can easily conceal his lunch inside an attaché case. Morgan suggested saucily that while a wife might include a small thermos of martinis, she should be careful not to fill the thermos "unless you want him to be a menace to navigation all afternoon."[40]

MIDNIGHT LUNCHES

Perhaps the most unusual lunch party is the "lunch" that denizens of the upper Midwest, particularly Minnesota, enjoy together late at night. This cheerful gathering is described in a novel by Elizabeth Hay: "It's the first Saturday in June . . . the Haarings are coming, the Gallots and the Wolfes, the teacher Miss Stevenson, the postmistress Wanda Thurston. They arrive by car and on foot, bringing for the midnight lunch roast ham, roast pork, pickled cabbage salad, pickled beets, and bread—all crowned by Lucinda's two sponge cakes and Mrs. Gallot's lemon meringue pies. There will be cards and singing and eating and talk."[41] Several women who grew up in the 1950s in the town of Hardwicke, Minnesota, remember the lunches being associated with birthdays and card parties. Some recalled that the food was mostly cold—and perhaps this is why the late-night supper was called a lunch. There were traditionally rolls, sliced meats, Jell-O, cakes, and lots of different kinds of pickles, including "sweet pickles, dill pickles, beet pickles, bread and butter pickles, watermelon pickles, society pickles, icicle pickles, [and] turmeric pickles." The range of flavors included in this list belies the persistent stereotype of Midwestern American food as bland, as do the occasional hot dishes two women remember as appearing at midnight lunches, one known as "Shipwreck Hot Dish," and another fancifully titled "African Chow Mein." Numerous recipe websites attest to the continued popularity of this hot dish, a mixture of ground beef, rice, celery, cream of mushroom soup, and cream of celery soup.[42]

The custom of late-night lunch, if not African Chow Mein, seems to have crossed the border, as a Norwegian woman who emigrated to Alberta, Canada, as a young child in 1910 recalled midnight lunches as a normal part of the Norwegian immigrant community's life. She recalled, for example, that Christmas always involved a pageant acted out by local children, a visit from Santa Claus, and "after a sumptuous midnight lunch, the floor was cleared for dancing that lasted until daybreak." In another context, this particular woman, Ellenor Ranghild Merriken, used the word *lunch* seemingly to mean a little something cold to eat, not a meal. Referring to bachelor emigrants who had come to Canada to set up farms before finding wives, she noted that they were always welcome at her home for meals or "if they happened to miss mealtime, there was always coffee and lunch."[43]

WHERE LUNCH STILL COMES HOME

In the post–Civil War nineteenth century, New England lunch was still an at-home affair for the middle class. One twentieth-century cookbook author has used her grandmother's recollections and cookbooks to re-create a lavish menu for the meal, typically held around noon from Monday to Saturday and a few hours later on Sundays. Green pea soup with diced salt pork was followed by boiled ham with cake icing and egg sauce, a dish for which the cook coats a boiled ham with beaten egg whites, sprinkles it with sugar and breadcrumbs, and broils it for a short while. This sweet/salty dish was accompanied by potato croquettes and escalloped tomatoes, homemade bread and freshly churned butter, coleslaw, pickles, sweet 'n' sour, and catsup. For dessert there were "Dan'l Webster Pudding, Boston Cream Pie, and tea or coffee. This meal was followed by a lighter supper around sunset. The man who ate this lunch was of the class that did not have to perform hard labor, so any torpor that his feast produced would have been acceptable. Although

Anglo-Americans never incorporated the siesta into their foodways, they nonetheless regularly ate themselves into a post-meal snooze in the nineteenth century.

Contributors to a community cookbook published in Sacramento, California, in 1920 recommended some simpler home lunch fare. Cabbage and garlic sausage reflected the presence of German immigrants in northern California, while "Pink Poodle," a traditional white sauce made pink with the addition of canned tomato sauce and served on toast, represented new, distinctly American fashions in food. A recipe for a hominy casserole that called for canned hominy, Worcestershire sauce, and "Del Monte sauce" reflected the growing use of commercially processed goods in American cooking and cookbooks during this era.[44]

While weekday lunches at home of this sort are no longer the norm in American life, in other parts of the world, people do preserve the tradition of eating at home in the middle of the day. A pair of researchers studying the role of sleep in modern life noted that "the Dominican Republic is known as the 'nap capital of the Caribbean'" because it is customary to follow lunch with a siesta. A New Yorker visiting the island remarked, "This sleepy, steamy three-hour calm between coffee-hopping Dominican mornings and rum-infested Dominican nights is excellent proof of the relationship between food and human biological rhythms."[45] Large lunches enable the rest that is necessary to prepare for a long night of lively entertainment.

An American who lived in the Dominican Republic recalled that in fact the term used for the midday meal was the siesta meal, not lunch. Local women at home were responsible for this meal: "Starting around 10 A.M., I'd start to smell the garlic, then the beans, and finally the chicken being fried for the Siesta meal. Moms, grandmas, and great-grandmas would gather in the kitchen in the mid morning to start preparing for Siesta." Having already gone shopping at the local farmer's market, they were ready to prepare "the necessary meat or vegetables for that day's feast." In honor of their work, "From noon to 2 P.M. everyday my little town would shut down and everyone would go home to enjoy a feast and a quick nap."[46]

Cultures without the habit of siesta sometimes judge communities who nap after lunch as lazy or not ambitious.[47] Even within one culture, views on siesta can be in conflict. In the nineteenth century in Japan, two contradictory sayings about after-lunch napping existed simultaneously. One valorized the practice: "A short nap after a meal is a universal remedy," while another condemned it: "If you sleep immediately after a meal you get dull-witted."[48]

English writer Alec Waugh even managed to disagree with himself over the issue. Writing at the age of thirty about living in the West Indies, Waugh condemned the siesta. He noted that most Europeans did siesta in the tropics, and "if you have eaten heavily and taken alcohol at lunch, no power on earth can keep your eyes open." For himself, he found no benefit in the practice, and he preferred "to lunch lightly, to avoid alcohol till sundown, and after lunch to write letters, play chess or patience," or some other occupation that "requires one to sit upright in a hard chair." Many years later, in editing this section of his letters for publication, Waugh added the note, "The siesta is now an essential part of my day's pattern, not only in the tropics." Nature had perhaps won out over Waugh's valiant efforts to remain English abroad.[49]

In Carole Counihan's interviews with modern Tuscan families, she found a continuing commitment to lunching at home. One man noted, "Lunch and supper are still today the family meeting place. We are all used to eating together at the same time every day. . . . The children talk about their issues, we talk about ours; we can argue, we can fight. However, it's great in my opinion, great to get together, and to do it while we're eating makes it even better. It is the only time when there is a dialogue in the family."[50] Although, as Counihan notes, northern urban Italians have been adopting a more Anglo-American approach to lunch—keeping it short and staying at work—in the 1990s eight out of ten Italians still ate lunch at home. By 2003, she found that "many Florentines reported increasing consumption of *pranzo* [lunch] away from home." *Pranzo* included a first course, a second course, and a fruit course, all of which, Counihan reminds us, "meant that someone had to be home to cook and clean up after" lunch "and that someone was almost always a woman."[51]

A woman who had grown up in a Tuscan family without much money recalled, "For lunch, a little thin soup—minestruccia—made of water and herbs. We always ate lunch at home, just to have a little something hot. We always had minestra; you know, that's what they made in those days . . . soup made with a bouillon cube or with many greens. Oh, God, in those days that's how we always ate. We ate bread, bread, so much bread."[52]

A Sicilian cookbook recommends a summer *pranzo* of pepper caponata, rigatoni all'Amatriciana, "Capricious" Salmon, poached in white wine and served with cucumber and caper salad, and a dessert of chocolate and cheese tart with cinnamon. This rich and attractive meal, which is in great contrast to the Tuscan meal recalled above, would surely be followed by an afternoon nap.[53]

In contemporary western society, a new category of worker, the freelancer, has brought the workday lunch back into the home. Freelancing lunch can blur the boundaries between work and home, however, as one guide to working from home suggests: "Don't feel you have to do everybody's breakfast dishes, but you do have to be sensitive to potential [conflict]—are you creating more mess because you are taking coffee breaks and eating lunch at home, and if so, are you doing proportionately more of the chores?"[54] What was once known as your family's kitchen has suddenly become your office lunchroom, but it must metamorphose back again before dinner.

HOME FROM SCHOOL

Despite the growing availability of on-site cheap or free school lunches in the United States by the late 1940s, many families continued to feed schoolchildren at home. If home was close enough to school and someone was home at lunchtime, this could provide a nice pause in the school day and a chance for families to reconnect, if only partially. The *Better Homes and Gardens New Cookbook* of 1951, a very popular guide to American mainstream lifestyles, noted, "Lunches are planned to fit the individual family. The amount of planning necessary depends on how many members of the family are home for lunch and the number of school lunch boxes to be packed." When family members were home for lunch, the fare should be kept simple: "For the noonday meal at home, it's best to have one hot dish. It may be soup accompanied by a crisp salad, cookies and a beverage." Should this seem too Spartan, "an interesting and attractive lunch may consist of a casserole made from leftovers accompanied by a fruit dessert and beverage." The idea that a simple family lunch at home could and should aspire to attractiveness reflected expectations that a woman at home was obligated to treat domestic work as artistry.[55]

Ruth Holberg offered an example of one woman who took this charge seriously. The woman, Ruth Howard, made her children's lunch the night before so that "when her two little girls come home from school at noon, they get party sandwiches, deviled eggs, and bologna slices rolled with cream cheese. They take their lunch, tucked into little baskets, and eat at the old-fashioned desks in their playroom." Howard perpetuated for her daughters the idea of lunch as a social, festive meal, much as she probably did for local friends of her own age.[56]

In the contemporary Middle East, school includes a snack time, but lunch waits until students come home. During a break between lessons, children either eat small snacks such as fruit or sandwiches prepared by women in their families or take money given to them by their parents to buy " sandwiches or pastry from the peddlers flocking around the schools." The sandwich, considered a lunch in itself in Anglo-American food culture, is merely a snack in the Middle East and North Africa. The same snack peddlers who haunt schoolyards also linger in the business districts, supplying late morning snacks to working people.[57]

Home at last, if children are the only members of their family present, they will be served light meals by household servants, a bit of bread and cheese or some soup. If other family members are home, then lunch is a real meal, perhaps composed of leftovers from previous meals. Rice and stews as well as bread make up these meals. Urbanization is making it harder for many people in the region to return home for lunch, which in turn supports the emergence of lunch restaurants and peddlers to serve city workers who are far from home during the day.

In France, too, a tradition of schoolchildren lunching at home persists. Although French schools provide lunch, even including a cheese course, students often have the option of returning home. One American woman who married a French man and raised her children in Paris was at first skeptical about this tradition, but she grew to value it highly. Having considered the *"cantine*, or school lunch" in her child's Parisian school "the best thing the French school system ever invented" because it freed her from doing any lunch work, author Harriet Welty Rochefort was not "overly enthusiastic" when her ten-year-old decided he would rather come home. And it also turned out that he had a very French vision of what lunch at home meant. "Benjamin was not going to be satisfied with the sandwich I tried to foist off on him. No, the kid . . . expected a real meal with salad or *pate* or sausage or sardines or something to start with and meat and potatoes or something hot in the middle and yogurt at the end." She complied, noting that her French husband firmly believed that a sandwich was not a meal and would actually say that he had not eaten lunch if he had only had a sandwich.[58] Rochefort discovered that she enjoyed the lunchtimes that she spent at the table with her son.

WEDDING LUNCHES

The 1913 edition of the often-reprinted British guide to *Manners and Rules of Good Society* informed readers that "the wedding breakfast is now termed a luncheon," signaling yet another movement of the meal in the expected order of things. Because the timing had changed, this guide explained, the beverages had, too. Where wedding breakfast guests had made do with coffee and tea, the wedding luncheon's attendees could have champagne. Appropriate dishes for this repast were soup and hot and cold entrees including chickens, jellies, mayonnaises, and salads. In the United States, chicken salad was a popular dish for wedding luncheons, reflecting the cultural affinities between Britain and North America. Fruit and a wedding cake—with the bride cutting the first slice and the butler cutting all the rest—as well as many bottles of champagne completed the meal.[59]

When Marthe, the stepdaughter of French painter Claude Monet, got married in 1900, the ceremony was followed by a six-course luncheon at Giverny, the painter's famous country home. There were hors d'oeuvres, turbot in hollandaise sauce or prawn sauce (guests chose), roast venison and turkey, lardoons fried in marrowbone, crawfish, pate de foie gras, the ubiquitous French green salad, and a dessert of praline candies and ice cream. As great a lover of food as of art, Monet paid rich culinary tribute to the newlyweds.[60]

A survey of Canadian mainstream cooking designates White Wedding Salad as "a must for bridal showers or luncheons" in the mid-twentieth century. The White Wedding Salad, also called the Bride's Salad, was a dessert dish made of chopped pineapple, grapes, bananas, marshmallows, and toasted almonds chilled in a thin lemon-flavored custard and served cold in lettuce cups garnished with mint.[61]

In the 1961 edition of *Betty Crocker's New Picture Cookbook*, one of the most popular cookbooks in American history, the "Bridal Luncheon" is a cup of bouillon, hot crabmeat salad served on tomato slices, "tiny celery sticks," and toasted English muffins. The recommended dessert for this fairly simple celebratory meal was the Aloha Chiffon Cake. This masterpiece, dreamed up "after a delightful holiday in Hawaii" taken by a Betty Crocker staff member, consisted of a chiffon cake cut into three layers and reassembled with whipped cream filling flavored either with crushed pineapple and colored green with food dye *or* flavored with coconut and colored red. The outside of the cake was covered in whichever filling had been chosen—green or red—and then sprinkled with a layer of crumbled peanut brittle. That this was far from the traditional multilayer fruitcake with fondant frosting signaled a more playful approach to even the solemn events in life.[62]

Ruth Langland Holberg recommended a wedding luncheon for twenty-five or fifty, which she confidently believed could be prepared by one "businesswoman" with a few friends and relatives helping. The happy couple would be toasted with champagne punch, then lunch on chicken mousse, seafood in patty shells, stuffed tomatoes, and hot rolls. The wedding cake, served with coffee, was not the responsibility of the very busy friend: "In this department," Holberg confessed, "I retire. Order the fanciest and most glamorous cake your bakery can supply."[63]

INSTITUTIONAL LUNCHES

Mass cooking has existed since at least the days of the first monasteries and convents in Europe, and it seems to have for the most part maintained its reputation for being unappetizing. Some of the first mass-feeding institutions that were not associated with the religious life were the workhouses and poorhouses that became an infamous feature of British life in the second half of the nineteenth century. Reviled in print by Charles Dickens, they strove to feed large numbers at low costs and even lower levels of satisfaction.

In the poorhouses of England in the first half of the nineteenth century, local authorities determined dinner (lunch) fare. Poorhouse dietaries included three meals each day. Breakfast, usually gruel, was served at 6:00 in the summer and 7:30 in the winter. Dinner/lunch was from 12:00 to 1:00, and supper, a bowl of thin soup, was taken at 6:00. While breakfast and supper were nearly always the same things, day after day, dinner/lunch menus varied. For the English "pauper," then, dinner offered the one spot of culinary uncertainty—perhaps even a chance to hope for something new and pleasant—during the day. Most diets for poorhouses listed different rations for men and women, although there were no clear rules as to what proportion of a man's diet a woman should get. Women's rations were always slightly less than men's because officials assumed that women were smaller and would engage in less physical labor than would men.[64]

By the 1860s it was common for those designated "able bodied" to receive different rations from those designated "aged and infirm." While in the north of England, oatmeal played a central role in workhouse rations, for most of the country, "bread was the basis of most workhouse diets." While most paupers had bread and either gruel or porridge for both breakfast and supper, "dinner was the meal which varied the most during the week. In most workhouses only four basic types of dinner meal were served—meat and potatoes, pudding soup, and bread and cheese." The one meal of meat that most paupers enjoyed once a week typically arrived as part of dinner. This meat was typically boiled, though in some places roasted, and usually served with potatoes. In some poorhouses, the potatoes and meat were boiled together as stew known as scouse. Occasionally, other root vegetables such as carrots, turnips, or a rare onion made it into the pot.[65]

Paupers could also expect to sample suet pudding and rice pudding for dinner during the week. While suet pudding consisting of a boiled or steamed mixture of suet, flour, and water was commonly served until the 1850s, the simple dish had been embellished with a few raisins and even an accompanying sauce by the 1870s. If raisins were added, the simple suet became a plum pudding, a special treat.

While poorhouse lunches were in some sense intended to make the poor aspire to something better by punishing them for their poverty, other kinds of institutions only inadvertently drove diners away with the poor quality of their food. College students and soldiers are two groups who have been served notoriously bad food that they have, ironically, paid for, either through tuition or military service.

The complications of mass cooking have tended to produce fare that was not especially exciting to those who ate it, even when the intent was to please. The 1910 *Manual for Army Cooks* produced by the U.S. Quartermaster General's Office provides sample menus for the midday meal, identified as "dinner," that suffered somewhat from repetition. A cream of potato soup is followed by boiled potatoes with boiled sauerkraut and boiled corned beef. The spiced muffins with caramel sauce that complete the meal are mercifully left unboiled.

The lunch menus in the army manual are interesting for the way in which they reflect contemporary middle-class American foodways. Each lunch begins with a soup and includes meat, starch, and vegetable dishes as well as sweets. Soups were typical of the Anglo-American repertoire—pea soup, clam chowder, cream of tomato, cream of celery, but they also included macaroni and spaghetti soup, reminders of the mainstreaming of Italian foodstuffs if not actual recipes. Soldiers were offered meat on a regular, almost daily basis for their lunch and dinner meals, but at the later meal, beef, clearly leftover from lunch, was used to make hashes and fritters rather than served in a joint or slices. Lunch thus appears to have been the heavier meal of the day. Army desserts also reflected the American love of puddings and pies, including apple tarts, coconut pudding, baked apples, rice pudding, vanilla ice cream, and the southern classic, sweet potato pie.[66]

Meals in the field, however, lacked these comforting delicacies, being pared down to the savory essentials. A typical menu was cold boiled beef, pickles, bread, and coffee; another was fried bacon, cold tomatoes, bread, and tea. On just one happy day, soldiers might pause in their marching to enjoy bacon, rice pudding with jam, bread, and coffee. When the army cook found himself on a transport train, he could offer soldiers something not much better than field meals, food that was a little plainer than what they ate in camp. Cold sliced corned beef with canned peas, bread, and coffee would do for an army on the move by rail. On a transport ship, where cooking space was extremely limited, the manual's author noted that a particular cake recipe "has been handled on board the transport with marked success." Fifty pounds of sugar, twenty-five pounds of fat, four hundred eggs, one hundred pounds of flour, and ten cans of baking powder were flavored with a whole bottle of lemon extract to produce a cake that could cheer the homesick and anxious soldier or sailor.[67]

The twenty-first-century army is famous for its Meals Ready to Eat, or MREs, but most soldiers are not lunching in emergency situations. Those who live in barracks are fed in "chow halls," while those in family housing are given meal allowances. A 2011 article about chow halls suggested that requirements of the army food program might not be doing soldiers any favors nutritionally. At lunch, chow halls were required to serve "at least two hot entrees, with one sauce or gravy, . . . along with a deli bar featuring three types of meat; a short-order grill with four items; 'two additional hot short-order entrees (pizza, fried chicken, and so forth)'; French fries; onion rings; assorted chips and pretzels, and at least four desserts."[68] An "army wife" reported on her personal blog a chow hall daily special of "Ribs or Fried Cat fish with sweet potato casserole, mac and cheese, collared [sic] greens, and hush puppies." For dessert, there were chocolate chip cookies and carrot cake with cream cheese frosting. In the midst of this richness, she was glad to see a salad bar.[69] In 2011, the army initiated a new campaign to help soldiers eat more healthily, assisted by a switch from frying to baking and reminders around the chow hall to "go green." When First Lady Michele Obama visited a chow hall during lunch, however, she ate with a soldier who had chosen a plate of ribs, which the diner explained was not her usual lunch, but a special reward for achieving a goal.[70]

The army has also established relationships with fast food chains, allowing them to set up on foreign bases. Thus, American soldiers in Afghanistan enjoyed fast food meals from Burger King, McDonalds, Pizza Hut, and many other chains until General Stanley McChrystal abruptly ordered the American-owned food franchises closed for security reasons. This left Tim Hortons, the Canadian donut emporium, one of the few reminders of "life at home" for American soldiers. McChrystal was famous for eating only one meal per day, an evening meal, disdaining both breakfast and lunch. His successor, David Petraeus, rescinded the order a year later, a move that would endear him to the soldiers, who had quickly tired of chow hall meals.

The other great mass-feeder in American culture, the college dining hall, only came to be in the late nineteenth century. Older colleges, such as Harvard, had provided food in common dining halls for students, but repeated regulations forbidding students to eat outside the common halls make it clear that most who could afford to avoided these places. The dining hall had its antecedents in England, where Oxbridge students similarly developed a habit of avoiding communal dinner—lunch—to eat privately with friends either in their rooms or in local pubs.

At Wellesley College, behavior in the dining hall was the source of controversy at the end of the nineteenth century. One alumna wrote in 1894 in the college magazine that the subject of lunch in the dining hall had been "burning, and boiling, and bubbling" within her ever since it had been mentioned in a recent magazine article. She felt certain that memories of the lunch hour were "correspondingly bitter" to all alumnae. The scene as she recalled it was one of anarchy. Each table was loaded with "various odds and ends, chiefly gathered from yesterday's dinner." A typical collection might be a plate of cold meat, a plate of bread, a plate of gingerbread and a few pieces of pie. From this collection, students served themselves on a first-come-first-served basis, giving no thought to the hunger or preferences of those to follow. Students came and went as they liked, usually in a rush, and they frequently read at the table to prepare for afternoon lessons. The entire performance reminded the aggrieved alumna of "the feeding of the animals in a menagerie."[71]

As educational pioneers in the United States adopted a university model based partly in British and partly in German history, they included grand dining halls, but they tended not to exert pressure on students to eat in the halls. In this way, universities newly and disruptively established in quiet rural towns could offer local entrepreneurs a business opportunity while still charging students for their meals. Lunch counters and lunch wagons ringed the edges of campuses to offer alternatives for the student who did not relish cafeteria fare. These establishments were open much longer hours than dining halls, too, which brought them loyal customers in the small hours. A typical example is Louie's Lunch Truck, a red van that serves students at Cornell University just as many midnight milkshakes, sandwiches, and coffees as it does lunch at lunchtime. That the college permits this competition to its own meal program is typical of the symbiosis of food purveyors and college dining.

WHITE HOUSE LUNCHES

In his memoir of his years in the White House, presidential chef Walter Scheib revealed the politics of lunch in the seat of power. Hired by the Clinton administration, Scheib developed a set of menus for Hillary Rodham Clinton with her input. Clinton regularly assembled her staff for lunch, a group that Scheib came to know fondly as "Hillaryland." The menus he devised for Rodham Clinton and her staff were light but also interesting, including diverse textures and flavors and seemed to please both the First Lady and her staff. Wrap sandwiches and salads were popular fare.[72]

President Bill Clinton typically ate his meals from the navy commissary, which was closer to the Oval Office than was Scheib's kitchen. Not wanting to put Scheib to too much work, the president was happy to eat whatever happened to be on the somewhat utilitarian commissary menu.[73]

When Clinton's second term ended and George W. Bush's family arrived, Scheib's world was profoundly disrupted. While First Lady Laura Bush simply adopted the lunch menus he had created for her predecessor (without knowing that this was what she was doing), the new president had very specific ideas about his own lunch. In his memoir of his time as White House Chef, Scheib dedicated a special chapter to this change of affairs titled "What's for Lunch? A Daily Guessing Game." While Scheib and his staff had some inkling that George W. Bush's "tastes were more limited" than his wife's, "we had no idea what a creature of habit he was. There was a handful of things the President wanted for lunch and he almost never deviated from that list." The short list of acceptable lunches was bacon-lettuce-and-tomato, grilled cheese "made with Kraft Singles and white bread," and peanut butter and honey sandwiches. Occasionally he deviated from this trio to have a hamburger, "cooked between medium and medium rare, on a bun with lettuce and tomato on the side." Bush had strict rules for how his simple lunches were to be served: "All sandwiches were to be served with Lay's potato chips; White bread was to be replaced with white toast for sandwiches; No grilled cheese sandwich was complete without a dish of French's yellow mustard on the side." Despite the seeming simplicity of this regime, the president made lunchtime a challenge for his chef. Usually taking a midday run in the White House gym, the president would arrive, sweaty and unannounced, in the kitchen doorway at lunch time. Rather than request the meal he wanted, Bush always asked, "What's for lunch today?"[74]

In the early days of the administration, Scheib recalled, "I entertained the idea that the President might join his wife for lunch. I always told him what she was having. I might say 'Well, Mr. President, Mrs. Bush is having Grilled Salmon with Endive and Watercress Salad.' Usually that was the end of the discussion. The President would say 'Aw, I don't want that. Can I have so-and-so instead?' So-and-so would be one of his go-to items, such as a peanut butter and honey sandwich."[75]

Once Scheib had learned that Bush only ever wanted one of these particular sandwiches for lunch, he began to respond to the president's rejection of his wife's lunch with "Well, Mr. President, today we also have a BLT." However, the president could not be satisfied so easily: "Inevitably, this didn't work either, because the President would decide he was in the mood for a different dish from his personal play list. If we had a BLT, then he wanted a peanut butter and honey sandwich. If we had grilled cheese, then he wanted a burger." Finally, Scheib established a special setup in another kitchen in which kitchen staff could immediately assemble any one of the president's four possible lunches. He referred to this move as "Outfoxing the President," a triumph of lunch politics.[76]

LUNCH AWAY
FROM HOME

L unch is the meal most commonly eaten away from home, which means that most of us are both participants and audience for a public theater of lunch. Our Tupperware containers spin in office pantry microwaves, revealing to co-workers the secrets of our private kitchens. If we are students of any age between kindergarten and college, we typically eat our lunches at group tables, dining from trays on material cooked in mass quantities for a common palate. On construction sites, we open our lunchboxes or purchase goods from a tricked-out pickup truck and hunker down amid the materials of our trade to take a break. In the fields, we search for shade and eat what we have brought along, looking out over rows yet to pick and weed.

As one cookbook author explained in 1956, "The carried lunch is a familiar sight in any community in America—the school child bounces along swinging a lunch box, the career girl dashes to the bus with the lunch bag tucked under her arm, the laborer swings off to work with his lunch box. And many times the brief case of a business man conceals a lunch."[1] While it is true that carried lunches remain familiar in America and most industrialized societies, there are also greater numbers and wider varieties of places to buy lunch, so that the carried lunch is now more a matter of frugality than of necessity.

Rules and folklore have sprung up around our contemporary lunches, such as that it is impolite to reheat fish in public and that lunch ladies produce mystery meat from the corpses of students assigned to detention. Lunch is also typically considered a casual meal, taken with groups of coworkers or alone, not the stage for romance or grand display.

As chapter 1 revealed, a midday meal break has often but not always been part of work life. While some agricultural workers in Asia and Africa dined only in the morning and evening, lunch has been common since the early nineteenth century in Europe and the Americas, where midday breaks were built into the daily schedules of industrialization and played important roles in the development of urban business culture as well as of middle-class leisure. In this section we will look at workplace lunching around the world, focusing on the twentieth century and especially the contemporary period. Environmental, cultural, and logistical limitations have shaped how lunch breaks occur and what is consumed.

LUNCH ON THE TOWN

In England and in America, there was no strong tradition of lunch at home with the family, so no strong pull out of the urban center at midday. The employer class, as well as the clerks who were responsible for the mountains of paperwork that supported industrial manufacturing economies, created a demand for lunch restaurants. By the 1850s, lunching out was considered a normal part of city life, and by the last quarter of the nineteenth century, there were many different types of eating places, catering to different classes in the major cities of Europe and America.[2]

One Englishman, Edmund Yates, observed a transformation of customs surrounding working lunches. Employed by the London post office in the 1850s, he witnessed the delivery, each day, of lunches for the staff, ordered individually from local inns and pie shops. This created such a distraction to workers, as delivery boys threaded through rows of desks spreading the scents of freshly cooked food, that Yates's supervisor ended the practice by allowing his clerks to leave for lunch. They were given fifteen minutes.[3]

While women who worked in factories left work to buy takeout lunches from local restaurants or carts, middle-class women also made use of the nineteenth-century city during the daytime, particularly in the fourth quarter of the century when department stores opened to serve this new consuming class. Middle-class women also patronized the cultural venues, such as museums and lecture halls, that were part of the modern city. In need of pick-me-ups while shopping or appreciating art, middle-class women created a market for a particular kind of lunch venue, one that offered light dishes as well as more substantial fare in a setting deemed respectable. Merely to feed customers was not enough—restaurants that wanted women's patronage had to assure that no lady in their dining room could be perceived as a prostitute in search of customers. To this end, one English magazine offered its readers a list of restaurants where a woman might eat "without a thought of being considered 'fast.'"[4] In order to create the atmosphere of propriety, some restaurants *only* admitted women, and most used an open plan for seating—no obscuring booths or nooks or curtains—to make sure that everyone could see that nothing could be hidden.

While the menus of restaurants and tearooms that catered specifically to women featured many more desserts and confections than did those that served men, they also typically included hearty options such as roast beef sandwiches for those who needed more sustenance. While some attributed the love of sweets to an essential weakness in women's nature, one trade journal, *The Caterer*, in 1878 blamed the marketplace, noting that respectable women had very few options and that "there are scarcely any refreshment rooms save the pastry-cook's shop open to them." For the readers of *The Caterer*, this absence offered potentially lucrative opportunities.[5]

Figure 4.1. *Tables for Ladies.* Source: Edward Hopper, 1930. Art Resource, New York. © The Metropolitan Museum of Art.

Figure 4.2. *Lunch*. Source: Hamilton Williams, 1907. New York Public Library.

Figure 4.2a. Vantine's Tea Room at 879 Broadway. Source: The Museum of the City of New York/Art Resource, New York.

A critic of women's eating in public feared that Whitley's, one of London's first lunch restaurants patronized by middle-class women, would degrade the entire gender by encouraging them "to acquire such things as soups, cutlets, omelets, macaroni, fritters, and so forth . . . [and to] revel in the accomplishments of cruets full of sherry or claret or Lilliputian bottles of champagne." The semi-satirical attack both gives us insight into what men could expect to eat for lunch in their clubs and into contemporary fears that a hearty lunch with liquor could tarnish a woman's femininity, perhaps even turn her into a man.[6]

In Tokyo, the culture of department store lunchrooms arrived in the second half of the 1920s, as the city rebuilt after an earthquake in 1923 and began to include more Western-style structures and institutions, considered attractively modern by the urban population. As part of this emulation of Western ways, in the Ginza shopping district department stores offered Anglo-American style tearooms. These restaurants were furnished with tables and chairs rather than the traditional Japanese tatami mats. This allowed women to keep both their shoes and coats on while eating, a practice considered more refined in this period. The perceived elegance of the experience allowed more women to feel that it was appropriate to eat in public, as long as they patronized department store tearooms.[7]

For some women in London at the end of the nineteenth century, the difficulty of finding appropriate places to eat lunch led to the establishment of women's clubs, modeled on the very popular men's clubs that did not admit women except as guests. The Lyceum, created to serve women of the intellectual class, was beloved by its members. Londoner Arnold Bennet remarked, "All the women I know seem to have joined" the club "and they are all so proud of it that they are all asking me to lunch there." The Lyceum, in particular among women's clubs of the era, served to connect professional women with each other in a time when little support was forthcoming from society at large.

Other eating clubs, historian Rachel Rich notes, were created to serve "the increasing number of young white-collar working women, who needed to live respectably in town while earning their livings in offices and shops." Because women were expected to prefer modesty in all things, women's clubs avoided the louche atmosphere and bill of fare that were the draw of men's clubs. Members of men's clubs typically lunched on soup, chops, and puddings with brandy and cigars to finish the meal/waste the afternoon. Women's clubs provided members with somewhat lighter dishes, little alcohol, and no cigars.[8] The success of the Lyceum was followed by the establishment of many women's clubs in London, New York, and other cities, some with distinct themes, others serving just as men's clubs did, to provide a place for lunch during a day in the city. When the American Portia Club, a group of female lawyers, attended their third annual luncheon, which they held at the St. Regis hotel, they were served a multicourse menu, printed in French, which included celery, radishes, and olives to start, a consommé, a fish dish, a *tournedos de beouf*, served with vegetables and potatoes, a salad *nicoise*, and finally a *Bombe Royal* and *friandises*, or pudding and cake. There were no wines listed with the courses, and the lunch concluded with coffee.[9]

In early-twentieth-century Istanbul, middle-class women could not be seen eating alongside men. Those "gentle ladies who had come downtown to shop" were nonetheless able to enjoy the food of a popular restaurant by retreating "to take their places seated on the upper storey . . . of some baker of savory pastries," where, crucially for their honor, "one side of the area [was] enclosed by a wooden lattice."[10] As in western Europe and the United States, pastry shops were seen as safe spaces, unlikely to attract molesters or women of questionable repute. The ladies of Istanbul, however, only came to the bakery for its veneer of respectability—they wanted real food for lunch.

From their respectable perch in the balcony, they ordered food from the famous Ekonomi restaurant, buying dessert from the baker who harbored them during their meal. Popular dishes were "sautéed chicken, a vegetable casserole, and pilaf with quail." The substance of fashionable masculine dining, if not the style, were thus accessed by savvy women in this era.[11] Just as middle-class and elite men had established their own urban lunch venues, in private clubs and public chophouses, women of these classes also established the legitimacy of their presence in the city at midday by helping to establish and then to patronize lunch venues.

The kind of American women who had leisure to lunch in the restaurants that catered to "ladies" were satirized in Stephen Sondheim's 1970 musical, *Company*. Sondheim's bitter Joanne sings mockingly of her own social crowd: "Here's to the ladies who lunch—everybody laugh./ Lounging in their caftans/ And planning a brunch/on their own behalf." Not gainfully employed, these "ladies" instead rush to the gym, to plays, to classes, "too busy to know that they're fools." The term has retained this negative connotation, resurfacing in a 2013 *New York Times* article about women professionals who meet for lunch at a few popular Manhattan lunch spots. Cautioning the reader, "Don't make the mistake of referring to these midday regulars as a new breed of 'the ladies who lunch,'" the writer explains that this generation of women meet for "power lunch," not because they have nothing better to do. Indeed one declares, "Lunch is always about business for me."[12]

LUNCH ON THE CLOCK

In England after World War II, urban lunches in the middle of the workday were still the only time that ordinary people ate away from home. Evening dining was still associated with the privileged classes exclusively. An impressive number of these workday lunches were provided in institutional settings. A survey in 1950 found twenty-five thousand eating places in British businesses. These establishments were defined by their class clientele as canteens for the working class, restaurants for middle management, and dining rooms for the executive crowd. Twenty years later there were almost as many, leading some observers to believe that the days of the brown bag lunch were in decline.

A study conducted in 1973 found that canteens were available for two-thirds of workers and that of those, half regularly used them. Those who did not use the canteen either brought lunch from home, actually went home for lunch, or visited a local pub or café. Significantly, the study found that most canteen users chose a substantial dish such as roast meat, fish and chips, meat pies, or sausages for lunch, suggesting that this might be their biggest meal. Lunchtime dessert, however, seemed to be on the wane, as one person remarked, "The days of Spotted Dick and Bread Pudding are fast disappearing." This was probably due to the weight-loss fads that permeated Anglo-American culture in this era as well as to the internationalization of British foodways, which provided more sweet options.[13]

For companies unable to afford employee cafeterias, a new system of issuing workers lunch vouchers emerged after the war. The vouchers could be redeemed for a bargain meal at local independent restaurants, giving workers more flexibility in their choice of lunch material and venue than canteens provided. As of 2004, vouchers were offered for food at thirty-three thousand establishments, including markets as well as restaurants, and one hundred thousand people used them each month.[14]

BLUE-COLLAR LUNCH

One mid-twentieth-century American cookbook writer declared "the worker and the school child" to be "the two members of the family most likely to be lunching out of a box." Published in 1946, just after the end of the Second World War, the book maintained a connection between national defense and lunch hour sustenance: "Make the luncher happy at the prospect of eating, and you have contributed to his health—and to a happier household. And in doing that you have contributed to the health and morale of the whole country."[15] The author's use of the term "worker" here connotes the kind of labor that was essential to the war effort—heavy physical labor—rather than the desk-based labor identified as white-collar work.

Working men had a long history of lunchbox dining before this period; they and their families were aware of its special features. In an early-twentieth-century Quebec lumber camp, for example, climate played a role in lunch preparations. A cook recalled that "the men who were going into the brush to cut logs were given a lunch to take with them." This lunch, "carried in cloth bags," was "meat sandwiches" and "more salt pork until freeze up, when they could keep beef frozen." Weather provided refrigeration during the cold season, and before that, salt preserved the food. To accompany either the salt pork in summer or the beef in winter were "lots of pie" and tea. During the morning's work, lunch would typically freeze solid and "had to be thawed out over a campfire until it was soft enough to eat" around noon. Tea, meanwhile, was reboiled "in a honey pail," something like the syrup buckets that many used as lunchboxes. The lumbermen ate from "'shanty dishes'—enameled bowls without handles, which warmed the hands cupped around them." According to one historian of Canadian foodways, the fire pit that was used to thaw lunch materials was known as "the dinner hole."[16]

The daughter of a miner from Cobalt, Canada, remembered environmental effects on her father's lunch. During her early-twentieth-century childhood, "it

Figure 4.3.   Miners' lunch buckets. Source: Smithsonian Museum of American History.

was a treat for the children to see what Dad had left in his lunch pail after a shift underground." While "cookies softened after a shift in the mine" in a way that the girl found appealing, "sandwiches were not palatable, having absorbed an unpleasant flavour and being unrefrigerated in the humid and hot atmosphere." These effects surely gave miners an incentive to dine early.[17]

A person from Appalachia similarly recalled the mines' effects on his coal-mining father's lunchbox from the early years of the twentieth century: "After a short time every coal miner's bucket smelled of the coal mines. You could scrub and scrub and scrub but when you pulled that sandwich out, it smelled of coal." These buckets were divided into an upper and lower compartment, the lower containing tea and the upper several sandwiches and a piece of fruit.[18]

While lunchboxes had been associated primarily with workers and children, the 1940s brought a change. During the Second World War, families saw more members than before, often including mothers, leaving home and eating lunch from boxes. Even those not employed in munitions factories might be busy with supportive activities from the early morning to the late evening, and thus in need of easily transported meals in boxes. The lunches suggested by the author of the 1946 book, then, were to be eaten in school or factory cafeterias or on the factory floor. Photographs from the war industries show workers perched for lunch on the wings of airplanes they are busily constructing. Nonetheless, the lunch maker was urged to plan "the menus that go into the boxes as devotedly as you plan the most important guest dinner," including such dainty touches as a folded paper napkin, "little waxed paper packages of salt, and sugar or lumps of loose sugar."[19]

Reflecting recently popularized findings of nutritional science, this author also instructed her readers to think of lunch as providing "one-third of the day's food needs." Imagining a planned diet that portioned out the day's nutritional and dietary needs evenly across three meals, she provided guidelines that included one half-pint of milk, in the form either of straight milk, cocoa, or milk-based soup; at least one full serving of vegetables and fruits; one full serving of protein; and one full serving of enriched grains, typically in the form of bread. For good measure, she also suggested each meal contain butter or margarine with added vitamins.

Where factories provided food in their on-site cafeterias, food was typically intended to serve as good fuel for an afternoon's hard work. At the cafeteria set up for engineers by Ford Motor Company in West Dearborn, Michigan, the cooking staff actually experimented with new foodstuffs, specifically soybeans. One employee recalled eating soy bread and soy biscuits and drinking soy milk for lunch in 1941, a time when these would all have been novelties. The initiative was part of Ford's broad interest in efficiency that extended beyond manufacturing into global agriculture.[20]

STOPPING FOR LUNCH

For those who work in transportation, lunch may be the only stationary part of the workday. In London, a unique form of restaurant, known as a tea stall, has come into being to serve the city's taxi drivers, for whom a long stop is a lost fare but a cup of tea is essential. These small food trucks provide hot tea and simple meals to many people on the go. One blogger waxed poetic about the clientele:

> If you have been working on one of the surrounding construction sites since dawn, this is where you escape to get your cup of tea and bacon sandwich. If you are a cab driver or a courier, driving around London all day, you can turn up and Paul will greet you by name, like a long lost friend. If you seek company and you have little money and nowhere else to go, you will be welcome here. Even if you are a peckish schoolboy that skipped the duff school lunch, you can drop by for a sausage sandwich on the way home. All of these I witnessed yesterday—when I joined the regulars at Paul's Tea Stall for a couple of hours.[21]

The blogger captured the interesting reality that although a stall may serve a population on the go and may itself be mobile, it can nonetheless provide a sense of comfort and continuity.

In mid-twentieth-century Calcutta, rickshaw drivers, another population on the move, paused to sit on roadside curbs to eat a simple lunch of roasted chickpea flour mixed with water and mustard oil and formed into balls. This they ate from tin plates with "some hot green chilies and maybe an onion or two" as condiments. When lunch was complete, they washed their plates in a public tap and stashed them in shelves built into the rickshaw. Then, as one observer recalled, they unfolded their head coverings and lay down upon them for an afternoon nap.[22]

Workers on a major new highway project in India find themselves necessarily moving further from established lunch spots and so patronize "the typical makeshift unit of a tarpaulin roof on bamboo poles, a table and a bench, a couple of portable kerosene stoves, lidded aluminum pots, and large kettles." Here one observer saw road crews consume platefuls ladled from "a mound of noodles, gleaming with oil and streaked with reddish brown sauce. Bits of chopped vegetables and even rarer shreds of omelets dotted the pile." This lunch, quick to eat, cheap to buy, and filling, reflects a growing trend in India for food in the Chinese style.[23] While there is a sense of improvisation to tea stalls and noodle carts of the world, they are nonetheless responsive to (as well as contributing to) food trends in the communities they serve.

Even those whose lives usually allow for a sit-down lunch sometimes have to take meals on the go. Calcutta native and cookbook writer Chitrita Banerji recalled lunch on a train trip in her youth. She and her cousin "watched with lip-smacking anticipation while our mothers took out the tiffin carrier . . . containing our home-cooked dinner." Banerji describes the tiffin, a set of linked metal boxes, as "possibly the best innovation to come out of the British colonial era." In her case, family tiffins contained "the traveling Bengali's traditional nourishment—soft, airy luchis [a kind of bread]; slow cooked potatoes flavored with cinnamon, cardamom and asafetida; kasha mangsho [mutton curry] . . . and an assortment of sweets."[24] By packing their tiffins before leaving home, the women of Banerji's family were able to bring their culture with them. They thus made travel less disruptive, but perhaps also less educational. Lunch, as suggested in chapter 2, can be a time to learn. It can also be a time to teach social norms and mores.

One of the most interesting traveling lunches is the collection taken on "stakeouts" by photojournalist Phil Giriodi, who learned from several occasions during which he was trapped without lunch while waiting for a story to break. To forestall such crises, he and a soundman "ordered a custom case that could accommodate the following: 1 small red tablecloth, red and white checked; 1 brick fine smoked cheese; 1 small jar lumpfish (poor man's caviar); 2 cans diet coke (poor man's Merlot); 1 box whole wheat crackers; 2 cans tuna or chicken; 1 medium size bag fine quality cookies; 2 large paper napkins." The case was sturdy enough to withstand rough baggage handling, and the brick of cheese was replaced "if it wasn't used in a few days."[25]

LUNCH ON THE STATE

When the Bolshevik Revolution brought change on a massive scale to Russian society, the citizen comrade's lunch was considered an important issue. In rejection of the bourgeois display that the urban lunch hour had become by the early twentieth century, leaders in the new government eagerly established state-run cafeterias. These cafeterias would serve many virtuous purposes. Reflecting the feminism that was part of early Bolshevik philosophy, the "attack on the private kitchen was first made in the name of women's emancipation." Sending all children to public school and opening all employment opportunities to women freed women from the need to be at home preparing a hot lunch for children. In addition, "to its advocates, communal dining was the form of dining most appropriate for a communist society. Not only would state cafeterias and communal kitchens inculcate collectivist values . . . but they would also utilize scarce food resources in the most efficient manner." Instead of the willful wastefulness of the capitalist lunch, there would be only sensible management of resources and a sense of equality-in-cuisine that would support true brotherhood among Russians.[26]

In the same spirit of communitarian rationality, a cookbook, *At the Common Table*, offered recipes to feed workers on collective farms. For lunch there was a choice of borscht or another unidentified soup, and for the main course either groats (a porridge made of wheat, barley, or rye) or noodles with butter—modest fare.[27]

Germany also experimented with state-run dining halls during this era in response to food shortages brought on by the First World War. Seeking an efficient way to get food to people, city governments established *Volkskuchen* or "people's kitchens," where food could be purchased to go or eaten on site. Despite the good intentions of the programs, however, they seemed to many to signal the "loss of the bourgeois custom, central to proper German living, that the family enjoy the warm midday meal together, around the table at home." Many women were apparently too embarrassed by the association with prewar soup kitchens for the poor even to purchase food to bring home, although this would have helped them both to feed their families and preserve the tradition of lunching together. The only successful program was instituted in Hamburg where "stew cannons," a custom predating the war, rolled through the streets in poorer neighborhoods. These large, mobile cauldrons of stew supplied hot food (ladled out rather than shot at customers despite their names) that could be eaten on the street or taken home to share with others.[28]

In Berlin, only an extreme shortage of potatoes in the 1916 harvest forced large numbers of people—152,000 out of 2.5 million in the winter of 1917—to patronize the public dining halls.[29] At the same time that many Germans steered clear of public dining halls, those who worked in factories seem to have flocked to the company canteens whether or not they had a financial need to do so. Using superior supplies donated directly from the army, factory cafeterias provided workers with a lunch that seemed to reward them for their labor in the war industries rather than to be embarrassing charity.[30]

SCHOOL LUNCH

Worldwide, lunch appears to be a common site for cultural change. This makes sense because it allows even children to perform awareness of the social meanings of food as it relates to culture. In Taiwan, for example, a teacher reported that students "refuse to eat the hamburgers ordered" through the school kitchen, "because they are not as tasty, or as prestigious as McDonald's." In order to eat more "prestigious" burgers, these students "demand that their mothers buy from McDonald's and deliver these hamburgers to school at lunchtime." Parents may also arrange with fast food chains, such as Wendy's and Lotteria, from Japan, to deliver lunches directly to schools. In contrast to American school health advocates, who are currently attempting to ban highly processed foods from schools, one school principal favored the arrangement as "promoting hygiene and etiquette."[31]

School lunch fashions have certainly changed since the 1970s, when one American child living in Tokyo rebelled when his mother sent him to school with his home nation's archetypal lunch, a peanut butter and jelly sandwich, carrot sticks, and an apple packed in a brown paper bag. Having witnessed the beauty of bento, he cried, "I want a cute lunch like the other kids." Wanting her son to feel at home in their new country, the American mother quickly picked up tips from the many bento magazines available to Japanese lunch makers and gave her son a bologna sandwich in the shape of a little boy's face, "bologna bangs and all." He approved the new regime.[32]

Schools present a distinct kind of work environment, worthy of special attention, both because the workers in these environments are young and because the didactic environment gives food added meaning. In the early days of public education in North America, students and teachers brought their lunches from home. These meals were carried in repurposed metal pails, which were often reused yet again as heating vessels. Through the nineteenth century, lunch pails were set in or near wood stoves in the morning so that their contents could be warmed in time for a midday break. Less lucky students ate cold lunch from folded napkins or kerchiefs, and the most unfortunate simply endured hunger pangs while the smells of other children's warming lunches filled the air. Lunch pails revealed variations in socioeconomic status.

In urban Scotland, during this same period, public school lunches did not coincide with breaks in the factory workday, leaving the children of working-class families to let themselves into the family's rooms to forage. This arrangement did not support a cooked lunch—time was short and children's skills limited. Thus working families abandoned the traditional meal of oatmeal porridge in favor of hunks of bread spread with jam, a less nutritious solution.[33]

Free lunch programs began in England in the 1840s as a form of charity directed at the children of the poor, in an acknowledgement that while parents might—according to the morality of the time—be blamed for their own poverty, children were innocent victims. In some cases, school lunches were used to lure those who would otherwise have worked instead of attending school, those who "needed to be tempted into education and discipline with the promise of food."

Advocates of this practice included the Destitute Children's Dinner Society and the Charity Organisation Society's Penny Dinner movement. Some services required a very small monetary contribution from parents, which did not actually cover the costs of the food but was intended to teach impoverished adults a sense of responsibility they were thought to lack.

The usual dish supplied for "dinner," the midday meal, was soup, the favorite substance of those who need to cook for large groups on small budgets. Soups were pottages made with root vegetables and grains and often thinned for economy's sake. An investigation of factory conditions revealed that for the many children who were not tempted into schoolhouses by the promise of meals, lunch was "the poorest and most meager fare," of bread and butter carried in handkerchiefs that served as lunchboxes. This meal was washed down with "a sprinkling of tea and sugar," and occasionally, on lucky days "a little potato pie, with a few pieces of fat bacon on it," that must have seemed like a lunch for kings in comparison to the usual daily fare.[34]

By the late nineteenth century, it was clear that private charities were unable to feed all of the schoolchildren who were going hungry. In 1906, Parliament enabled local governments to raise funds to feed needy children in schools. Although the voluntary nature of the program caused it to develop unevenly, by 1912 approximately one hundred thousand children were receiving cheap or free meals in London, and more than twice that number in the rest of the country. In one pilot program, established in 1907, lunch menus included "potato and onion soup, hashed beef with savoury balls, Yorkshire cheese pudding, shepherd's pie, fish and potato pie with parsley sauce, rice pudding, baked jam roll," and other dishes familiar to the foodways of lower-middle-class English families in this particular region. For the poorest children, used to a diet of bread, butter, and tea, school lunches were an introduction to a whole new, more rich and varied cuisine.[35]

Typical school lunches for children in Appalachia in the early twentieth century were of a similar type, but they were brought from home. "Soup beans," a specialty of the region, cold fried chicken, ham-filled biscuits, cornbread, corn, and pieces of pie filled the pails that children brought to school during the few months each year when their parents could spare them from work at home. One historian of the region recounts that trading was a lively part of the lunch hour, as "one child trades a biscuit for another's jam cake while another child traded blackberry pie for cornbread," giving all children the opportunity to sample the cooking of the community's mothers. In some schools, teachers had to add the job of trade mediator, while others tried to prohibit the practice.[36]

Teachers were also sure to notice who had lunch and who did not, and many managed to stretch their own meals or to bring a little extra for the child whose

Figure 4.4.   Child eating lunch during the noon hour at school in Breathitt County, Kentucky. In his lunch pail were cold potatoes, cornbread, and mush. Source: Prints & Photographs Division, Library of Congress, LC-USF33-031059-M1.

family could not afford to send food. This informal supplement, wholly dependent on the teacher's ability and willingness to share, was often all that stood between underfed children and simple starvation. Painful as it might have been in the moment, however, teachers' awareness of their students' hunger actually helped to bring positive change in the form of subsidized school lunches.

The spread of public schooling revealed childhood poverty in ways that had remained hidden before and that provoked reform. In 1906, John Spargo published *The Bitter Cry of the Children*, an exposé of the plight of economically disadvantaged young people in the United States. His stories of hungry students led New York City officials to initiate a school lunch program. One student whom Spargo interviewed was only able to buy lunch for herself when her father had five cents to spare. With this five cents she almost always bought a cup of coffee, "because coffee is hot, sir, and I was so cold." Without the nickel, which her father could not always afford, she went hungry.[37] Inspired by Spargo's work and the improvement in student health where lunch programs were introduced, thirteen states and Washington, D.C., instituted school lunch programs by 1917.[38]

Another element of Spargo's tale of the little coffee drinker that is important to note is that in urban areas parents often sent students to school not with lunches but with lunch money. This tradition, continued when school lunches were instituted, made weaker children easy marks for bullies who could supplement their own lunch funds by taking others'. All children, too, became the prey of candy sellers who set up their shops as close to schools as they could manage. Like the saloons that popped up around factory neighborhoods in the nineteenth century, sweet shops always appeared in close proximity to schoolyards, seeking out the addict.

When public education became more centrally and generously funded throughout the United States and Canada in the early twentieth century, one-room schools were replaced with larger institutions that typically included kitchens and dining spaces, referred to as lunchrooms because that was the meal most often eaten in them.

In a transitional period, however, before the introduction of school cooks and lunchrooms, teachers in Appalachia in the 1950s were given the work of cooking for their classes. While government funding provided the food, it largely did not stretch to providing cooks, so "the already-busy teacher had to pick up the food, prepare and serve it, record who ate it, and collect money from those who paid." Running a lunch business as well as a classroom, the rural teacher might well have considered herself overworked.[39]

When cafeterias became common in public school buildings in the United States in the 1960s, teachers were freed to focus on pedagogy while hired cooks prepared meals, served the students, and collected fees. As teachers retreated to staff lunchrooms, and students trooped off to noisy cafeterias, however, a tradition of conviviality, of eating together in the classroom, that had made school just a little bit more like home and less like an institution came to an end.

The 1946 School Lunch Act provided the means for school districts to offer free and cheap lunches to all students. Although nutritionists had been advocating for the program for many years, the immediate impetus for it came from the disturbing results of physical exams given to draftees during the war years. A significant number were found to be malnourished, making the nation anxious that it might not have the physical strength to be successful in war. After the war, however, the program was developed equally as a way to help American farmers manage crop surpluses and as a way to feed American schoolchildren.

These two interests were not always aligned, and from the beginning the interests of agriculture dominated. The program's public mission was to feed nutritious meals to the nation's children, but, as one historian of the program notes, "In the end, nutrition science provided a convenient and appealing justification for a school lunch program that was designed primarily as an outlet for surplus food." When farmers had surpluses that were not especially nutritious, school dieticians just had to make the best of what they got.[40]

While trained dieticians retained management of school lunches, child nutrition could remain the top priority, but changes in Department of Agriculture policy in 1969 allowed schools to contract with private industry suppliers for their lunches, saving the government and school districts money but turning school lunches into a for-profit business in which the customer's palate rather than her health was the primary focus. As private companies like Sedexho moved into the school lunch business, schoolchildren became customers rather than beneficiaries, and the nutritional value of school lunches declined precipitously.[41]

In 1980, school lunch nutrition became a national joke when changes in the funding to lunch programs caused nutritionists to seek new definitions for materials to fill criteria. Some were easy to accept, such as including pasta in the category of "breads," but others, such as the suggestion that pickle relish might be counted as a vegetable, were not. Although no member of Ronald Reagan's administration ever identified ketchup as a vegetable, he was widely credited with making this claim. The idea that Reagan would anoint ketchup part of an adequate diet for the nation's children caught on quickly because he often seemed out of touch, and even openly hostile, to the poor and working class.

In the early twenty-first century, a movement to once again make child nutrition the main goal of school lunches has emerged, often teamed with programs to teach environmental sustainability. The movement's most notable spokesperson is Alice Waters, a restaurateur and originator of the Edible Schoolyards project.

Two lunch activists, Ann Cooper and Lisa Holmes, describe the project as "an across-the-board rethinking" of the city of Berkeley, California's, school lunch program. The model for the nationwide movement is the garden at King Middle School, in Berkeley, about which Cooper and Holmes write, "watching students work in the garden, cook in the kitchen and eat the fruits of their labor" for lunch is "a joyous experience for teachers, parents, and even just passersby." Not a mere lunch program, Edible Schoolyards brings a far-reaching philosophy to the table.[42]

The issue of student choice is also important to contemporary thinking about school lunches. In one Kentucky school, where meals are prepared "from scratch," meaning that no part of any meal is delivered to the kitchen precooked, students are offered several meal choices every day. Among the offerings are dishes typical for the region such as country-fried steak and those most broadly popular in American foodways: pizza and hamburgers. Younger children are allowed to choose their own meals but are served by staff while older children both choose for and serve themselves. The model of choice is one that echoes the world of lunch options in the consumer culture beyond the school walls.[43]

In modern France, the school lunch has been so integrated into contemporary foodways that not only are menus posted but at least one school even offers parents suggestions for what they might make for dinner that would complement their child's school lunch. For example, one American parent in Paris found that on a day when children were lunching on a hardboiled egg, steak *hache*, mashed potatoes, and camembert with fruit, the school suggested radishes, moussaka, and petit Suisse for dinner.[44]

In England, as in the United States, World War II produced the recognition that poor nutrition was rampant in the nation, a problem made worse by wartime rationing. Postwar policymakers pushed for a school lunch program with patriotic justifications. New programs shifted the emphasis from needy children to all children, providing free or low-cost meals of one thousand calories to 1.75 million students each day by 1945.[45] Those calories came in the form of traditional British favorites, or as one writer recalled, "fatty roasts, spam fritters, over-boiled peas, and tapioca puddings (otherwise known as frogspawn)."[46]

In the United States the National School Lunch Program provided thirty-one million cheap or free lunches every day in 2011. Legislation that went into effect in the 2012–2013 school year reduced sodium, increased the amounts of fruits, vegetables, and whole grains available for lunches, and adjusted calorie counts for different age groups.[47]

While for some, simple nutrition is the focus of the midday meal, the more economically privileged may indulge in other lunch worries, such as how not to look like a loser in the cafeteria. As a 1993 British cookbook advised, "The choice of container in which to carry lunch to school will depend on what is 'in' at the moment." At some schools it might be the norm to wrap the lunch simply, while at others "the bright and shiny lunch box is 'in.'" Rather than teaching their children to disdain consumer goods trends, parents were implicitly encouraged to help them fit in by providing the culturally appropriate lunch receptacle. Innovation in foodstuffs was also discouraged with the gentle warning, "the school lunch may not be the best place to introduce new foods and flavours" because "it is likely that such foods will be swapped or end up in the rubbish bin." The caution draws attention to a singular aspect of the lunchbox experience, that school lunch often involves a barter market seldom seen among adults.[48]

For children in India in the late twentieth century, "there was no such thing as school lunch," so children carried tiffin boxes containing "small sandwiches, fruits, and sweets."[49] One woman recalled that when her family moved from

India to Australia in the early 1980s, they took this custom with them. The perceived strangeness of her "lunch consisting of rice, and *dahl* and yogurt [in] a *tiffin-dubba*—a split-level metal lunch container" made her feel like an outsider. After beseeching her mother successfully first for a plastic lunchbox and then for a tuna sandwich like those that her classmates carried with them, the girl was ultimately foiled when she found that, "my mother had 'Indianized' my lunch and created a bright yellow tuna fish sandwich filling spiced with green chilis, cilantro, chopped onion and turmeric."[50] As delicious as this might sound to the adult reader, its eccentricity was anathema to the teen.

The social importance of school lunches and the great variety of ways in which different cultures prepare this meal led one school-aged blogger to collect images of school lunches from around the world. On her site, "Never Seconds," Scottish student Martha Payne invited her peers across the world to share their meals virtually. The site proved immensely popular as people of all ages took an interest in what was revealed. Among the lunches posted were an Estonian meal of cabbage and beet salad, baked zucchini with cheese and tomato, rye bread, and a cup of coffee. Japanese schoolchildren posted pictures of lunches with many dishes—rice, soup, fried fish, and cooked vegetables in broth.[51]

The World Food Program of the United Nations also posts images and information about its school feeding program, which serves meals such as a nutritious stew served to schoolchildren in Indonesia that is cooked on site and made from cornmeal, coconut milk, mung beans, sweet potato, brown sugar, and banana.[52] The simple mugs and bowls in which many of the world's hungriest children take what may be their one substantial meal of the day—their school's free lunch—present a stark contrast to the bright and technologically advanced vacuum bags with Velcro fastenings that seem to be the lunchboxes of choice for postmillennial children in the West.

THE LUNCHBOX AND THERMOS

The lunchbox as a single-purpose item is a relatively recent invention, as is the thermos, which sometimes travels inside the box, sometimes alongside it. For most of human history, when lunches were carried from home they were wrapped in pieces of cloth. There are many advantages to this system. A cloth is light, washable, can serve as a napkin, and is cheap, usually being a scrap torn from an old garment. Cloth lunch carriers, however, are limited in two important ways: They cannot carry contents that are hot or liquid and they allow odors to escape. In addition, being soft they may allow their contents to be squished. As metal packaging for mass-produced food became more common in the late nineteenth century, thrifty families used old tin cans to transport lunches to school. Because of their hard sides, these so-called lunch pails, sometimes actually pails with cloth tied over the top, allowed for the portable lunch to retain some of its heat and all of its form.

As both industrial labor and public schooling spread in the early twentieth century, the need for a reliable lunch carrier became an opportunity for commercial enterprise. In 1904, the first vacuum-packed thermoses were sold in American stores, enabling people to carry hot food from home and keep it warm until lunchtime. By the 1920s, tin boxes specifically for lunch were on the market, though they remained uniformly monochromatic until the postwar period.

The domed lunchbox, favored by adults, allows a thermos to be included, which in turn helps to keep food warm. As the sandwich became more distinctively the schoolchild's lunch and as schools provided milk cartons, however, student lunchboxes took on a square shape. If necessary, thermoses were carried separately. Lunchboxes retained an industrial aesthetic until the boom in consumer culture that arrived in America with the end of the Second World War. The realization that children could be treated as consumers, especially by using the medium of television advertising, spurred the growth of the novelty lunchbox market. Decorated with popular cartoon characters and superheroes, the lunchbox made a statement about a child's cultural preferences that few wanted to be left out of. Novelty lunchboxes are such a unique item in the history of material culture in the United States that the Smithsonian Museum has a rich collection of lunchboxes, seventy-five of which are on permanent display, appropriately next to the cafeteria.[53]

The author of the 1946 classic *The Lunch Box and Every Kind of Sandwich* advised readers, "Take care of the box so it gives the maximum of good service to your luncher. It must be washed and aired every day, frequently scrubbed with hot water and soda." The "valuable and useful vacuum bottles" are cared for according to manufacturer's instructions. "If its cork becomes smelly after long use, replace it with a new one. Be sure the bottle remains odorless, clean looking and immaculate inside and out."[54] No one likes the taste of soup in their coffee, or vice versa. Useful as the lunchbox was, there was one lunch setting in which it was not welcome—the picnic, where "its rigid limitations" were out of tune with "this pleasant occasion."[55]

Figure 4.5. Farm children on the way to school with lunch pails, Nebraska. Source: John Vachon, 1938. Prints & Photographs Division, Library of Congress, LC-USF33-T01-001230-M3.

WHITE-COLLAR LUNCH

The thriftiness that is implied by the adult who takes lunch to work, whether in a lunch bag or briefcase, is typically considered antithetical to the executive's persona. White-collar lunches are opportunities to make statements about one's wealth or ethics. Internet search company, Google, for example, provides lunch (and breakfast and dinner and snacks) free for all employees. The grand gesture seems to say, "stay with us, we value you so much that we will provide for all your needs," or it may say, "you don't need to take a lunch break—everything is right here. Just go on working." For those at the top of the corporate ladder, lunch gives an opportunity to set an example for those on the lower rungs.

A cookbook author asked readers in 1993 to "picture the busy executive at lunch time—a sandwich in one hand, financial report in the other. He, or she, may be deskbound with no time to go out in search of something for lunch, but will still need a well-balanced meal to provide energy for the afternoon's work. The executive lunch should be light but filling, high in energy and low in carbohydrates and fats." Readers were advised to "organize the packed lunch to fit in a briefcase," reinforcing the idea that the executive's lunch must fit in with other elements of his or her life. Only schoolchildren have the simplicity of lifestyle that can accommodate an entire bag or box for one purpose—lunch.[56]

Among the suggested meals for the busy businessman or woman were courgette salad, stuffed tomatoes, salmon wine spread (reflecting the executive's high social status), and a fruit trifle. Most specific to the case was the "executive kebab," a brilliantly conceived skewer of bite-sized pieces of cooked meat, apples, pineapples, pickles, and cherry tomatoes. What could be easier than keeping one hand on the keyboard while the other pokes a stick in one's executive mouth?

Although admitting that "many smaller businesses lack sophisticated kitchen facilities," this book also suggests menus for "boardroom lunches," meals to be shared during business meetings. The author left open the question of who in the office might be operating the electric sandwich toaster recommended as "a joy to use," or the "electric frying pan and small convection or microwave oven" identified as sufficient to the task. The lucky executive, or more likely secretary, given the role of cook, would be able to turn out a Danish smorgasbord, baked potatoes with a variety of fillings, or roquefort steak sandwiches, each main course accompanied by vegetable or fruit salad.[57]

By 1983, it was becoming more common for French workers, who had traditionally taken lunch breaks at home or in restaurants, to eat at their workplace. One study found that "20 percent of all workers . . . eat lunch where they work," and that to facilitate this behavior, "cafeterias and restaurants are found in many factories."[58]

Lunch habits are a little different in the countryside, as Peter Mayle, an Englishman who settled in Provence, noticed. There, "The people who work on the land are more likely to eat well at noon and sparingly in the evening." Although Mayle deems this habit "healthy and sensible," he regrets that "for us [it's] quite impossible." Thrilled by the bounty and quality of food in Provence, he and his wife found "there is nothing like a good lunch to give us an appetite for dinner." Indeed, Mayle's very popular book's first sentence is "The year began with lunch," referring to a lavish New Year's Day lunch in Provence that marks the beginning of his new life in France.[59]

PICNICS

Although lunch has been a meal often eaten outside in human history, it was not until the eighteenth century in Europe that the outdoor lunch became the picnic, a minor adventure. The term "pic nic" originally was synonymous with "hodgepodge," and a picnic meal was assembled from parts brought by different diners. The first uses of the word to mean a meal outdoors are found in the early nineteenth century.[60] It seems likely that both rising levels of wealth and urbanization in Europe made this behavior possible. Europeans of the elite classes, with time on their hands and a romantic nostalgia for "simple" rural pleasures, had the resources and longings to make picnics enjoyable.

Figure 4.6. *The Spinnie.* Joseph Goodyear after William Harvey, c. 1800–1839. Source: © The Trustees of the British Museum.

Cultural historian Michel Jeanneret argues that picnics only make sense in reaction to the tensions of modern life: "The commonplaces of pastoral poetry on the joys of leisure and simplicity are known to everyone. Taking lunch on the lawn, sipping wine or milk, eating cheese or strawberries, all this expresses an ecological worry about progress—or, transposed into our own terms, a deep concern about industrialization and globalization." Picnics, Jeanneret surmises, are our bulwark against the mechanization of existence.[61]

A century earlier, a decidedly less philosophical writer declared, "Half the fun of a long drive into the country is stopping in some cool, attractive spot for the picnic luncheon." For the author of *The Automobile Lunch*, the car was most valuable as a vehicle back to nature. She asks, "What could be more welcome or altogether tempting than a dainty and delicious luncheon served al fresco?" While suggesting cold dishes—"a variety of sandwiches—perhaps cheese, tomato and caviar: a salad, a bit of sliced cold meat or fried chicken garnished with parsley, and some small cakes and a bit of sweets"—the author also reminded readers that the car made it possible to return briefly to the stone age because its trunk could carry all the tools necessary for cooking out or barbecuing. One could even build a fire "with the dry kindling which has been brought along in the motor."[62] The idea of carrying nature to nature in a car nudges the auto picnic into the realm of the ridiculous.

In 1949, British author Georgina Battiscombe declared the picnic a uniquely English art: "A picnic is the Englishman's grand gesture, his final defiance flung in the face of fate." It was a defiant gesture, Battiscombe explained, because "no climate in the world is less propitious to picnics than the climate of England, yet with a recklessness which is almost sublime, the English rush out of doors to eat a meal on every possible and impossible occasion." In more clement parts of Europe, people "have adopted the café habit," so that the "continental . . . indeed eats and drinks out of doors, but with the protection of an awning overhead and the safe retreat of a restaurant at his back." Not so the English, who exposed themselves daringly to the elements, even if this resulted in a "picnic basket in a wet and wasp-haunted field."[63] English essayist Osbert Sitwell agreed that the idea of a picnic was "enticing," but he cautioned "it is often more pleasurable in reality to *think* of a picnic, while steadfastly remaining in your own dining room, than to attend one."[64]

This propensity seemed especially absurd to Battiscombe when it was applied to picnicking associated with the point-to-point meeting, a popular horse race run in April, despite the fact that "the chilly . . . English spring is surely the last season during which any sane person would want to eat a meal out of doors." Like Jeanneret, Battiscombe associated picnics with a reaction to urban modernity. Explaining that "the English have not always been thus demented," she blamed the Romantics and "the nature cult popularized by Rousseau."[65] Looking back through English history, Battiscombe declared, "The Elizabethan age is barren of picnics"; she gives evidence of just one attended by the Virgin Queen herself, at which diners enjoyed "neats' [calves'] tongues powdered well, then gambones of the hog [hams], then sausages and savoury knacks [possibly a term for a 'tricky' or elaborate dish] as well as cold loins of veal, cold Capon, Beef, and Goose with pigeon pies, and mutton cold."[66]

Neats' or calves' tongues appear to have been very popular picnic fare; the protagonist of *The Pennyles Pilgrimage* carried "In my Knapsack (to pay hungers fees) . . . good Bacon, Bisket, Neates-tongue, Cheese" and by way of condiments, "Roses, Barberies, of each conserves." Essayist Samuel Pepys likewise took some bottles of wine and beer and neats' tongues along on a river barge outing.[67]

Arguing a strong connection between Romanticism and outdoor meals, Battiscombe designated Sir Walter Scott "a prince among picknickers." An avid fan of fishing, Scott set bottles of wine to chill in streams and served his picnic guests "salmon boiled, salmon grilled, salmon roasted." Two other Romantics, William Wordsworth and his sister Dorothy, were also constantly on the march through nature, setting out with "cold mutton in our pockets" to traverse "rough hill-country roads in the depth of winter." The Wordsworth family took the national habit of picnicking in bad weather to the extreme.[68]

The British took their willful picnicking with them when they colonized India. Jennifer Brennan, who grew up as part of the British Raj, remembered that "when thrown on their own resources for amusement, the *sahib* or *memsahib* invariably organized a picnic. Even on the plains, during the cold weather, the nearest clump of trees, orchard, or garden became the venue for an al fresco meal." Indeed, these were "one of the chief forms of social activity" for the British living in India. While the picnics were often impromptu and usually potluck (in the sense that participants brought food their servants had prepared), they were not entirely rustic, for "a picnic in the days of the Raj often included snow-white tablecloths, silver cutlery, crystal glasses and finger bowls!" Reflecting British power in the region, picnics also involved "many uniformed servants lurking discreetly behind the trees, ready to run forward at a moment's notice to serve more refreshments or pour out more champagne." Making the outdoors even more like the indoors, Brennan's aunt was often known to say, "I'll bring the gramophone and records" to whatever picnic had been planned.[69]

The food as Brennan recalled it represented a thorough mixing of English and Indian foodways: "cold ham or tongue, *naan* bread or *parathas*, 'steamroller' chicken, potato cutlets or rissoles, sausages, spiced beef, lettuce, tomatoes and fruit, such as Alfonzo mangoes and *behr* (a small red plum the size of an olive) for dessert." Lemonade, ginger beer, and cold beer were carried along in thermoses; champagne, as has been noted, was also on hand.[70]

As Romanticism began to reshape European notions of nature, one solitude-seeking Englishwoman set out to hike the British countryside with a frugal lunch. Nelly Weeton recounted, "I put my maps, memorandum book, three boiled eggs, and a crust of bread into a work-bag, and thus equipped sallied forth," in one day hiking thirty-five miles on such simple fare. A Victorian vicar likewise wrote in his diary of setting off to ramble with "my luncheon in my pocket, half-a-dozen biscuits, two apples, and a small flask of wine." When he picnicked in company, however, "the usual things" were "cold chicken, ham and tongue, pies of different sorts, salads, jam and gooseberry tarts, bread and cheese." And to drink, "cups of various kinds went round, claret and hock, champagne, cider and sherry," as if the better part of the liquor cabinet and wine cellar had also longed to get out into nature.[71]

Hunting provided a reason other than national perversity for English people to brave the elements. The traditional hunt breakfast usually took place at noon, drifting into the realm of lunch and famously including many dishes arrayed buffet style. Along with the domestic dishes of pork chops, veal chops, lamb chops, roast beef, and ham, hunters also typically feasted on game—venison pies, roasted pheasant, and jugged hare.

Southern food historian John Egerton notes that the hunt breakfast was a tradition Englishmen brought with them to North America when they colonized the region in the seventeenth century. As one experienced in such meals notes, "The Hunt Breakfast, to the uninitiated, is a misnomer. It never takes place in the morning. Rather, it's offered following the hunt and sometimes doesn't begin until four or five in the afternoon."[72] For this deceptively named meal, a cookbook published by the Colonial Williamsburg foundation recommended a bountiful meal of Tidewater specialties: scrambled eggs with Virginia ham, scalloped oysters or pan-fried oysters, hash browns, fried apples, grits, buttermilk biscuits, and muffins. In the colonial era, such a feast would have followed the English model more closely and included many more meat dishes.[73]

A Californian contributed his own distinctly West Coast version of the hunt breakfast to a 1949 cookbook, *Dining with My Friends*: frozen grapefruit with sloe gin; orange avocado omelet; baked ham steak with pineapple; apple pancake; braised sweetbread; calf's liver in wine, and kidney lamb chops with truffles. Though they might smile at the thought of lamb chops, the ancestral English foxhunters would surely turn in their graves at the thought of orange avocado salad or grapefruit juice.[74]

In Germany, hunters took this meal, *jagd frühstück* (a direct translation of "hunt breakfast") "in the open air, with their fingers, in order that they may lose no time," and one cookbook writer noted that "gentlemen usually prefer eating this [meal] about the middle of the day." Given the extremely informal nature of the meal, she did not advise packing knives and forks or tablecloths, as all would come back unused. Her suggested menu required the cook to cut small loaves of bread in half and "to fill them with different sorts of meat, veal, ham, pork-rolls and sausages, or cheese." Although each gentleman was to be given four of these sandwiches, this would not be enough: "A large cold pie or sausage should also be always sent, as well as a cake cut up . . . apples, eggs, pepper, and salt must also not be forgotten." To accompany this nice array of finger food, she prescribed, "both red and light white wine, as well as Port and Madeira," with punch and mulled wine added if the day were cold.[75]

Fascinatingly, this author described a sliding scale of lunches, making suggestions for feeding the gamekeepers and drivers as well as the hunting gentlemen. Gamekeepers were allowed "as much bread and butter as for their masters," which seems generous except that it was to be "of a commoner sort" and accompanied by "only one kind of meat and cheese." For drinks, they could each have "half a bottle of ordinary wine." Drivers could only have beer, brown bread, sausages, cheese, and apples—a ploughman's lunch.[76]

As picnics became more fashionable in the middle of the nineteenth century, advice manuals reflected the trend with specifically designed menus as well as suggestions for the social makeup of the picnic. One British guide advised that all foodstuffs be entrusted to the care of "only one, dear old lady." Such persons would be found to have remarkable talents of organization, never forgetting the mint sauce or breaking the dressing bottle, and "who else could have so piled tart upon tart without a crack or a cranny for the rich red juice to well through?" Such attention to detail even prompted the writer to declare in imaginary awe: "Observe her little bottle of cayenne pepper!" Ready for any picnic eventuality, the dear old lady was a true Victorian heroine.[77]

An American in interwar France happily joined in local customs in outdoor dining. Samuel Chamberlain remembered that, despite looming world events, "June 1939 was beautiful, a perfect month of clear, crystal days, when every Parisian family waited eagerly for the long week-end and the early Sunday morning sortie into the country." On Sundays, "elaborate precautions were taken to fill the hamper with delicacies for the classic *déjeuner sur l'herbe*. And Madame did not forget the St. Emilion to go with the cold bird, or the chilled bottle of champagne to accompany the *fraise de bois* which the children would collect in the forest before the *pique-nique* began." Locals and day-trippers in his village visited the shops, loading up on bread, charcuterie, pastries, and newspapers to carry off with them into the countryside.[78]

An American author regretted that in the United States, "Picnic menus sometimes suffer from lack of imagination on the part of the man or woman who packs them." Although sandwiches and salads could be "delicious," the well-thought-out picnic "may be luxurious, more like a generous buffet supper at home." The most heartfelt suggestion was to "take along a whole roast chicken or a small turkey and the sharp knife needed to carve it limb from limb." No need for much cutlery, however, because "picnickers like to eat cold roast bird in their fingers; it tastes better than any other way." Among the alternatives to the usual picnic basket that this author proposed were "a jar of smoked turkey pate or, if you're in the millionaire class, caviar." Whatever the economics of the meal, one "essential" of the picnic "spread is plenty of hot coffee and the sugar and cream to go with it." Presuming perhaps, that eating in the open air had a soporific effect, this marked the author as distinctly American—French picnickers would have taken wine and the English a thermos of tea.[79]

Recalling a childhood in the first half of the twentieth century in Baghdad, one writer recommended the four-thousand-year-old city as "a delightful spot for a picnic." Her parents had hired horse carts to pull guests and food to a site in a garden, where "Aziz the cook would start the fire and Ahmas would begin setting the Persian rugs out. They were covered with a huge tablecloth on which the dishes were set. Sometimes we had stuffed baby lamb or chicken with rice, or *dolmah*, or *fesenjan*. There were many types of salad, and *doogh*, which was the yogurt drink we had most often for lunch." The famous sweet ice, *sharbat*, "was served too as well as roasted nuts and seeds—pumpkin seeds, watermelon seeds, and pear seeds." As with American picnics, no rural relaxation was complete without caffeine, so by the end of the meal "the samovar was ready and bubbling with its freshly brewed tea."[80]

Consistent with this tradition of luxurious picnicking, the most important celebration of the Iranian calendar, Noo Rooz, ends its twelve days with a picnic. Noo Rooz is the New Year holiday, which in Ancient Persia began on the vernal equinox and is still observed on this day, March 21. After the twelfth day, it is traditional to go out for a picnic in order to scatter herbs that have been gathered for the festivities but are now well on their way to drooping or drying out. The herbs are tossed into running water, and then everyone settles down for lunch. The meal will be more than bread and cheese, however. As one participant notes, "Not for Persians a sandwich and a flask of tea," the simple picnic associated with the English. Instead,

> The complete *sofreh*, including the table cloth, cutlery, crockery, glasses, condiments, bowls of *mast-o khiyar* (yogurt with cucumber), fresh herbs, and pickles are all loaded up. A large saucepan of cooked *sabzi polow* (rice with herbs) is taken, along with a small portable paraffin or gas heater on which to heat it up. The hot *polow* must of course be served with fried fish, wedges of herb omelet, and lemons. In some regions, the new season's tiny broad beans are boiled whole in their pods, drained and sprinkled with crushed angelica seed or dried mint. In others, romaine lettuce leaves are dipped in a sweet vinegar syrup.[81]

Working against the sandwich-and-mug-of-tea stereotype of an English picnic, an English cookbook published in 1993 suggested many interesting contemporary dishes for picnics—curried beef rolls, Parmesan drumsticks, bobotie quiche—but also offered a section of precautionary advice "for safety's sake" that seemed to belie an earlier assertion that "just the suggestion 'let's have a picnic,' seems to make life suddenly more carefree." Readers were warned that although "a warm summer's day is perfect for a picnic," that same warmth could lead to food poisoning without careful monitoring of temperatures. Among the great heaps of "picnic musts" suggested, including cutlery, glasses, condiments, and a barbecue, was also a first aid kit. Nature, though subdued beneath a washable tablecloth, was still nature, red in tooth and claw.[82]

Safari chef Josie Stow's customers deliberately confront the wild side of nature. For the intrepid set, she presents a menu that blends African foodstuffs and foodways with the expectations of the mostly Western adventurers: "onion and poppy seed bread, bowls of chilled soup and a carved wooden platter with a riot of colorful salads . . . thinly sliced venison bresaola, grilled sweet potatoes with ginger and lime dressing, a green bean, baby corn, olive and basil salad and roast beetroot and carrot salad. This is followed by blue cheese, green fig preserve and a thin, crisp bread called a shraak," allowing for one local element in what is otherwise a European-style meal. For packed lunches to take into the bush, she recommends pizza made in an oven built in a vacated termite mound. Although the kitchen equipment may be wildly different from place to place, the simple slice of pizza is an archetypal lunch.[83]

In Japan, the season of *sakura hanami*, when the nation's cherry trees blossom, is also a time for lunching outdoors. One cookbook author notes that during this time, "whole cities become one vast picnic blanket. . . . Friends, co-workers, and families eat, drink sake, and sing beneath the floral canopy." For such occasions, the author recommends that multicultural picnic favorite, fried chicken, as well as some more specifically Japanese sushi balls and steamed edamame served in the pod.[84]

As a hierarchy of foods developed in Mexico in the nineteenth century, picnics received special attention. The European style of the *comida*, historian Jeffrey Pilcher writes, "push[ed] national dishes to the periphery." Tamales and enchiladas became suitable for "light brunches to be eaten privately in the morning." Dishes that seemed more Spanish were reserved for the evening, when one might have guests. Local foodways thus ceded importance to those of the former empire. Because these food rules did not apply so stringently outside the metropolis, however, middle-class Mexicans still felt free to enjoy "the *tamalada*, a picnic expressly for eating tamales." Spending an afternoon outside the town, Mexico City residents could relax their guard to lunch on tamales and drink *atole de leche*, made with cornmeal and milk.[85]

LUNCH IN RESTAURANTS

While dining out with one's family in the evening was still seen as something of an adventure in the early twentieth century, lunch in restaurants had become a necessity for most urban workers in Europe and North America. The growth of cities had pushed business and residential neighborhoods too far apart for lunch at home to be an easy option. As discussed in chapter 1, different establishments served different classes and categories of workers, with men of the business-owner class dining richly and often in elegant settings, while clerks and middle managers ate in establishments more valued for their speed than their cuisine.

In 1916, playwright Frank Dumont satirized the offerings of the ubiquitous lunch counter in his play *The Depot Lunch-Counter*. To set the scene he described a counter "with plenty of fruits, sandwiches, bags of peanuts, pies, bottles of catsup, knives, forks, plates and everything to indicate a railway lunch counter." There were to be high stools at a counter with a coffee urn behind it and "on the walls are numerous placards announcing the refreshments, viz. . . . 'Pig's Tootsies,' 'Bosom of Veal,' 'Ox's Narrative,' 'Hot Butter.'" Utensils were ten cents extra, and customers were exhorted, "Don't go elsewhere to be poisoned—eat here." Dumont's lunch counter would have been easily recognizable to audiences in its clutter and dubious cleanliness. Lunch counters existed for quick business, not to impress clientele with their fixtures.[86]

N. S. Macintosh, the supervisor of "half a hundred successful cafeterias and cafeteria fountains," a professional term for lunch counters, gave detailed advice for "profitable cafeteria management" in a 1935 guide for industry professionals.

Different strategies were needed in different kinds of locations and at different times of the day. Macintosh paid special attention to "outgoing orders," what we now think of as to-go or takeout during the lunch hours. In business districts, "The chief requisite . . . is speed and in order to obtain this it would be well to specialize in certain sandwiches." It was a good idea to keep the variety small but to make sure it was "made well and satisfying." Assigning particular sandwiches to particular days of the week saved time for the harried business-district worker.

If the cafeteria happened to be in a neighborhood where "many office workers prefer to send for their lunches" rather than eating in the restaurant, "a small carton of either the coleslaw or potato salad may be included in the price of the sandwich, this being figured in the cost." What looked like a "freebie," generating customer loyalty, was not.[87]

Good dishes for lunch were "croquettes, stews, and meat pies," because "lunches must take care of cheaper cuts of meat, the parts which cannot be used for the more expensive dishes and what is left from roasts after carving is done for the dinner trade." As in private homes, lunch was often a by-product of last night's dinner. There would also always be demand at lunchtime for "salad combinations and assorted cold cuts with salad accompaniments." Salad in this era referred to "composed" cold dishes such as chicken salad and ham salad, typically served on lettuce leaves or, more glamorously, in tomato halves.[88] Orders to go or for delivery had to be packaged, a problem that, in this era before commercial plastics, limited the kinds of food that could leave the restaurant. While the paper carton associated with Chinese food was first patented in 1894, it does not seem to have been used until later in the twentieth century and even then remained tied to the one particular market. Wax-paper packages, folded by the restaurant staff, were all that was available in most restaurants, so only sandwiches and hamburgers could feasibly be taken out.

In 1942, the popularity of sandwiches for lunch still seemed relatively new to restaurant manager Pierre J. Berard. He estimated that "sandwiches have increased in popularity each year for the past 18 years," and another food industry professional agreed that, "sandwiches are getting to be one of the most popular items on the luncheon menu." They were displacing the slices of roast beef, turkey, or pork that had been served usually with potatoes and gravy and the above-mentioned croquettes and fritters since the appearance of cheap lunch businesses in the late nineteenth century.

For the lunch-counter sandwich, Berard informed readers, white bread was preferred a dozen to one over wheat, and the five sandwiches that a seasoned professional always kept on the menu were "ham and swiss cheese, [cream] cheese and jelly, peanut butter and jelly, peanut butter and pimento cheese, lettuce and tomato." Under "Standard Profit Makers," Berard listed ham sandwiches, cold roast beef sandwiches, and hot roast beef sandwiches, served open. These three served as transitional dishes between the roast meats of lunchtimes past and the primarily cold sandwiches of the future.[89]

The grilled cheese sandwich that was to be considered a lunchtime classic by the late 1960s was not one of the regular moneymakers. Berard did, however, include a recipe for a "toasted melted cheese sandwich" which was made with two slices of buttered bread, four slices of American cheese, and browned "under a hot flame."[90] This recipe was a new variation on an older dish, the toasted cheese sandwich, which was open-faced. The sandwich craze was really made possible both at home and in restaurants by the introduction of sliced bread and electric toasters. American cheese, which was packaged in a bread loaf–sized square, fit perfectly into this technological convergence. Presliced bread and loaf-shaped cheese made it much clearer how many sandwiches could be made from existing supplies. The lunch-counter owner never ended up with an irregularly shaped piece of cheese or heel of bread with these two ingredients.

Focusing on the technical side of lunch-counter management, N. S. Macintosh was also very particular about the physical setup of the lunch counter. Both hooks for men's hats and undercounter "package shelves" for women's shopping bags were seen as essential. On the other side of the kitchen door, "salad preparation is usually accorded a separate part of the kitchen," the domain of "the salad girl," who must "take care of the sandwich mixes, the bread and butter, gelatine desserts . . . [and] must make her mayonnaise, her other types of salad dressings."

That the work of making food typically associated with women customers' lunches seems to have been assigned to a female worker reinforced the idea, prevalent in the 1930s, that both food consumption and food production were gendered behavior.[91] By the twenty-first century, lunch customers were being categorized along different lines. An industry guide published in 2003 explained, "Luncheon customers can usually be classified in two groups: business people who have a short lunch and want quick service, and casual diners who want more leisurely service. The duty of the waitperson is to avoid keeping customers in the first group waiting for service, and to avoid making those in the second group feel they are being rushed."[92] While we often focus most intently on what we will have for lunch, it is worth noting that our hungers create both opportunities and challenges for a whole cohort of people who see the lunch rush from the other side of the deli counter, school lunch line, or commercial kitchen.

LUNCH IN THE ARTS
AND POPULAR MEDIA

Two of the most controversial works of art in the Western world have to do with lunch. Eduard Manet's *Déjeuner sur l'Herbe* and William Burroughs' *Naked Lunch* both upset contemporaries with iconoclastic representations of everyday life, and both were censored in their time. Both pair lunch with nudity, although in the case of Burroughs, this only goes as deep as the title. Still, Burroughs chose the title for its shock value. According to his own account, the title was proposed by Jack Kerouac and meant to invoke "a frozen moment, when everyone sees what is on the end of every fork." Still somewhat cryptic, the explanation itself suggests that we seldom pause in our lunches to consider what we are eating, a vision of lunch as the hurried and unremarkable meal.[1]

That for both artists, living several generations apart, the idea that lunch without clothes would be shocking indicates how much lunch is associated with the ordinary and normal. While breakfast and dinner are both often private, allowing for states of undress, lunch is broadly assumed to be a public and therefore a respectably clothed meal.

Artists and writers as well as film and TV producers have used the normality of lunch to comment on their times, sometimes richly portraying the ordinary in its own right, sometimes juxtaposing unexpected elements against the meal.

PAINTED LUNCH

Art historian and critic James Yood notes that as a genre, still lifes have "been a major—perhaps *the* major—vehicle for artistic ruminations on the edible world." Still lifes first appeared in abundance in European painting in the early seventeenth century, when "the mundane activities of humankind—in which, of course, food plays no small role—were no longer considered to be beneath observation; instead they were sought out for their universal appeal."[2]

An early example of the celebration of everyday life, Pieter Bruegel the elder's *The Harvesters* offers a portrait of Dutch peasants picnicking in the middle of a workday. The painting, completed in 1565, was created to represent the fall in a series of paintings of the four seasons that were commissioned by a successful merchant who lived near Antwerp. Although in comparison to Manet's later picnic painting, *The Harvesters* seems quite tame, it had radical aspects that make it and the other surviving works in the series important to the history of art. By painting the seasons without allegories and without religious motifs, Bruegel helped chart a new course for art. Real life could be portrayed as rich and interesting even in its most ordinary moments. In part, this attention to the real was made possible by the influence of Protestantism in Bruegel's part of the world. Protestant teachings of the time forbade the creation of religious idols and discouraged the painting of religious figures as a little too close to idolatry. Freed from the traditional subjects of art and living in a part of the world newly intrigued with material goods, painters of Bruegel's and later generations turned their keen eyes on their countrymen, both rich and poor.

By portraying the rural laboring class, Bruegel not only provided future generations of cultural historians with great insight into the lives of the ordinary folk; he may also have been making his wealthy patron feel good about his own social status at the time. Almost lost in the background of the picture are some of the boats that helped this patron make his fortune, the fortune that he could afford to spend on magnificent decorations such as Bruegel's series of the seasons.

Bruegel's peasants are entirely absorbed in their lunch, one even napping face up to the sky as they sit in the middle of the frame. Nothing could be less like the religious paintings that had preceded Bruegel's time or the formal portraits of wealthy people that became popular in this era. The simple repast of the field worker achieved a kind of dignity as it was centered like a hub amid the cycles of the seasons.

Bruegel's lunchers are eating slices of bread and cheese taken from a basket, which one of them must have carried into the fields. They also have bowls of

Figure 5.1. *The Harvesters.* Source: Pieter Brueghel the elder, 1565. Art Resource, New York. © The Metropolitan Museum of Art.

porridge, spoons, and large jugs of beer. The pear tree under which they are sitting seems to have dropped some fruit to add to the feast. The bread that sixteenth-century Dutch peasants ate would have been dense, chewy, rye or coarsely milled wheat bread, while their cheese would have been semihard and only slightly sharp, like an edam of today. We can be sure of the importance of beer to the meal when we notice that a man is carrying two more jugs up a hill toward the picnic and that yet another jug is hidden amid the wheat, perhaps to keep cool.

Although they are all humbly dressed and seated on hay bales, the harvesters are gathered around a white cloth set on the ground, a picnic blanket, effectively, that serves to give a touch of formality to their otherwise very relaxed gathering. In Dutch homes, it was typical to cover the table in a cloth on which were placed bread and salt. Sometimes the bread served as a plate. Bruegel's peasants, then, have brought their indoor customs outside with them.[3]

Men and women eat together with no apparent hierarchy. Their appetites are clearly hearty, as each person (aside from the one who is asleep) is either eating or reaching for something to eat. The relish with which they eat suggests that they have been working hard and that they enjoy their food.

Bruegel emphasizes the momentary nature of lunch by painting the harvesters as just one small group who pause while the work of the harvest continues around them. Other workers have either already taken a break or will when this group gets up. For some in the picture this will be the first meal of the day, as traditionally Dutch people had taken their first meal late in the morning and their second (a smaller meal) just before bed. By the late 1500s, when Bruegel completed the work, it had become more common to eat a breakfast in the morning and a lunch in the middle of the day. This probably remained a luxury of the elite for some time, however, before trickling down. That breakfasts were to some degree trendy is reflected in the high popularity of the breakfast table as painting subject in the seventeenth century.[4]

Frans Hals, a master of the generation that followed Bruegel, portrayed the lunch of the class who owned the land the harvesters worked in his 1616 *The Company of St. George Banquet*. Here, well-dressed men in stiff lace collars gather on chairs around a table. An open window in the background tells us that this is a daytime banquet, more like similar events in China during this era than what early-twentieth-century Americans associate with the term banquet. On the table are many small plates, representing the diversity of diet available for elite lunches. Delicate glassware is filled with wine, a great contrast to the heavy jugs of beer Bruegel's peasants hoisted to their mouths. And perhaps most interestingly, all of the diners are looking at the painter, whereas Bruegel's harvesters did not, going about their own essential business. Visible on the table are a roast chicken, white bread rolls, and olives.

Luncheon was well established as a fashion of the elite by 1735, when French painter Nicholas Lancret could expect his audience to understand the title of his painting *Luncheon Party with Ham*. Despite its prosaic name, the painting portrays a scene of louche disorder as a party of wealthy young men dine out of doors but in great style. They are seated at a table, dressed in the finest style with a white cloth, china, and wine buckets. They are attended by five servants, one of whom appears to be African—a further marker of the lunchers' high social status. They are also attended by a woman, who stands with one arm around one of the diners, one of her hands intimately close to his chin. The men have loosened their neckties and unbuttoned their shirts. They are clearly drunk, several slouching in their chairs as one of the party stands on his chair with a foot on the table pouring wine from on high into a small glass. It is hard to be sure just how many empty bottles are arrayed in front of the party on the ground because some have been broken in the festivities, as has a plate. A cat and dog are about to start fighting over scraps. On the table, as promised by Lancret's title, is a large baked ham, half eaten. There are also a few crusts of bread, a plate that may have held crawfish, and servants approaching with plates of fresh fruit, signaling that we are near the planned end of the meal.

The classical architecture that sits in the background of the luncheon indicates that the scene is probably the grounds of an estate, placing the lunchers within the landed aristocracy, a social class who were especially given to public performances of excess during this era. In 1737, French painter Carle van Loo captured a similar scene in his *Halt in the Hunt*. Here a group of richly attired men and women sit together on the ground or on low benches to enjoy a picnic spread on cloth on the grass. The proportion of bottles to lunchers is much less extreme than in Lancret's painting, but there is clearly much drinking going on nonetheless. There is some interest in the actual food as one man cuts into a pie and several other picnickers reach toward a plate offered by a uniformed servant. Two other servants, one African, manage more hampers of food, and a large ham and several roasted rabbits wait on platters on the cloth. As if to comment subtly on the indecency of aristocratic lunchtime excesses, van Loo has included a dog licking its private parts in the foreground of the painting.

The Dutch fashion for "little breakfast paintings" or *onthijtje* was in decline when Spanish still-life artist Luis Egidio Menéndez painted his *La Merienda*, or the *Afternoon Meal*, in 1771, but he followed Dutch conventions in portraying the ingredients, primarily in their raw state. Menéndez gives us cantaloupe, apricots, pears, grapes, and some bread for lunch. We also see a flask of wine in

Figure 5.2. *Le Déjeuner de Jambon*. Source: Nicholas Lancret, 1735. © RMN-Grand Palais/Art Resource, New York.

the background and some covered pots. Perhaps the real sustenance is hidden in these. The background is a slightly wild, certainly uninhabited landscape rather than the traditional Dutch tabletop or shelf. Menéndez typically painted foods out of the kitchen context, but his *Merienda* is unusual in that it offers a sort of explanation for the scene: A picnic basket sits in the middle of the picture, enclosing a white napkin folded over something we cannot see. A few bowls are nested together in the basket, too, The melon has been cut into, but the two small breads are intact, and the wine bottle full, a combination that creates a little ambiguity about what point we are at in the meal.

Menéndez's work hovers between the utilitarian, though also pleasant meal, of Bruegel's harvesters and Lancret's louche lunchers, portraying elegance and plenty but no bad behavior, indeed no lunchers at all. By the nineteenth century, and largely through the work of the Impressionist painters, picnics had become a middle-class pastime, rather than the just the default of the working class and the extravagance (all those servants to carry all that stuff!) of the economic elite. Even as they celebrated Bohemian lifestyles, the impressionists recorded bourgeois culture in the form of an outdoor lunch.

IMPRESSIONS OF LUNCH

For painters of the Impressionist school, who became active in the 1860s in France, lunch seems to have been the perfect meal, portrayed and really celebrated in many of their works. Lunch offered an opportunity to be leisurely in public and thus to advocate by example for a lifestyle loosened from strict bourgeois rules of behavior. Of the three main meals, lunch was also the most likely to be eaten outside, in season, and so the only meal that brought the diner into the natural world that Impressionists delighted in. Because they loved to paint out of doors, painters such as Renoir and Monet were highly susceptible to picnicking. Eating informally on the grass allowed them to pause without having to pack up and enabled them to sustain the charm of the outside world, broken only much later when the light was finally too dim for painting.

Manet's naked lunch was a sort of apotheosis of the Impressionist love of lunch, taking the theme of relaxed codes to its extreme by unbinding the two women who appear in the painting from all or most of the clothing that kept them proper in the eyes of society. To lunch in the nude, in public, was to defy prudism in the name of pleasure. Equally loose was the *déjeuner* itself, which consists of a tumbled basket of fruit and a small round bread, not much more than a roll. Far from the formal luncheon that bourgeois French families ritually consumed each day, Manet's morsels were a mere gesture toward a meal. There is slightly more on the table in his 1869 *Luncheon in the Studio*, where we can glimpse a half-filled glass, an open beer bottle, a coffee cup, a half-peeled lemon, and some oyster shells.

When Monet created his own version of the *Déjeuner sur l'Herbe*, he not only dressed all the participants but also provided a much more substantial lunch. *The Picnic*, in which Monet reworked Manet's theme of an midday meal in the woods, showed a roast chicken, a ham, a large raised meat pie, a loaf of bread, a collection of cheeses, and four bottles of wine. Civilizing Manet's disorderly meal further, Monet's version included china plates and wine glasses spread on a white tablecloth.

Yet another Impressionist picnic is featured in James Jacques Joseph Tissot's *Holyday*, painted in 1876. It is a multigenerational group picnic, with the younger adults taking center stage. As a man in a fez stretches out between two young women on the edge of a picnic blanket, a small child is partially seen along one edge of the canvas, near to where an elderly couple sits in chairs. Perhaps the viewer is supposed to think that picnicking belongs to lovers, rather

Figure 5.3. *Le Déjeuner sur l'Herbe*. **Source: Eduard Manet, 1863. © RMN-Grand Palais/Art Resource, New York.**

Figure 5.4. *Lunch on the Grass.* **Source: Eduard Manet, 1863. © RMN-Grand Palais/ Art Resource, New York.**

than to families, because as well as the ménage à trois depicted in the center of the painting, another male-female couple loiter intimately behind a tree in the background. The material repast is laid out on a white cloth: A raisin-studded cake has been cut into, some slices of what look like a delicate ham wait on a plate, there is a joint of meat, a plate of grapes, two teapots, and four glass torpedo shaped-flasks, associated with carbonated water, fanned out on the picnic blanket. The meal seems to be taking place in a public park, so we can assume that the intimacies of the moment will not go too far, especially with the elderly couple as chaperones, but there is still a tension between propriety and pleasure on display over lunch.

Renoir's most famous depictions of lunch chronicle the social life of the Restaurant Fournaise, on the Seine, where patrons could rent boats and also dine on the riverside. His attention to foodstuffs is closer to Manet's than Monet's. In both his *The Rower's Lunch* and *Luncheon of the Boating Party*, Renoir portrays only fruit and wine as lunch fare. Like Manet, he presents the Bohemian life as one outside the norms of sensible meals. He also seems more interested in the habits of lunchtime than in its foods in his *The End of the Lunch*, in which all food has been removed from the table; all that remains to complete the meal is the cigarette that a young man is lighting and the tiny glass of cordial one of his female companions is about to sip. Far from gearing up to go back to work, the pair seems intent on drawing out the pleasures of relaxation.

We do not have to take Renoir's as a reliable culinary witness, however, because a contemporary researcher finds that the restaurant served lunches of "tiny deep-fried river fish, freshly caught crayfish, and *matelote*—a stew prepared from the daily catch of river fish such as pike, perch, carp and eel—served

Figure 5.5. *Holyday*. Source: James Tissot. Tate, London/Art Resource, New York.

with mimosa salad and followed by the local specialty, a tart made with the delicious variety of *verte bonnes*, greengages that grow" in the region.[5] French writer Guy de Maupassant, who also patronized the Restaurant Fournaise, gave some of his characters a picnic, purchased from the restaurant and composed of fried fish, sautéed rabbit, salad, and dessert.[6] Perhaps Renoir worried that if he painted such delicious bounty his viewers would be distracted by their own hunger and pay no attention to his talent.

A menu designed by Impressionist painter Jean-Georges Huyot for the popular café Le Chat Noir reveals the lunch food more typical in the city. At Le Chat Noir, painters and anyone else could choose from oysters, a few soups including onion soup and consommé, cold sliced meats and sausages, and sandwiches of roast beef, ham, anchovy, caviar, sausage, and cheese. There were also a few omelets and egg dishes as well as salads and assorted fruits. The salads seem to have been less of the leafy variety and more substantial. Potato, anchovy and potato, and camembert were three of the choices. A few specialties included two types of terrine, chateaubriand, and roast beef. The menu suggests that lunch portions may have been smaller than dinner portions because prix fixe meals were offered at 2 francs 50 for lunch and 3 francs for dinner.[7]

While many of the most famous painters of the era spent their days in and around Paris, dining at cafes like Le Chat Noir, Monet preferred to live in the country, where he generously entertained his many friends. Monet employed a cook named Marguerite whose talents were much appreciated in the painter's circle. The main meal of the day in Monet's household was lunch, according to writer Alexandra Leaf. Lunch took place at 11:30 and "was usually composed of a hot first course, perhaps stuffed tomatoes or mushrooms *au gratin*, followed by a meat or fish dish, a cooked vegetable, a salad, and dessert." Much of the material for the meal had been grown in the artist's own garden.[8] Monet enjoyed food so much that he actually kept a cooking journal. His friend Henri de Toulouse-Lautrec also gave much thought to meals. Toulouse-Lautrec believed that lunch should properly "consist of only two main dishes, one rather more elegant that than the other," so that it stood out as the centerpiece of the meal. The two main dishes could be accompanied by side dishes that complemented their flavors.[9]

As the Impressionists' interest in everyday life spread beyond France, lunch appeared in the work of other artists, particularly as English and American painters took a new interest in the effects of industrialization and the lives of the working class. In 1874, British painter Eyre Crowe portrayed a group of young women factory workers taking their lunch break in *The Dinner Hour*. Eyre's women drink from small bowls, suggesting that their many thermoses may be filled with soup, while covered picnic baskets do not reveal their contents to the viewer. Although the crowd is appealing and the scene bright, Crowe seems to be challenging his audience to think about the situation realistically. His working women are fine today, while the sun shines and they can sit on a wall to eat from their lunch pails, but what will happen on a rainy day? Or when winter comes? The artist paints many of the women as physically close to each other, suggesting a very important feature of the factory lunch hour. Time away from bosses gave workers a chance to bond with each other, providing emotional support and also political support in opposition to unfair working conditions.

A much later work, *South Beach Bathers* by John Sloan, painted in 1907–1908, also portrays a working-class lunch party. In this case, however, the young people are at the beach, on a day off from work, and able to enjoy lunch at more leisure. Instead of sandwiches or scraps from a lunch pail, they eat freshly cooked hot dogs on a blanket in the sun while enjoying physical intimacy with each other in a state of greater undress than would have been usual during the workweek.

The American painter Winslow Homer portrayed an important moment in late-nineteenth-century lunch rituals—the blowing of the "dinner horn," a simple tin horn that summoned workers home from the field to their midday meal. Homer's 1870 painting shows us a young woman, standing with her back to us. She is dressed in white clothes that billow a little in a wind and, with her silver trumpet, make her look somewhat angelic. She may have apron strings around her waist but she shows no overt signs of having cooked, maintaining her ethereality. Perhaps Homer intended us to think how much like a call to paradise the dinner horn can seem in the middle of a workday. Or perhaps he meant to valorize the work of farm women who provide meals for workers. Homer repeated this figure in several works during his life, suggesting that it was important to him to tell the simple, daily story of lunch.

MODERN ART LUNCH

For a performance piece, Red Grooms made a boar's head out of papier mâché, then stuffed it with dry ice and pieces of bologna. He stood around and made sandwiches for the audience. When cookbook compilers Madeline Conway and Nancy Kirk asked him about the piece, they learned that "Red is sure the image of what he wanted, but he is not sure of its meaning." Grooms offered a more practical, though also idiosyncratic lunch dish, titled confetti egg salad, which mixes hardboiled eggs, black olives, diced salami, pimientos, and mayonnaise.[10] His contemporary, painter Alex Katz, enjoys sandwiches of strange combinations, such as "bologna, bananas, chocolate bits with lettuce on rye," but he also believes "American cheese on white [bread] is the ultimate. To me as a kid it represented the straight world," an intriguing concept for Katz, whose mother was partial to "remnant pies," constructed of a week's worth of leftovers between two pie crusts. He also enjoys classic New York sandwiches, "corned beef on rye and liverwurst with mustard on rye are also absolutes."[11]

Painter Willem de Kooning emigrated to America in 1926, from Holland. The first meal he remembered eating in America was a lunch: "Lunchtime I went to a place on River Street and I saw on the bill of fare that I could read 'Hamburger,' so I said, 'Hamburger.' The next day I took a hamburger and on the following day I took a hamburger, and then I thought I'd change and ordered a sirloin of beef and tried to say it but the waiter gave me the hamburger anyway," a choice that was perhaps better for de Kooning's finances, as he had not yet achieved fame and was working as a house painter. His wife, the artist Elaine de Kooning, in contrast had little interest in lunch, declaring, "Three meals a day is preposterous," and eating small snacks of fruit and cheese throughout the day instead.[12]

Philip Guston, an American painter, used the motif of a sandwich often in his work. Art critic Arthur Danto suggests that Guston's sandwich was both a symbol of domesticity and richer than that. Referring to Guston's later work, Danto mused, "An artist who leaves us with a painting of a thick salami and cheese sandwich on seeded rye as one of his last works cannot be reduced to a single narrative theme, political or poetic."[13]

PERFORMANCE ART LUNCH

As noted earlier, the very ordinariness of lunch—just a bite to eat, nothing special, only twenty minutes—seems to lend itself to playful reinterpretation. In 2011, an arts group known as "a razor, a shiny knife," made performance out of the very dreary fact that so many New Yorkers end up eating their lunch on the subway, hurrying between appointments. Commandeering one car on the L train (L for lunch?), the organizers suspended counter space over the car's seats and served a lunch of multicourse haute cuisine complete with foie gras torchons, fillet mignon, and chocolat pot de creme. Each course boarded the train separately at a different station, amounting to an amazing feat of culinary choreography.[14]

WRITTEN LUNCH

In the introduction to the *Canlit Foodbook*, a collection of writing about food by Canadian authors, Margaret Atwood (who edited the book) noted some artistic meal biases. While it was easy enough to assemble pieces about breakfast (especially by poets), her luck ran out with the next meal. It was unclear why, but "for some reason nobody seems to write much about lunch." Atwood speculated that "perhaps it's too late in the day for poets and too early for novelists."[15] Lacking any literary descriptions specifically about lunch, Atwood does include poems and fiction about soups, salads, and sandwiches, which are common North American lunch foods.

Poet Michael Ondaatje, a contributor to the collection, declares, "Since my wife was born / she must have eaten / the equivalent of two-thirds / of the original garden of Eden. / Not the dripping lush fruit / or the meat in the ribs of animals / but the green salad gardens of that place." He imagines that if she were Eve, even in the moment of expulsion from the garden, she would be nibbling on her fig-leaf clothing, turning the expulsion from Paradise into a stroll through a salad bar.[16]

John Thompson provides a recipe for onion soup in the form of a poem: "In this kitchen warmth I reach / for the bouquet / of thyme and sage, drifting / in the heat . . . I cup the onion I watched grow all summer: / cutting perfectly through its heart / it speaks a white core, pale / green underskin, the perfections / I have broken." As the poem concludes, a close friend joins him and "we turn from our darkness, / our brokenness, / share this discovered root, / this one quiet bread / quick with light, thyme." A simply made onion soup becomes a deeply restorative shared moment.[17]

The onion makes another appearance in fiction-writer Brian Doyle's Onion Sandwich, made by a character in his novel *Up Low* for a character named Baby Bridget. The first step is to "cut the middle slice (1/2" thick) out of each onion. Throw the rest of both onions out in the yard." This perfect onion slice will be enjoyed with "a loaf of fresh, hot, homemade bread from some farmer's wife whose dress smells like milk." To make the sandwich, Doyle instructs us to "plaster the bread with butter. / put on the onion slices / pour salt to her [Baby Bridget] / get a beer and some mayonnaise. / Put lots of mayonnaise on the onion slices. / Close the sandwich with the heel of your / hand, press. / Eat." In case the eroticism of the recipe has been overlooked, the narrator adds, "it was quite a romantic" meal.[18]

Atwood also discovered a picnic lunch in Nellie McClung's *Clearing in the West*, at which so much food was prepared that there was even some left over for supper. The picnic was set on tables outside, and there were "raisin-buns and cinnamon rolls, curled like snail shells, doughnuts, and cookies (ginger and molasses), railroad cake; lettuce cut up in sour cream, mustard and sugar, cold sliced ham, home cured, and mother had made half a dozen vinegar pies, using her own recipe." The narrator's mother had dreamed of making fruit pies for the occasion, but in hard times she had not been able to afford any. Instead, she "made her filling out of molasses and butter, thickened with bread crumbs, and sharpened and flavored with vinegar and cinnamon. Her one regret was that she had not the white of an egg to make a frosting, but we had no hens that year." Although her cook's pride may have suffered from the lack of meringue, she had at least managed to bring pies to the picnic. A local storekeeper also distributed oranges and bananas, both rare treats that had to be imported into western Canada by train.[19]

Lunching and Dining with Jane Austen

Meal habits were a very important part of the performance of social class in the time when Jane Austen lived. It is natural, then, that a writer famed for her attention to detail would devote much time to portraying the meanings of meals. Scholar Maggie Lane, who has devoted an entire book to understanding how Austen used food to convey meaning, reveals that Austen's attention to the timing of "dinner," a meal in the afternoon that came before supper, reflects a society in transition. By making her less fashionable characters take their dinner earlier than those more in touch with power and wealth, she lets the dinner hour tell us something about her characters. In a letter to her own sister, Austen reflected on the later dinner preferred by the fashionable: "We dine now at half after three, and have done dinner I suppose before you begin.—We drink tea at half after six.—I am afraid you will despise us." In her unfinished novel, *The Watsons*, a character shows her honesty and lack of pretension by admitting to an aggressively fashionable young man that her family keeps "early hours," meaning that they have dinner at three. When, another day, he is asked to share the family's supper at six, he is unwilling, because of the semantic issue: "For a man whose heart had long been fixed on calling his next meal dinner," it was "insupportable" to eat a meal called supper first. Going home to a lonely meal when he could have been in good company, the man is revealed to be a fool.[20]

While Austen herself gives no recipes, one writer suggests a menu that might have been served when Austen's Emma visits the estate of her neighbor Mr. Knightley to pick strawberries. Emma, Knightley, and the meddling Mrs. Elton, along with a host of other local characters, might have dined on rice and chickpea salad, a fish "shape" or cold jellied mousse, cucumber slices in vinegar, and chocolate-dipped strawberries. While these are not all exactly era-appropriate dishes—English people seldom ate chickpeas before the late twentieth century, for example—they might help a reader channel the kind of summer day on which the visit took place.[21]

Dickens and Lunch

While Charles Dickens's characters may be more memorable for their hunger than their meals, they did occasionally get their hands on some lunch. Dickens uses his portrayal of this meal to establish class and character for the many men, women, and children who crowd the streets of his books. In an early phase in the life of David Copperfield, for example, the young hero is working at a wine merchant's warehouse. There, "I paid sixpence . . . for my dinner, which was a meat pie and a turn at a neighboring pump" for water. During his lunch hour, he was left to wander, there being no attractive place to sit. This meal, in its simplicity and loneliness, foreshadows Copperfield's experiences in the warehouse. When another character in this novel sets sail from England, her friends come to see her off and dine on "preserved ginger and guava and other delicacies of that sort for lunch," as if they were tasting a little of the adventure that lies in her future.[22] For the gentlemen of *The Pickwick Papers*, lunch is a bit more English. As Sam Weller, a young assistant to Mr. Pickwick, unpacks the hamper for a group picnic, he remarks, "Weal pie," meaning veal, "Wery good thing is weal pie when you know the lady as made it and are quite sure it ain't kitten arter all, though, where's the odds, when they're so like weal the very piemen don't know the difference?" Along with the suspect pies, Pickwick and his friends eat a knuckle of ham, cold slices of beef, tongue, and bread and drink beer and punch from pitchers. The plenty of the meal and its ample supply of alcohol reflect the group's economic stability, but the chance of kittens in the pie lend it all the comic touch that is the soul of the narrative.[23]

Concerned as he was with portraying the life of London in his time, Dickens was particularly skilled at re-creating a special sort of "business lunch," that which cannot stop for business. In *Great Expectations*, for example, we find two men at lunch separately, neither seeming willing to give the meal any respect as a pause in work. Mr. Jaggers, the lawyer and Pip's guardian, is described as taking his lunch "standing, from a sandwich-box and a pocket flask of sherry," and "he seemed to bully his very sandwich as he ate it." Jaggers, as a surprising precursor to Gordon Gekko, clearly believes that lunch is for wimps.

Keeping up with his employer, Jaggers's clerk, Wemmick, is seen "at his desk, lunching—and crunching—on a dry hard biscuit; pieces of which he

threw from time to time into the slit of his mouth as if he were posting them."
He, too, has no time to waste on luncheon.[24]

In the interests of saving time, or because they do not have full households
of their own, or sometimes are in transit, Dickens characters often eat at inns
or order food delivered from inns. In *The Old Curiosity Shop*, for example,
when Mr. Swiveller is "inwardly reminded of its being nigh dinner time,"
in other words, feels his stomach rumble, he "dispatched a message to the
nearest eating house requiring an immediate supply of boiled beef and greens
for two," as he is entertaining a friend. When the food arrives, his friend remarks on the rather rough nature of the cooking: "I like this plan of sending
[potatoes] with the peel on; there's charm in drawing a potato from its native
element (if I may so express it) to which the rich and powerful are strang-
ers." For this character, Dick, cheap food from city inns had its own special
charms. Characters also frequent the food shops of the city, those descendants
of the medieval-era pie stalls, which offered fare that had not changed much in
several hundred years. In *Little Dorrit*, Dickens shows us what might tempt
the hungry at lunchtime. In "a dirty shop window in a dirty street," Fanny and
her uncle note, the window is

> made almost opaque by the steam of hot meats, vegetables, and puddings. But
> glimpses were to be caught of a roast leg of pork, bursting into tears of sage and
> onion in a metal reservoir full of gravy, of an unctuous piece of roast beef and
> blisterous Yorkshire pudding, bubbling hot in a similar receptacle, of a stuffed
> fillet of veal in rapid cut, of a ham in a perspiration with the pace it was going at,
> of a shallow tank of baked potatoes glued together by their own richness, of a truss
> or two of boiled greens, and other substantial delicacies.[25]

In Dickens's novels, the wandering ways of meals, noted in Jane Austen's
work, persist. Dickens writes of both lunch and dinner as well as supper. When
a time is noted, dinner is taken in the afternoon, whereas supper seems to be
a late-evening meal. Tea, of course, complicates matters, appearing at times to
be another term for late-afternoon dinner. In one passage, David Copperfield
takes a dinner of chops, vegetables, potatoes, and pudding and is then offered
supper later in the day. When he visits his friend Mr. Micawber in a hotel "at
the appointed dinner hour, which was four o'clock," he enjoys "a beautiful
little dinner," which included "quite an elegant dish of fish; the kidney-end of
a loin of veal, roasted; fried sausage-meat; a partridge, and a pudding." Beautiful, certainly, but not really little. Copperfield and Micawber drank wine and
"strong ale" with the meal and then punch, mixed by Mrs. Micawber, after they
had finished eating.[26]

Cooking about Books

In 1995, bibliographer Norman Kiell wrote, "The literary glorification of food may be lurching towards its logical conclusion. 'Since restaurants and their dishes are now reviewed in a more indigestibly Proustian style than most books,' the *Times Literary Supplement* reports, 'should not restaurants actually sell books as well, enabling one to eat an *Omelette Arnold Benett*, say to the accompaniment of *The Old Wives' Tale*?'"[28] In fact, as Keill's own bibliography attests, there are many cookbooks dedicated to literature, sometimes to individual authors.

A cookbook that provides recipes for food mentioned in James Joyce's works, for example, lists six lunches from Ulysses, which seems to include the most midday meals of all the writer's works. The novel's hero, Leopold Bloom, lunches on a sandwich of gorgonzola and mustard on "clean white bread," accompanied by a glass of burgundy. Another character has cold veal and ham "mixed sandwiches," which the cookbook's editor advises should be made on soda bread with mayonnaise. For a "midnight lunch" that Bloom and his wife are invited to at another couple's home, the host recalls, "There was lashings of stuff we put up: port wine and sherry and curacao, to which we did ample justice. Fast and furious it was. After liquids came solids. Cold joints galore and mince pies."[29]

Cookbook writer Craig Boreth used both Ernest Hemingway's diaries and his fiction to create a collection of menus and recipes tied to the Nobel Prize–winning writer's life. For instance, readers can make for themselves a meal that Hemingway and his wife, Hadley, cooked at home rather than spending money at a café. The young, intellectual couple was trying to save money so that they could rent books from the lending library at the world-famous Shakespeare and Co. bookstore in Paris. Our penny-pinching booklovers lunched on radishes, veal liver, mashed potatoes, endive salad, and an apple tart, a distinctly French meal for two Midwestern Americans.[30]

When Hemingway joined fellow Midwesterner F. Scott Fitzgerald on a driving trip in France, the two enjoyed a quintessentially French meal at a hotel in Lyon, lunching on "excellent truffled roast chicken, delicious bread and white Macon wine." With another American writer, John dos Passos, Hemingway had a more elaborate lunch, enjoying rollmop herring, *sole meuniere, civet de lievre a la cocotte* or "jugged hare," *marmelade de pommes*, and three bottles of wine—one for each course.[31]

Some of the most delicious lunches recorded in fiction are those in children's books. Carol MacGregor collected accounts of meals in children's stories in her *Storybook Cookbook* and included recipes so that children could make these meals themselves. Readers are reminded that after a long journey to her grandfather's house, Joanna Spyri's beloved character Heidi was hungry. Her grandfather set to work toasting a piece of cheese in the fireplace of his mountain home, holding it out "on the end of a long iron fork[,] he moved it this way and that, until it was golden yellow on all sides." In the meantime, Heidi rushed about the cottage, setting the table with a loaf of bread, two plates, and two knives. Impressed with her initiative, Heidi's grandfather declares, "Now, this is nice that you can think of things for yourself," and he placed the toasted cheese on two slices of bread. This version of a toasted cheese sandwich makes the reader feel that Grandfather's home is a cozy and familiar place, and it also suggests that Heidi and her grandfather are going to be good partners in housekeeping. MacGregor's recipe for "Heidi's Toasted Cheese Sandwiches" notes that "cooking has advanced quite a bit since Heidi's day," and she recommends toasting a cheese sandwich in a hot buttered frying pan in an oven rather than roasting a piece of cheese directly in a fireplace.[32]

From the *Wind in the Willows*, MacGregor takes a cue from the bountiful picnic that Rat offers Mole as they float down the river in Rat's boat. In Rat's "fat, wicker picnic basket" are, Rat explains, "cold chicken . . . coldtongue-coldhamcoldbeefpickledgherkinssaladfrenchrollscresssandwidgespottedmeatgingerbeerlemonadesodawater." Rat is about to continue the catalog when Mole cries out "in ecstasies: 'This is too much.'" MacGregor's cookbook only offers a recipe for cold ham, but she encourages readers to add their own "picklesandlemonadeandfrenchrollsand—."[33]

Extrapolating from the beloved stories of Finnish children's author Tove Jansson, *Moomins Cook Book* includes many intriguing lunches. A "vegetable patch summer soup" recalls Moominmamma's devotion to her garden, while "Little My's Peppery Spaghetti" seems to reflect that character's waywardness. Although classified as an evening meal, it can be assumed that the Snork Maiden's berry soup would also make a nice, light lunch. The recipe is simple enough: "'Didn't you bring a bottle of juice?' the Snork Maiden asked Sniff" as they are wandering in the woods in search of water, "'Give it to me.' And with that she poured the juice into a saucepan and boiled up some berry soup. 'That settles it,' she said."[34]

At a midsummer garden party, "great barrels of mead were rolled out" around noon, and everyone drank some from small bark cups, eating "onion, anchovy, and marmalade sandwiches," for lunch. The cookbook mercifully offers recipes for both marmalade sandwiches *and* onion and anchovy sandwiches, not blending the three ingredients, as the original text suggests.[35]

Adventure stories for children often include picnics, or lunch along the way, because they generally take place in the daytime—the part of the day best known to children—and eating away from home in the freedom-from-rules associated with picnicking appeals to children's natural desire to escape the world ordered by adults. J. R. R. Tolkien satisfies this interest in traveling food with his invention of *lembas*, the special cakes of the Elves, which appear in his Lord of the Rings trilogy. Giving those who eat them both physical sustenance and courage, the lembas are specifically offered for use in emergencies and given to travelers. Frodo and his friends are warned that the cakes stay sweet only when unbroken and wrapped in leaves, just as the Elves provide them. Referred to as "waybread," lembas is a kind of mystical picnic dish.[36] The Hobbits, when at home and not on a world-saving quest, are famous for their "second breakfasts," which might also be called "first lunches"; they occur regularly between breakfast and lunch.

The now obsolete term *déjeuner à la fourchette*, which meant an early lunch of fairly substantial ingredients, inspired a satirical poem in 1844. The poet begins joyfully, "What a beautiful day! Had the weather been wet, / What a damp on my dejeuner a la fourchette." Clearly hoping to gain social capital from the event, the narrator is sorry to see a dowdy old woman arrive first, aware that she will not understand the new fashion in meals and will think that noon, the time arranged, is too late for breakfast. Unfashionably dressed and too early, she is "a blot on my dejeuner a la fourchette." When all the fashionable people send regrets, the narrator wishes she had cancelled the event. The meal proceeds, a grand picnic with musicians and an assortment of tents—"*This* tent for the dinner, and *that* for the tea. / (Though *breakfast* they *call* it, no dinner they'll get / Except at my Dejeuner a la Fourchette.)" Apparently, the guests are going to stay for several meals, all under the confusing umbrella of the French term. As the champagne runs out, the sky darkens, and strong breezes blow out the fireworks and lanterns, the hostess muses on the expense of the fashionable entertainment: "I'm sure that my husband will never forget / The cost of my Dejeuner a la Fourchette."[37]

Twenty years later, the author of the *Cook and Housewife's Manual* turned to poetry to list the menu of a typical déjeuner à la fourchette:

There are the sausages, there are the eggs,
and the chickens with close-fitted legs,
And there is a bottle of brandy,
And there's some of the best sugar candy
Which is better than sugar for coffee.
There are slices from good ham cut off,—he

Who cut them was but an indifferent carver,
he wanted the delicate hand of a barber.
And there is a dish
Buttered over! And fish, trout and char,
Sleeping are
The smooth ice-like surface over,
there's a pie made of veal, one of widgeons, and there's one of ham mixed
    with pigeons.[38]

The déjeuner à la fourchette had come a long way from what were supposed
to have been its frugal and rationalist beginnings.

Lunch and Character

In *Little Women*, Louisa May Alcott's novel of New England childhood, lunch
serves as a test of maturity for characters. Amy, with pretensions to elegance,
has invited her rich friends over for a lunch party. When she first mentions the
idea, her mother, Marmee, suggests that "cake, sandwiches, fruit, and coffee
will be all that is necessary, I hope." Amy has a grander lunch in mind: "Oh,
dear, no! We must have cold tongue and chicken, French chocolate and ice
cream, besides." Marmee offers that perhaps Amy's rich friends will not be
impressed by such fare, as it is ordinary to them, and that something more
simple might be "pleasanter to them, as a change if nothing more." But Amy
is unwilling to conform to her social reality and offers to pay for the fancier
meal herself.

When the day arrives, rain keeps the crowd away and the family dines on the
treats Amy has prepared. The next day had been set as an alternate, but by then
there is very little tongue left and the housecat has eaten the leftover chicken,
Amy feels she must go into town to get a lobster with which to make salad, a
ladylike lunch dish in the nineteenth century. Traveling home from the market
by omnibus with a lobster and a bottle of dressing in a basket, Amy is mortified
when the crustacean is revealed to an elegant young man of her acquaintance.
Because well-to-do women of her era did not do their own marketing, the fact
that she is carrying home groceries may reveal her family's "genteel poverty"
to the gentleman, who is just the kind of person Amy, the social climber of the
family, wants to impress. Amy triumphs, however, by being both forthright and
clever, acknowledging that the lobster is her own, but distracting the young
man by immediately teasing him with the question, "Don't you wish you were
to have some of the salad he's going to make, and to see the charming ladies

who are going to eat it?" Amy is able to distract from her own role as marketing drudge by painting a bold picture of the decorous meal she has in mind.

Thus, for the young man, Mr. Tudor, "the lobster was instantly surrounded by a halo of pleasing reminiscences and curiosity about 'the charming young ladies' drove his mind from the comical mishap." Amy, with the poise of a society matron, transformed herself in a few words from a cook to a lady who lunched. Unfortunately, after all the trouble Amy takes, only one of the twelve girls she has invited shows up. This, too, Amy bears with poise, showing that, although the youngest of the family, and often the least sympathetic, she has the potential for gracious maturity.[39]

When Tom Sawyer and his friends set out on their ill-fated afternoon of cave exploration, Becky Sharp packed a picnic for Tom and herself to share. While Twain does not tell us what was in the basket, one writer muses that "the meal, according to the custom of the country, probably included fried chicken . . . accompanied by thin, sliced, buttered bread, sweet pickles or watermelon pickles and a luscious cake." Given the shortage of fresh fruits out of season, this may have been a fig layer cake, "a favorite in those days." During Mark Twain's own Missouri childhood, which he used as a background for his Tom Sawyer stories, families had their heaviest meals at noon, lunching on soup, roast mutton, beef, or ham, with gravy, chickens, ducks, or wild game, side dishes of potatoes and onions, as well as many jellies and jams, which were served with meat, following British tradition. These bountiful lunches ended with cakes, pies, and puddings.[40]

Twain himself once offered a confession of his own less-than-diligent nature through the description of a midday meal. In a letter to his brother, from 1860, he described a delectable lunch in New Orleans. Twain was at this time a pilot of a riverboat on the Mississippi. "Yesterday," he told his brother, "I had many things to do, but Bixby and I got with the pilots of two other boats and went off dissipating on a ten dollar dinner at a French restaurant." Lest his brother tattle, Twain jokingly inserted, "Breathe it not unto Ma!" Then he catalogued the meal: "We ate Sheep-head fish with mushrooms, shrimps and oysters—birds—coffee with burnt brandy in it, &c &c, —ate, drank & smoked, from 1 P.M. until 5 o'clock." By then, at the end of a four-hour lunch, "the day was too far gone" to do any of the many things he had earlier planned.[41]

One hundred and fifty years later, Twain fan Andrew Beahrs visited New Orleans in search of the great writer's "dissipating" meal. Following leads through Twain's texts, Beahrs was on the trail of *Twain's Feast*, as he called the resulting book. In New Orleans, he found the sheep-head fish a rare and highly prized commodity. One chef waxed eloquent on the fish: "Sheep-head—oh my goodness, that is just out-of-this-world good. . . . We buy absolutely as much as we can get—forty pounds, eighty pounds, whatever" the restaurant can get from suppliers. After some time, Beahrs is able to try some and finds it "like lump crabmeat, fresh and sweet and bathed in a creamy pepper sauce, and it's exactly as good as it sounds." What may be even more delicious to the writer, though, is to taste part of Twain's feast.[42]

In more contemporary children's fiction, lunch continues to fascinate. The very popular *Captain Underpants* features a title, *Captain Underpants and the Invasion of the Incredibly Naughty Cafeteria Ladies from Outer Space (and the Subsequent Assault of the Equally Evil Lunchroom Zombie Nerds)*, in which human lunch ladies accidentally create a green slime that eats "everything in its path" and are then replaced by wicked extraterrestrial lunch servers who turn children into zombies. Scholar of children's literature Annette Wannamaker theorizes that such a tale "serves as a site for fantasies of power and control," as the story disrupts the tedious normality of institutional lunch, and also as "narrative device serving to seduce the beginning reader into the Symbolic in ways that make reading seem inviting and mildly subversive." In other words, the chaotic lunchroom scenes are intellectually tasty to beginning readers, making them hunger for more texts.[43]

Jarrett Krosoczka has turned the age-old fear of lunch ladies inside out, creating an extremely popular series of graphic novels for young readers that showcase the secret superpowers of a lunch lady. Krosoczka has himself become a hero to lunchroom staff, who are proud to hear him honoring their work: "They are far from the nasty old lady slopping goulash on the tray. They are the most positive, cheery people I have ever met."[44] His hero's tagline is "Serving Justice . . . and Lunch!" The lunch lady of Krosoczka's series, along with her cheerful sidekick Betty, a fellow lunch lady, is a tireless champion of a group of students known as the "lunch bunch," and not just in terms of nutrition. The lunch lady will go out of her kitchen and out of her way to save them from all kinds of outlandish enemies, such as "math mutants" and a "cyborg substitute."

Emile Zola's characters in *The Belly of Paris* are entirely ensconced in a world of food. They work at the public market, Les Halles, which was once vital to the city of Paris, as Zola's title suggests. One day, the character Cadine invites her friends to "an enormous lunch" served in the midst of the market, but secluded among "four walls of wicker" made by using market baskets for cover. Zola tells us not only each item consumed, but where in the market it came from, giving us a tour in a lunch and prefiguring on minute scale the locavorism of the twenty-first century. On the table, made from an overturned flat basket, the lunchers eat "pears, nuts, cream cheese, prawns, fried potatoes, and radishes. The cheese came from a fruiter . . . and was a present. A fried-food man . . . had sold them two sous worth of potatoes on credit. The rest of the meal, the pears, the nuts, the prawns and the radishes, had been stolen from various parts of Les Halles. It was a wonderful banquet."[45]

Poet's Lunch

The poet Frank O'Hara called his most well-known collection *Lunch Poems*. The legend is that these were poems he came up with during his lunch hour and quickly typed out, perhaps even on display typewriters in office supply shops. The idea of lunch-hour poems suggests that they are casual and serendipitous, like the meal of lunch itself, which people often say they will "grab," as if it they were going to see a sandwich floating by. O'Hara's poem most directly related to the urban lunch scene—he lived and worked in Manhattan—is "A Step Away from Them." The poem begins, "It's my lunch hour, so I go / for a walk among the hum-colored cabs." On his way, he sees construction workers at lunch: "laborers feed their dirty / glistening torsos sandwiches / and Coca-Cola, with yellow helmets / on. They protect them from falling bricks, I guess." O'Hara's observation that the workers do not take off their hardhats for lunch gives readers the idea that they are barely pausing in their work for the meal. O'Hara continues his stroll through Times Square, observing the life of the city, commenting, "It is 12:40 of / a Thursday. / Neon in daylight is a / great pleasure." Amid these musings, "I stop for a cheeseburger at JULIET'S / CORNER," which makes him think of the Italian actress Giulietta Masina before he adds to his order a "chocolate malted." Done with this part of lunch, he wanders on, stopping for "a glass of papaya juice / and back to work." O'Hara's lunch poem is both the quintessential New York City lunch experience and a uniquely personal journey, punctuated with associations and reflections—"my heart is in my / pocket, it is Poems by Pierre Reverdy"—that are specific to the poet himself.[46]

LUNCH IN FILMS AND TV

Since the 1980s, when restaurant culture became a national form of entertainment in the United States, there have been many food-focused films produced both in the United States and abroad but enjoying huge popularity among American viewers. Among these movies, dinner tends to steal the show, but lunch has long played a role in movie plots, serving to gather characters for a moment in the midst of the action. Some of these important lunches are discussed below.

In Charlie Chaplin's 1936 *Modern Times*, a spoof of industrialization, a "feeding machine" salesman demonstrates his product on Chaplin, a factory worker. The machine is supposed to eliminate that great time waster, the lunch break, by automatically feeding workers while they keep working. Chaplin is picked out from a crowd on their break—he appears to be eating an apple—and strapped in. At first all goes well; the soup bowl neatly tips a little soup into Chaplin's mustached mouth, then the table turns and a pair of tongs feed him cubes of meat. Between each dish, a buffer wipes his mouth. But the machine quickly malfunctions when it turns to corn and the poor worker's face is nearly rubbed off by a piece of corn on the cob that will not leave him alone. Smoke and flashes of light come out of the feeding machine, and it continues to malfunction, pouring soup in Chaplin's lap and tossing pie into his face. At last it is turned off and the factory owner rejects the machine not because it has abused his employee, but because "it isn't practical."

When the slavery-era romance *Gone with the Wind* proved to be a box office success, the film studio that had produced it thought to capitalize on its success by publishing a cookbook. This cookbook explains that "'Gone with the Wind' told of a style of living, as well as a romantic drama. A way of living and playing and eating that thrilled us all." One particular scene that most viewers would remember features Mammy lacing Scarlett O'Hara into her corset. On her way to a barbecue picnic lunch—at which guests will learn of the outbreak of the Civil War—Mammy admonishes Scarlet not to eat much. Instead of eating in front of others at the picnic, which she claims would be unladylike, Scarlett is advised to eat some pancakes before she leaves home. The *Gone with the Wind Cook Book* advises "young girls" that such behavior is no longer necessary, for "ladies may eat heartily in public today and still be ladies." The luncheon party recommended here, though lacking plates of roasted meat, seems filling enough: broiled oysters, chicken pilau, a vegetable salad, biscuits, and Sally Lunn followed by eggnog ice cream and Lady Baltimore Cake.[47]

Encouraging readers to think about "what picnics they must have had at Tara," and admitting that most readers "can never actually experience . . . the real Georgia barbecue—fresh pork and mutton by the pit-full, roasted over hickory log coals and spiced by the sharp barbecue sauce," the *Gone with the Wind Cook Book* helpfully offers recipes for barbecued spareribs, "juicy baked glazed hams," and the kind of fried chicken that, in "a big iron kettleful was always found at most barbecues just as it was on that eventful barbecue day at Twelve Oaks so many years ago."[48]

Quite the opposite of an antebellum barbecue, the automat captured the imagination of many moviemakers, seeming to represent modernity or perhaps alienation. It could also be used to excellent comic affect, as many directors have proved. Preston Sturges's 1937 *Easy Living*, made in the midst of the Great Depression, featured a free-for-all, sparked when an automat staff member, played by Ray Milland, tries to help out a hungry young woman, Jean Arthur, by giving her free lunch, a gesture most of the film's viewers would surely have seen as heroic, given the national crisis. In a scuffle with the policeman who catches him at it, Milland accidentally throws a lever that opens all the automat's slots and sets rivers of hot coffee and milk pouring from spigots. The customers make a run for the free food and someone takes the news outside, encouraging all who can to loot the restaurant.

Director Delbert Mann set another comic scene in the automat in his 1962 Doris Day and Cary Grant romantic comedy, *That Touch of Mink*. In an early scene in the film, Doris Day's character, Cathy, visits an automat in midtown Manhattan, where her friend Connie works. Buying a token for a salad, Cathy calls for her friend through the open slot and receives a much more substantial lunch—chicken pot pie, baked potato, Jell-O, and a piece of cake—without spending more money. As the two women chat through the slot, their conversation is punctuated by the passage of plates from one side to another. Soon after, in a case of mistaken identity, Connie reaches through the slot first to slap and then to throw pie at a man she thinks has wronged Cathy. One of the pleasures of the scene is that viewers get to see behind the scenes at the automat, as uniformed staff dash back and forth, refilling empty slots, something like the operators who once ran the telephone lines.

Probably the most often-referenced scene in the 1989 romantic comedy *When Harry Met Sally* is a lunch scene at Katz's Deli in which Sally, played by Meg Ryan, fakes an orgasm to prove to Harry that many of his partners may have done the same. When she finishes, a neighboring customer famously tells a waiter, "I'll have what she's having." What "she" was having was also important to the movie's plot. Sally has ordered a turkey sandwich on white bread with mayonnaise that symbolizes her WASP heritage and perhaps her cluelessness about others. Katz's is famous for pastrami, corned beef, and knishes, classic Jewish American cuisine, which Sally rejects by choosing something that one could order anywhere. She is missing out on what makes Katz's special and—at this point in the movie—also missing out on what makes her lunch date, Harry, her perfect partner.

While the orgasm gets all the attention in this scene, a closer look at Sally's lunch can reveal that the scene is either a knowing reference or an echo of a scene in Woody Allen's *Annie Hall* in which the WASPy Annie has lunch with the Jewish Alvy in a Jewish deli. While Alvy has corned beef on rye, Annie orders pastrami on white bread with mayonnaise, lettuce, and tomato, a culinary faux pas that Alvy is quick to notice.[49]

In the 1993 movie *Falling Down*, Michael Douglas's tightly wound character, William Foster, finally unravels over the boundary between breakfast and lunch. Arriving at a fast food chain, Whammyburger, modeled on McDonald's, Foster finds that he is five minutes too late to order breakfast and must choose from the lunch menu. When he takes out a machine gun, breakfast becomes possible. Deranged and not in control of his gun, he then switches his order to a burger and fries—a lunchtime meal—underscoring the senselessness of his psychosis. When he gets his lunch, he is infuriated to find that the real burger does not live up to the restaurant's advertisements, echoing the movie's theme that life does not live up to the expectations of our youth.

Although best known for initiating a global frenzy for cosmopolitans, *Sex and the City* also made the "girls' lunch" a regular event for its four characters. Their regular lunches take place in different restaurants, signaling that they are not stuck in their ways, like the characters of Seinfeld, who usually resorted to the same diner for all meals. By meeting for lunch, the four women of *Sex and the City* leave their evenings free for the activities suggested by the show's title. They meet in midday to share news, primarily of their romantic lives, but the public nature of the meeting place and its impersonality—none of the friends is cooking for the others—suggest that there is actually a limit to these friendships.

In a scene from the movie *Sex and the City*, Carrie Bradshaw announces her engagement to her longtime boyfriend at a restaurant, not privately, which triggers her friend Charlotte to scream with glee and then explain to the whole restaurant that Carrie has been waiting ten years for this proposal. The moment both celebrates Carrie's happiness but also puts her down, as someone perhaps not desirable enough to be chosen sooner. These "girls' lunches," like a kind of business lunch, can reveal the competitive edge to the characters' friendships.

Many movies and TV shows that feature teenaged characters have important scenes that take place in the lunchroom. The school lunchroom offers characters a moment of freedom from adult supervision, an opportunity that they usually exploit to create hierarchies of their own. In the 2004 film *Mean Girls*, for example, the cheerful new girl played by Lindsay Lohan is given a map of the lunchroom that explains which cliques sit at which tables. In her first foray, she is summoned to the table of "the plastics," adopted by them, and indoctrinated into their rules, proving that the lunchroom can be a dangerous place.

In the 1988 satire of teen movies, *Heathers*, another new student, Christian Slater as J.D., makes a notable first impression when he pulls a gun on two bullying jocks. The gun fires blanks, but the act so intrigues popular girl Veronica, played by Winona Rider, that she becomes involved with him, costing a few unpleasant teens their lives along the way.

Although its title suggests otherwise, the most important meal in the 1985 film *The Breakfast Club* is actually lunch. Each of the five characters is reflected in the lunches they bring to their Saturday morning detention. The sophisticated and popular Claire, played by Molly Ringwald, brings sushi in a neat black box, complete with a small pitcher of soy sauce. The lunch signals her uptight, perfectionist identity. In contrast, the loner played by Ally Sheedy takes apart her bologna sandwich, flinging the slices of meat around the room, and refills it with pixie straws and sugar crunch cereal, a rebellion against the idea of a balanced meal or mind. The jock, Emilio Estevez, has a notably large lunch, including several sandwiches, a whole pint of milk, a bag of potato chips, a bag of cookies, one apple, and a banana. He is focused on building physical strength. The nerd, Anthony Michael Hall, whose lunch receives a hands-on critique from Judd Nelson's rebel, brings peanut butter and jelly, apple juice, and soup in a cheerfully colored thermos, revealing that he is still as much a child as a young adult. The rebel himself brings nothing, reflecting his refusal to fit in with social expectations.

HOLLYWOOD LUNCH

Much like the power lunch of the New York business world, the Hollywood lunch has its own mores and lore.

Producer Hank Moonjean recalled the special arrangements of lunch at the MGM commissary in the 1960s. "As you entered, there were three long tables about thirty feet long, each with a telephone on it to receive important messages from the set. The first table was for all the key staff that was currently shooting a film." They were given immediate service for a lunch period that was often only thirty minutes. The second table was for directors and producers, and the third was for writers and visitors. A fourth table was set aside and known as "The Lion's Den," where sat the "very, very V.I.P.'s." If any member of the MGM studio was nominated for an Academy Award, everyone clapped when they entered the commissary. If they actually won, everyone stood to applaud.[50]

In 1986, one producer explained that "the art of ordering the Le Dome salad," a lunch dish at the once-popular but now closed Le Dome restaurant in

Los Angeles, "is who can ask for the most things to be left out, starting with the ham, bacon, cheese and chickpeas." A studio marketing executive noted that while in Chicago and New York, it is perfectly fine to order a second martini at lunch, this is "unacceptable" in LA.[51]

If lunch was "neutral ground," a place to meet where both players are on equal footing, lunch dates are a battlefield, as one producer found when a colleague looked into his date book and asked, "Is that the best lunch you can get?" The assumption was that everyone who is important will be lunching in public with other important people. If one was only "having lunch with somebody's errand boy . . . it's better to have it at a low-profile restaurant—Hugo's or the Ritz—where you can go and not be seen, rather than the Ivy," which has a reputation for being very popular with big names in the entertainment business.[52]

In 1991, movie producer Julia Phillips burned all her professional bridges with a tell-all memoir of the film business titled *You'll Never Eat Lunch in This Town Again*. The kind of lunch she was referring to was the Hollywood ritual in which two important figures "do lunch" together in a fashionable restaurant. The doing of lunch must necessarily be public so that the Hollywood press can begin to circulate rumors about what the lunch might mean. Lunch in these cases is always business. A *New York Times* reporter met Phillips in one of the few places that would allow her to lunch. Indeed, the maître d' of the Polo Club at the Beverly Hills Hotel seemed delighted by the attention Phillips might bring to his restaurant, claiming to have displaced a king to seat her in a preferred spot.[53]

Something of a lunch crisis occurred in 2007, when two major Hollywood companies, Creative Artists Agency (C.A.A.) and International Creative Management, moved to Century City, a neighborhood previously uninhabited by the movie industry. There seemed to be nowhere to lunch but a Panda Express and a Fuddruckers in the local mall. Desperate, a partner at C.A.A. called Tom Colicchio, the New York restaurateur, and begged him to establish a Century City outpost of his popular restaurant, Craft. Colicchio obliged and the lunching began.

One restaurant that predated the new arrivals was able to appeal to the Hollywood crowd, but first the restaurant staff had to learn who the new clients were. It is easy enough to recognize a movie star, but not so easy to recognize her agent when she is not with him. The restaurant requested headshots of all the agencies' executives so that its staff could be sure to treat them better than nobodies. Another restaurateur on the brink of opening a Century City lunch spot committed to putting up pictures of important executives in her staff room if it were necessary to ensure that waiters would know who to seat where—and when to back away from the table. A manager at another restaurant explained that waiters are trained "to mostly communicate via eye-contact. We don't want a waiter to try and take an order when someone is just about to sign a contract. Not good."[54] The phrase "let's do lunch," which really means "I don't want to have lunch with you," seems to have become standard in the 1980s, when it was well known enough for a satirist to suggest that if the devil were real and living in LA, there would be "no more diabolic threats. From now on it would be 'Let's do lunch sometime, have your girl call my girl.'"[55]

In a 2013 survey of top movie executives, the top three best places for a power lunch were the Soho House, a private club and British import with membership fees; the Polo Lounge, a perennial favorite; and e. baldi, an Italian restaurant, where the chef, Edoardo Baldi, manages the seating chart himself to be sure that everyone eats in the appropriate spot given their Hollywood hierarchy. Executives interviewed for the survey noted changes in Los Angeles lunch culture: "Lunch has lost many of its indulgences. Iced tea is the new martini. Just about everyone's on a special diet, regardless of whether the intent is to lose weight. It's rare to find people tarrying at their tables beyond an hour and a half. And folks are generally more conscious of cost." Instead of fighting over who got to indicate dominance by getting the check, lunch partners now split the costs evenly.[56]

LITERARY LUNCHES

The "literary lunch" is a tradition now seemingly out of fashion that dates back to the early nineteenth century. Literary lunches may be gatherings of writers or gatherings of readers who invite a writer to speak. An early American literary lunch club was the Bread and Cheese Club, a group featuring both writers and painters, who met at the New Street Bookstore, owned by the publisher John Wiley. James Fenimore Cooper was the original convener of the club in 1824, which also included Samuel Morse, William Cullen Bryant, and Asher Durand. The group, first known as "The Lunch," and "Cooper's Lunch," took the name "Bread and Cheese" from their system of voting, in which a piece of bread placed on the table was a vote to admit a new member and a bit of cheese a vote to reject him.[57]

The most famous literary lunch club was the Algonquin Hotel's "Round Table," a gathering of writers and performers that met weekly during the 1920s. Dorothy Parker, Harold Ross, and Robert Benchley were three of the best-known regular members of the group. A menu from a meal served at the club in

1920 survives, to give us some idea of what the famous club might have tasted. Although the food listed was probably beyond the means of most of the writers and actors who ate at the Round Table, we know that they could at least have aspired to lobster bisque, sautéed kingfish, chicken with ham, and Salad Louise. Knowing their lack of means but relishing the fame that their presence brought his restaurant, the Algonquin's manager provided the Round Table with free celery and popovers—an interesting lunch. They bought their own drinks.[58]

A more contemporary version of the literary lunch is that hosted since 1996 by the *Oldie*, a literary magazine in London. Once a month, three of the *Oldie*'s writers address an audience for ten minutes each over lunch. The meal takes place at Simpsons-on-the-Strand, where the menu offers classic English dishes, such as meat pie, dover sole, and breast of wood pigeon.

For another kind of literary lunch, in 1961, Ruth Langland Holberg recommended turkey and ham mornay followed by strawberry chiffon pie and coffee as "a delicious lunch, and an easy one. If you are entertaining an editor, with a discussion following, you won't be too exhausted to be at your mental best."[59] In a reversal of roles, Holberg noted, "A young editor sometimes prefers to serve luncheon in her apartment not far from the office when she wants to discuss a new book with an author and an illustrator." When the editor plays host, the meal is creamed mushrooms, baking powder biscuits, broiled tomatoes, apricot snow, and of course coffee. Most of this meal the busy working woman has prepared early in the morning before going to the office.[60]

In a 1969 article for the *New York Times*, writer Nora Ephron explained the centrality of lunching to the book business. In publishing, Ephron wrote, "One. Has. Lunch. A two or three hour lunch. In a restaurant. With someone else in the publishing business." Lunch was not just a meal but "a tribal rite indulged in by agents, editors, publicists, rights salesmen, book-club editors, critics, book review editors, and when they are invited, authors." There were, Ephron figured, three different kinds of lunch, one at which editors talked to agents, another at which editors talked to reviewers and book club editors, and a third at which editors talked to writers. Lunching patterns changed during an editor's career, being most intense in his or her early years in the business because they were the way in which editors found business. Imagining a prototypical newcomer to the editorial world, Ephron sketched a trajectory: "In time, a number of things will happen to our young editor. He will gain 15 pounds. He will meet all the agents he cares to. And the joy of spending someone else's money for a meal he could not otherwise afford will be mitigated by the suspicion that the institution of lunch is not worth the time it takes." He might then, like famous publisher Robert Gottlieb, attempt a full-scale retreat from lunch. Gottlieb tried to organize his fellow publishers and editors to quit lunching and donate the money they would have spent to the Student Nonviolent Coordinating Committee. However, as Ephron drily notes, they discovered that they could not deduct their donations to SNCC on their taxes but they could deduct their lunches, so the institution endured.

One editor explained the lunch phenomenon as particular to the industry: "This is the kind of business where the stuff you're paid for you don't really do during the day. I've never edited a book in the office—you do that work nights and weekends. Since you don't do that much during the day anyway, you might as well have lunch." And an average lunch budget of $75–$100 per week (in 1969) could make that "might as well" very pleasant. Another editor stood by the publishing lunch, for a more practical reason, celebrating them as "a great source of information about what is being written, what other publishers are doing, what might be written. . . . You find out more through lunch than through *Publishers Weekly*." This network of "scuttlebutt" existed at what Ephron described as "a small number of restaurants in the Fifties, with The Brussels seeming to be a current favorite." Just as in Hollywood, it was very important for lunch partners to be seen by others, so that lunch was never just a lunch, never just business, but always also a show for others to absorb and interpret. In her byline for this article, Ephron was identified as "a freelance writer who eats lunch at home."[61]

NOTES

CHAPTER 1

1. Shimon Dar, "Food and Archaeology in Romano-Byzantine Palestine," in *Food in Antiquity*, ed. John Wilkins (Exeter, UK: University of Exeter Press, 1995), 330.

2. John Wilkins describes this multipurposing of grains in Ancient Greece: "Grains listed by Camporesi are millet, melic, barley, vetch, buckwheat, oats, spelt and 'panic.' These foods, made by boiling flour in water or milk, were widely used in Greece in particular, and could produce 'porridge'; dried porridges that could be reconstituted in thick soups, or flatbreads cooked in the hearth." John Wilkins and Shaun Hill, *Food in the Ancient World* (Oxford, UK: Blackwell, 2006), 119.

3. Peter Reynolds, "The Food of the Prehistoric Celts," in *Food in Antiquity*, ed. John Wilkins (Exeter, UK: University of Exeter Press, 1995), 312–14.

4. Dorothy Thompson, "Ptolemaic Temple Workers," in *Food in Antiquity*, ed. John Wilkins (Exeter, UK: University of Exeter Press, 1995), 320–23.

5. Martha Carlin, "Fast Food and Urban Living Standards in Medieval England," in *Food and Eating in Medieval Europe* (London: Hambledon, 1998), 28.

6. Terence Scully, *The Art of Cookery in the Middle Ages* (Rochester, NY: University of Rochester Press, 1995), 118.

7. Alison Sim, *Food and Feast in Tudor England* (New York: St. Martin's, 1998), 86.

8. Scully, *Art of Cookery*, 119.

9. Scully, *Art of Cookery*, 119.

10. Scully, *Art of Cookery*, 119.

11. Scully, *Art of Cookery*, 119.

12. Donna Barnes and Peter G. Rose, *Matters of Taste: Food and Drink in Seventeenth-Century Dutch Art and Life* (Albany, NY: Albany Institute of History & Art/Syracuse University Press, 2002), 20.

13. Scully, *Art of Cookery*, 122.

14. Scully, *Art of Cookery*, 122.

15. Scully, *Art of Cookery*, 122.

16. Frederick W. Mote, "Yuan and Ming," in *Food in Chinese Culture*, ed. K. C. Chang (New Haven, CT: Yale University Press, 1977), 220.

17. E. N. Anderson, *The Food of China* (New Haven, CT: Yale University Press, 1988), 84.

18. Naomichi Ishige, *The History and Culture of Japanese Food* (London: Kegan Paul, 2001), 101–2.

19. Ishige, *History and Culture of Japanese Food*, 102.

20. Richard B. Mather, "The Bonze's Begging Bowl: Eating Practices in Buddhist Monasteries of Medieval India and China," *Journal of the American Oriental Society* 101, no. 4 (October–December 1981): 417.

21. Ishige, *History and Culture of Japanese Food*, 77.

22. Ishige, *History and Culture of Japanese Food*, 102–3.

23. Alice-Mary Talbot, "Mealtime in Monasteries: The Culture of Byzantine Refectories," in *Eat, Drink and Be Merry: Food and Wine in Byzantium*, ed. Leslie Brubaker and Kallirroe Linardou (Aldershot, UK: Ashgate, 2007), 109–13.

24. Talbot, "Mealtime in Monasteries," 114.

25. Talbot, "Mealtime in Monasteries," 114–15.

26. Talbot, "Mealtime in Monasteries," 117 (from Theleptos of Philadelphia).

27. Johannes Koder, "Stew and Salted Meat," in *Eat, Drink and Be Merry: Food and Wine in Byzantium*, ed. Leslie Brubaker and Kallirroe Linardou (Aldershot, UK: Ashgate, 2007), 62.

28. Carlin, "Fast Food and Urban Living Standards," 28.

29. Carlin, "Fast Food and Urban Living Standards," 32.

30. Deniz Gursoy, *Turkish Cuisine in Historical Perspective* (Istanbul: Oglak Yayincilik ve Reklamcilik, 2006), 8, 88.

31. Paulina Lewicka, *Food and Foodways of Medieval Cairenes* (Leiden, The Netherlands: Koninklijke Brill, 2011), 125.

32. Carlin, "Fast Food and Urban Living Standards," 39–40.

33. Beverly Cox and Martin Jacobs, *Spirit of the Harvest* (New York: Stewart, Tabori & Chang, 1991), 12.

34. Anne Mendelson, "The Lenapes," in *Gastropolis*, ed. Annie Hauck-Lawson and Jonathan Deutsch (New York: Columbia University Press, 2009), 26.

35. Jeffrey Pilcher, *Que Vivan Los Tamales!* (Albuquerque: University of New Mexico Press, 1998), 20–22; John C. Super, *Food, Conquest, and Colonization in Sixteenth-Century Spanish America* (Albuquerque: University of New Mexico Press, 1988), 71.

36. Super, *Food, Conquest, and Colonization*, 8.

37. Pilcher, *Que Vivan Los Tamales!* 12.

38. Barnes and Rose, *Matters of Taste*, xiv.

39. Quoted in Julie Lautenschlager, *Food Fight: The Battle over the American Lunch in Schools and the Workplace* (Jefferson, NC: McFarland, 2006).

40. W. J. Rorabaugh, *The Craft Apprentice: From Franklin to the Machine Age in America* (New York: Oxford University Press, 1986), 194.

41. Rorabaugh, *Craft Apprentice*, 99.

42. Rorabaugh, *Craft Apprentice*, 194.

43. Marjorie Myers Douglas, *Eggs in the Coffee, Sheep in the Corn* (St. Paul: Minnesota Historical Society Press, 1994), 97.

44. Carol Ferguson and Margaret Fraser, *A Century of Canadian Home Cooking* (Scarborough, ON: Prentice Hall Canada), 52.

45. Mrs. Inchbald, "Such Things Are" (1788), in *The British Theater* (London: Longman, Hurst, Rees and Orme, 1808).

46. Evangeline Bruce, quoted in Steve Zimmerman and Ken Weiss, *Food in the Movies* (Jefferson, NC: McFarland, 2005), 134.

47. Lady Morgan, *France in 1816* (London: printed for Henry Colburn, 1817), 174.

48. Christian Isobel Johnstone, *The Cook and Housewife's Manual, by Margaret Dods* (Edinburgh: Oliver and Boyd, 1862), 547.

49. David Burton, *The Raj at Table* (London: Faber and Faber, 1993), 17.

50. Lizzie Collingham, *Imperial Bodies* (Cambridge, UK: Polity Press, 2001), 156–57.

51. C. Anne Wilson, "Luncheon, Nuncheon and Related Meals," in *Luncheon, Nuncheon and Related Meals: Eating with the Victorians* (Dover, NH: Allan Sutton, 1994), 34.

52. Wilson, *Luncheon, Nuncheon*, 41.

53. Burton, *Raj at Table*, 89.

54. Flora Annie Webster Steele, *The Complete Indian Housekeeper and Cook* (Cambridge, UK: Cambridge Univeresity Press, 2010), 22

55. William Howitt, *Life in Germany: or, Scenes, Impressions, and Every-Day Life of the Germans* (London: Routledge, 1849), 107.

56. Graham Midgley, *University Life in Eighteenth-Century Oxford* (New Haven, CT: Yale University Press, 1996), 28.

57. Midgley, *University Life in Eighteenth-Century Oxford*, 31–32.

58. Jonathan Smith and Christopher Stray, eds., *Cambridge in the 1830s* (Cambridge, UK: Boydell, 2003), 51, 57.

59. Midgley, *University Life in Eighteenth-Century Oxford*, 33, 35.

60. Midgley, *University Life in Eighteenth-Century Oxford*, 35, 36.

61. Midgley, *University Life in Eighteenth-Century Oxford*, 45.

62. Wages for Lowell mill workers: http://milltimes.weebly.com/boardinghouse-living.html, accessed June 10, 2013.

63. George Edwin McNeill, ed., *The Labor Movement: The Problem of To-Day* (Boston: Bridgeman, 1887), 477.

64. Reverend Thomas Dixon Jr., quoted in *The American Heritage Cookbook* (New York: Simon & Schuster, 1964), 408–9.

65. *The Trained Nurse and Hospital Review* 32–33 (January–December 1904): 338.

66. Cleburne Cafeteria menu: www.cleburnecafeteria.com, accessed June 21, 2013.

67. Rachel Rich, *Bourgeois Consumption* (Manchester, UK: Manchester University Press, 2011), 74.

68. Rich, *Bourgeois Consumption*, 75.

69. Rich, *Bourgeois Consumption*, 80, 76.

70. Rich, *Bourgeois Consumption*, 78–79.

71. Ferguson and Fraser, *Century of Canadian Home Cooking*, 106.

72. David Welch, "Campbell Looks Way Beyond Tomato Soup," *Businessweek*, August 9, 2012, www.businessweek.com/articles/2012-08-09/campbell-looks-way-beyond-tomato-soup, accessed June 30, 2013.

73. Marion Gregg, *American Women's Voluntary Services Cookbook* (San Francisco: Recorder-Sunset, 1942), 146.

74. Oral memoir, www.galaxy.bedfordshire.gov.uk/webingres/bedfordshire/vlib/0. wla/wla_oral_memoir_wortham.htm, accessed October 15, 2012.

75. Oral memoir, www.galaxy.bedfordshire.gov.uk/webingres/bedfordshire/vlib/0. wla/wla_oral_memoir_henman_potton.htm, accessed October 15, 2012.

76. Ishige, *History and Culture of Japanese Food*, 161.

77. Katarzyna Cwiertka and Miho Yasuhara, "Beyond Hunger," in *Japanese Foodways, Past and Present*, ed. Eric C. Rath and Stephanie Assmann (Urbana: University of Illinois Press, 2010), 178–79.

78. Ruth L. Gaskins, *A Good Heart and a Light Hand* (New York: Simon & Schuster, 1968), viii–ix.

79. Pilcher, *Que Vivan Los Tamales!* 126.

80. Michael Korda, "Le Plat du Jour Is Power," *New York Times*, January 26, 1977, C1.

81. Mandy Stadtmiller, "Break the Lunch Crunch," *New York Post*, July 20, 2010, www.nypost.com/p/lifestyle/food/break_the_lunch_crunch_enESSXIsvUL4Rw9d9OxxUJ, accessed May 10, 2013.

CHAPTER 2

1. Uche Nworah, *Nigeria Confidential: A Blogger's Musings on His Country* (Bloomington, IN: iUniverse, 2009).

2. Aase Stromstad, *The Norwegian Kitchen*, trans. Mary Lee Nielsen (Oslo: Boksenteret, 1999), 17.

3. Sylvia Munsen, *Cooking the Norwegian Way* (Minneapolis: Lerner, 2002), 31.

4. Stromstad, *Norwegian Kitchen*, 8.

5. Stromstad, *Norwegian Kitchen*, 16.

6. Marty Klinzman, *The Lunch Box Cookbook* (London: New Holland, 1993), 7–16.

7. "The Sandwich That Changed Lunch Forever," http://www.dailymail.co.uk/femail/article-1268371/M-S-sandwich-celebrates-30th-anniversary-launch-changed-lunch-forever.html.

8. Julia Werdigier, "Rallying the Team to Cater to the Company's Strengths," interview with Pret a Manger chief executive Clive Schlee, *New York Times*, May 9, 2012.

9. Debra Samuels, *My Japanese Table* (Rutland, VT: Tuttle Publications, 2011), 150.

10. Samuels, *My Japanese Table*, 148.

11. Editorial, "Is Ma Deaf to Normal People's Pleas?" *Taipei Times*, May 17, 2012, www.taipeitimes.com/News/editorials/archives/2012/05/17/2003533002, accessed October 31, 2012.

12. Elaine Yi-lan Tsui, "Breakfasting in Taipei: Changes in Chinese Food Consumption," in *Changing Chinese Foodways in Asia*, ed. David Y. H. Wu and Tan Chee-Beng (Hong Kong: Chinese University of Hong Kong, 2001), 237.

13. Adam Roberts, "The Amateur Gourmet," http://www.amateurgourmet.com/2012/07/shaken-dosirak-at-kang-ho-dong-baekjeong.html, accessed November 2, 2012.

14. Emiko Ohnuki-Tierney, "McDonald's in Japan," in *Golden Arches East*, ed. James Watson (Stanford, CA: Stanford University Press, 2006), 164.

15. Stephanie Assmann, "Culinary Heritage in Northern Japan," in *Japanese Foodways, Past and Present*, ed. Eric C. Rath and Stephanie Assmann (Urbana: University of Illinois Press, 2010), 248.

16. Anya von Bremzen and John Welchman, *Please to the Table* (New York: Workman Publishing, 1990), 112.

17. Christopher Wanjek, *Food at Work: Workplace Solutions for Malnutrition, Obesity and Chronic Diseases* (Geneva: International Labor Organization, 2005), 13.

18. Janet Mancini Billson and Kyra Mancini, *Inuit Women: Their Powerful Spirit in a Century of Change* (Plymouth, UK: Rowman & Littlefield, 2007), 31.

19. Arthur L. Meyer, *Danish Cooking and Baking Traditions* (New York: Hippocrene, 2011), 2.

20. "Revolution in Dayparts: Lunch in the Foodservice Market," www.packaged-facts.com/Revolution-Dayparts-Lunch-1351325.

21. Allison Martell, "In Canada, Tim Hortons Aims to Eat McDonald's Lunch," *Reuters*, July 12, 2012, www.reuters.com/article/2012/07/12/us-timhortons-house-idUSBRE86B13C20120712, accessed June 14, 2013.

22. "Subway Tops McDonald's as No. 1 Worker Lunch Spot," www.businessweek.com/articles/2013-04-18/subway-tops-mcdonalds-as-no-dot-1-worker-lunch-spot, accessed June 14, 2013.

23. Madhur Jaffrey, *At Home with Madhur Jaffrey* (New York: Alfred A. Knopf, 2010), 12.

24. 24 Stuart Elliott, "The Pursuit of Happiness," *New York Times*, October 1, 2007.

25. Bertha Vining Montgomery and Constance Nabwire, *Cooking the East African Way* (Minneapolis: Lerner, 2002), 28.

26. Carl Keyter, *Feeding Customs and Food Habits of Urban Africans* (Johannesburg: S.A. Institute of Race Relations, 1971), 4.

27. "Kenyan Food," http://blog.kevinandpage.com/2011/08/Kenyan-Food, accessed November 2, 2012.

28. Cari Cornell and Peter Thomas, *Cooking the South African Way* (Minneapolis: Lerner, 2005), 31.

29. Jessica B. Harris, *The Africa Cookbook* (New York: Simon and Schuster, 1998), 356.

30. Pierre Tham, *Recipes from the Heart of Senegal* (New York: Lake Isle Press, 2008), 14.

31. William Crawford and Kamolalmal Pootaraksa, *Thai Home-Cooking from Kamolalmal's Kitchen* (New York: New American Library, 1985), 24, 145–69.

32. Virginie F. Elbert and George A. Elbert, *Down Island Caribbean Cookery* (New York: Simon & Schuster, 1991), 18.

33. Clifford A. Wright, *A Mediterranean Feast* (New York: Morrow, 1999), 304.

34. Harris, *Africa Cookbook*, 360.

35. Maideh Mazda, *In a Persian Kitchen: Favorite Recipes from the Near East* (Boston: Tuttle, 1960), 27.

36. Daisy Iny, *The Best of Baghdad Cooking* (New York: Saturday Review Press, 1976), 12.

37. Margaret Shaida, *The Legendary Cuisine of Persia* (Boston: Grub Street, 2000), 64.

38. Shaida, *Legendary Cuisine of Persia*, 142.

39. Mazda, *In a Persian Kitchen*, 15.

40. Patricia Moore-Pastides, *Greek Revival* (Columbia: University of South Carolina Press, 2010), 40–41.

41. Najmieh Ratmanglij, *New Food of Life: Ancient Persian & Modern Iranian Cooking & Ceremonies* (Washington, DC: Mage Publishers, 1992), 424.

42. Lynne W. Villios, *Cooking the Greek Way* (Minneapolis: Lerner, 1984), 18–23.

43. Janet Whittle, *Argentina Business: The Portable Encyclopedia for Doing Business with Argentina* (San Rafael, CA: World Press, 1998), 162.

44. "Italian Restaurants in Buenos Aires," http://www.lonelyplanet.com/argentina/buenos-aires/restaurants/italian, accessed November 2, 2012.

45. Maria Baez Kijac, *The South American Table: The Flavor and Soul of Authentic Home Cooking from Patagonia to Rio de Janeiro* (Boston: Harvard Common Press, 2003), 244.

46. Kijac, *South American Table*, 201.

47. Kijac, *South American Table*, 202.

48. Kijac, *South American Table*, 348.

49. Thalia Rios, "Bolivia," in *The Ethnomusicologists' Cookbook: Complete Meals from around the World*, ed. Sean Williams (New York: Routledge, 2006), 122.

50. Yvonne Ortiz, *A Taste of Puerto Rico* (New York: Dutton, 1994), xii, 61, 3.

51. Michael Roberts, *Parisian Home Cooking: Conversations, Recipes, and Tips from the Cooks and Food Merchants of Paris* (New York: Morrow, 1999), 49, 82.

52. Moore-Pastides, *Greek Revival*, 164.

53. Chen Yunpia, "The Altar and the Table: Field Studies on the Dietary Culture of Chaoshan Inhabitants," in *Changing Chinese Foodways in Asia*, ed. David Y. H. Wu and Chee Beng Tan (Hong Kong: Chinese University of Hong Kong, 2001), 20.

54. Shanshan Du, *Chopsticks Only Work in Pairs: Gender Equity and Gender Equality among the Lahu of Southwest China* (New York: Columbia University Press, 2003), 54.

55. Liu Junru, *Chinese Food* (Cambridge: Cambridge University Press, 2010), 139–45; 32–38.

56. Lodewijk Brunt and Brigitte Steger, *Night-Time and Sleep in Asia and the West: Exploring the Dark Side of Life* (New York: Routledge, 1918, 1923).

57. Jeffrey Alford and Naomi Duguid, *Beyond the Great Wall: Recipes and Travels in the Other China* (New York: Artisan, 2008), 30.

58. Brunt and Steger, *Night-Time and Sleep in Asia and the West*.

59. Glenn R. Mack and Asele Surina, *Food Culture in Russia and Central Asia* (Westport, CT: Greenwood, 2005), 122.

60. Phoebe Taplin, theMoscowNews.com, November 25, 2010, http://themoscow news.com/food/20101125/188231019.html, accessed June 25, 2013.

61. Chitrita Banerji, *Eating India* (New York: Bloomsbury, 2007), 80.

62. Vidyadhar Date, "Travails of an Ordinary Citizen: A Tale from Mumbai," *Economic and Political Weekly* 41, no. 32 (2006): 3473–76.

63. Banerji, *Eating India*, 57, 62.

64. Banerji, *Eating India*, 97–99.

65. Banerji, *Eating India*, 117–21.

66. Banerji, *Eating India*, 167.

67. Niloufer Ichaporia King, *My Bombay Kitchen: Traditional and Modern Parsi Home Cooking* (Berkeley: University of California Press, 2007), 281–84.

CHAPTER 3

1. Catherine Owen, *Culture and Cooking: Art in the Kitchen* (New York: Cassell Petter, Galpin & Co., 1881), 35.

2. Isabella Beeton, *Mrs. Beeton's Book of Household Management* (London: Bouverie, 1861), 9, 915.

3. Owen, *Culture and Cooking*, 35–36.

4. Owen, *Culture and Cooking*, 35.

5. Alice James, *Catering for Two* (New York: Knickerbocker Press, 1898), 193–95.

6. Mary Johnson Lincoln, *What to Have for Luncheon* (New York: Dodge, 1904), 5.

7. Ruth Langland Holberg, *The Luncheon Cookbook* (New York: Thomas Y. Crowell, 1961), 125.

8. General Mills, *Betty Crocker's New Picture Cook Book* (New York: McGraw Hill, 1961), 36, 279.

9. Holberg, *The Luncheon Cookbook*, 125.

10. Barbara Kafka, *Food for Friends* (New York: Harper & Row, 1984), 199–200.

11. Martha Stewart, *Favorite Comfort Food: A Satisfying Collection of Home Cooking Classics* (New York: Martha Stewart Living, 1999).

12. Jane Stern and Michael Stern, *Square Meals* (New York: Knopf, 1984), 116, 131.

13. Barbara W. Hill, *Cooking the English Way* (Minneapolis: Lerner, 2003), 37.

14. Callum G. Brown, *The Death of Christian Britain* (London: Routledge, 2001), 133–34.

15. Linda Brooks et al., *We Are Australians* (Australia: Linda Brooks, 2010), 17.

16. Nigel Slater, *Toast* (New York: Gotham Books, 2005), 47–48.

17. Robert Arbor and Katherine Whiteside, *Joie de Vivre: Simple French Style for Everyday Living* (New York: Simon and Schuster, 2003), 113.

18. Beth Tartan, *North Carolina and Old Salem Cookery* (Chapel Hill: University of North Carolina Press, 1992), 104–5.

19. John Egerton, *Southern Food: At Home, on the Road, in History* (New York: Knopf, 1993), 170–71.

20. Emily Post, *Etiquette* (New York: William Morrow, 2011), 305.

21. Lincoln, *What to Have for Luncheon*, 7.

22. Lincoln, *What to Have for Luncheon*, 8.

23. Lincoln, *What to Have for Luncheon*, 9.

24. "A Member of the Aristocracy," *Manners and Rules of Good Society: Or, Solecisms to Be Avoided* (London: Frederick Warne, 1913), 177.

25. Macaire Allen and Mary L. Allen, *Luncheon Dishes* (London: Kegan Paul, Trench, Trubner & Co., Ltd., 1891), 11.

26. Ruth L. Gaskins, *A Good Heart and a Light Hand* (New York: Simon and Schuster, 1968), xi–xii.

27. *Better Homes and Gardens New Cookbook* (New York: Meredith Publishing, 1951), chapter 19, 2.

28. Lila Perl, *What Cooks in Suburbia* (New York: Dutton, 1961), 74.

29. Perl, *What Cooks in Suburbia*, 65.

30. Perl, *What Cooks in Suburbia*, 77–83.

31. Perl, *What Cooks in Suburbia*, 102.

32. Perl, *What Cooks in Suburbia*, 103, 118–19.

33. Jane Stern, Michael Stern, Louis Van Dyke, and Billie Van Dyke, *The Blue Willow Inn Cookbook* (Nashville, TN: Thomas Nelson, 2002), 70.

34. Holberg, *Luncheon Cookbook*, 102.

35. Holberg, *Luncheon Cookbook*, 165.

36. Holberg, *Luncheon Cookbook*, 3.

37. Holberg, *Luncheon Cookbook*, 79.

38. Holberg, *Luncheon Cookbook*, 129.

39. Crosby Gaige, *Dining with My Friends* (New York: Crown, 1949), 7–8.

40. Jinx Morgan and Judy Perry, *The How to Keep Him (After You've Caught Him) Cookbook* (New York: Doubleday, 1968), 88.

41. Elizabeth Hay, *A Student of Weather* (Toronto: McClelland & Stewart, 2001), 72.

42. Gail Wiese, Denice Seeley, Marlys Edwards, Jan Thies, and Karla Brummer Tildahl, Facebook messaging with the author, June 2013.

43. Ellenor Ranghild Merriken, *Looking for Country: A Norwegian Immigrant's Alberta Memoir* (Calgary: University of Calgary Press, 1999), 142, 93.

44. Order of the Eastern Star, *Choice Recipes* (Sacramento: Order of the Eastern Star, 1920), 43.

45. Erin Chase, *The $5 Dinner Mom: Breakfast and Lunch Cookbook* (New York: St. Martin's, 2010), 151.

46. Brigitte Steger and Lodewijk Brunt, eds., *Night-Time and Sleep in Asia and the West: Exploring the Dark Side of Life* (London: Routledge, 2003), 60.

47. Chase, *The $5 Dinner Mom*, 151.

48. Stege and Brunt, eds. *Night-Time and Sleep in Asia*, 60.

49. Alec Waugh, *The Sugar Islands: A Collection of Pieces Written About the West Indies* (London: Bloomsbury Reader), 33.

50. Carole Counihan, *Around the Tuscan Table: Food, Family, and Gender in Twentieth-Century Florence* (New York: Routledge, 2004), 119.

51. Counihan, *Around the Tuscan Table*, 34.

52. Wanda Torbabene and Giovanna Torbabene, *Sicilian Home Cooking* (New York: Knopf, 2001), 29.

53. Anna Wright, *Making It Work at Home* (Richmond, UK: Westminster House, 2008), 120.

54. *Better Homes and Gardens New Cook Book*, chapter 2, 1.

55. Counihan, *Around the Tuscan Table*, 34.

56. Holberg, *Luncheon Cookbook*, ix–x.

57. Peter Heine, *Food Culture in the Near East, Middle East, and North Africa* (Westport, CT: Greenwood, 2005), 104–5.

58. Harriet Welty Rochefort, *French Fried: The Culinary Capers of an American in Paris* (New York: Thomas Dunne, 2001), 123–24, 36.

59. "A Member of the Aristocracy," *Manners and Rules of Good Society*, 140.

60. Pamela Todd, *Celebrating the Impressionist Table* (New York: Stewart, Tabori & Chang, 1997), 23.

61. Carol Ferguson and Margaret Fraser, *A Century of Canadian Home Cooking* (Scarborough, ON: Prentice Hall Canada, 1992), 108.

62. General Mills, *Betty Crocker's New Picture Cookbook*, 364.

63. Holberg, *Luncheon Cookbook*, 88.

64. Valerie J. Johnston, *Diet in Workhouses and Prisons 1835–1895* (New York: Garland, 1985), 109.

65. Johnston, *Diet in Workhouses and Prisons 1835–1895*, 110–12.

66. *Manual for Army Cooks* (Washington: Government Printing Office, 1906), 48–49.

67. *Manual for Army Cooks*, 144, 155.

68. Kristen Hinman, "Chocolate Milk at Every Meal," *Slate*, February 28, 2011, www.slate.com/articles/life/food/2011/02/chocolate_milk_at_every_meal.html, accessed July 3, 2013.

69. Daniela K. Pina, "The Adventures of an Army Wife," http://theadventuresofanarmywife.wordpress.com/2012/10/31/army-chow-hall, accessed July 3, 2013.

70. Mimi Hart, "First Lady: Army Health Initiative May Be a Model for Fitness and Nutrition," *USA Today*, January 27, 2011.

71. Matthew Rosenberg, "Afghan Forces Eat Up Return of Fast Food," *Wall Street Journal*, February 22, 2011, http://online.wsj.com/article/SB10001424052748703610 6045761586101111737164.html, accessed July 3, 2013.

72. *Wellesley College Magazine* 3 (1894).

73. Walter Scheib, *White House Chef: Eleven Years, Two Presidents, One Kitchen* (Boston: Houghton Mifflin Harcourt, 2007).

74. Scheib, *White House Chef*, 19, 67.

75. Scheib, *White House Chef*, 228–39.

76. Scheib, *White House Chef*, 236.

CHAPTER 4

1. Staff Home Economists, Culinary Arts Institute, *The American Peoples Cookbook* (Chicago: Spencer Press, 1956), 68.

2. Rachel Rich, *Bourgeois Consumption* (Manchester, UK: Manchester University Press, 2011), 142.

3. Rich, *Bourgeois Consumption*, 142–43.

4. Erika Diane Rappaport, *Shopping for Pleasure: Women in the Making of London's West End* (Princeton: Princeton University Press, 2000), 132.

5. Rich, *Bourgeois Consumption*, 157. Rich offers a different reading of this passage from *The Caterer*, in which the writer is entirely critical of women's foodways. Because the periodical was a trade journal, I would suggest that the aim of the article is to reveal new business opportunities for the readers, who might take the hint and open less sweet-centered midday lunch restaurants to serve women.

6. Rappaport, *Shopping for Pleasure*, 38.

7. Elise K. Tipton, "The Café," in *Being Modern in Japan*, ed. Elise K. Tipton and John Clark (Honolulu: University of Hawaii Press, 2000), 123.

8. Rich, *Bourgeois Consumption*, 198.

9. Menu, The Portia Club, 1905. The Buttolph collection of menus, New York Public Library.

10. Deniz Gursoy, *Turkish Cuisine in Historical Perspective* (Istanbul: Oglak Yayinevi, 2007), 20.

11. Gursoy, *Turkish Cuisine in Historical Perspective*, 20.

12. Jeff Gordinier, "Ladies Who Power Lunch," *New York Times*, September 3, 2013.

13. John Burnett, *England Eats Out: A Social History of Eating Out in England from 1830 to the Present* (London: Pearson Longman, 2004), 303.

14. Burnett, *England Eats Out*, 303–4.

15. Florence Brobeck, *The Lunch Box and Every Kind of Sandwich* (New York: M. Barrows & Company, 1946), 8, 3.

16. Elinor Thomas, *A Loving Legacy*, quoted in Dorothy Duncan, *Canadians at Table* (Toronto: Dundurn Press, 2011), 154.

17. Duncan, *Canadians at Table*, 170.

18. "Every Coal Miner's Lunch Bucket Smelled of the Coal Mines," www.appalachianhistory.net/2008/06/every-coal-miners-lunch-bucket-smelled.html, accessed June 12, 2013.

19. Brobeck, *Lunch Box*, 4, 6.

20. William Shurtleff and Akiko Aoyagi, *Henry Ford and His Researchers—History of Their Work with Soybeans* (Lafayette, CA: Soyinfo Center, 2011), 236.

21. "At Paul's Tea Stall," http://spitalfieldslife.com/2011/11/17/at-pauls-tea-stall, accessed May 23, 2013.

22. Chitrita Banerji, *Eating India* (New York: Bloomsbury, 2007), 53.

23. Banerji, *Eating India*, 54.

24. Banerji, *Eating India*, 47.

25. Phil G. Giriodi, *Breakfast in Paris, Lunch in Rome, Dinner in London* (Mustang, OK: Tate, 2010), 132.

26. Mauricio Borrero, "Communal Dining and State Cafeterias in Moscow and Petrograd, 1917–1921," in *Food in Russian History and Culture*, ed. Musya Glants and Joyce Toomre (Bloomington: Indiana University Press, 1997), 163.

27. Halina Rothstein and Robert A. Rothstein, "The Beginnings of Soviet Culinary Arts," in *Food in Russian History and Culture*, ed. Musya Glants and Joyce Toomre (Bloomington: Indiana University Press, 1997), 190.

28. Belinda J. David, *Home Fires Burning* (Chapel Hill: University of North Carolina Press, 2000), 139–141, 148, 154.

29. Davis, *Home Fires Burning*, 139–41, 148, 154.

30. Davis, *Home Fires Burning*, 157.

31. David H. Y. Wu, "McDonald's in Taipei," in *Golden Arches East: McDonald's in East Asia*, ed. James Watson (Stanford, CA: Stanford University Press, 1997, 2006), 131, 133.

32. Debra Samuels, *My Japanese Table* (Rutland, VT: Tuttle Publications, 2011), 144.

33. R. H. Campbell, "Diet in Scotland: An Example of Regional Variation," in *Our Changing Fare*, ed. T. C. Barker, J. C. McKenzie, and J. Yudkin, 47–60 (London:

MacGibbon and Kee, 1966), quoted in Sidney Mintz, *Sweetness and Power* (New York: Penguin, 1985), 128.

34. Burnett, *England Eats Out*, 32, 36.

35. Burnett, *England Eats Out*, 114–15.

36. Mark Sohn, *Appalachian Home Cooking* (Lexington: University Press of Kentucky, 2005), 72–73.

37. John Spargo, *The Bitter Cry of the Children* (New York: MacMillan, 1915), 70.

38. Ann Cooper and Lisa Holmes, *Lunch Lessons* (New York: HarperCollins, 2006), 34.

39. Sohn, *Appalachian Home Cooking*, 74.

40. Susan Levine, *School Lunch Politics* (Princeton: Princeton University Press, 2008), 39.

41. Levine, *School Lunch Politics*, 150–78.

42. Cooper and Holmes, *Lunch Lessons*, 66.

43. Sohn, *Appalachian Home Cooking*, 74–75.

44. Harriet Welty Rochefort, *French Fried: The Culinary Capers of an American in Paris* (New York: St. Martin's, 2001), 126.

45. Burnett, *England Eats Out*, 248.

46. Laura Mason, "Learning How to Eat in Public: School Dinners," in *Oxford Symposium on Food and Cookery Proceedings: Public Eating* (London: Prospect, 1991), 209.

47. National School Lunch Program Factsheet, www.fns.usda.gov/cnd/Lunch/AboutLunch/NSLPFactSheet.pdf, accessed June 26, 2013.

48. Marty Klinzman, *The Lunch Box Cookbook* (London: New Holland, 1993), 7.

49. Banerji, *Eating India*, 81.

50. Anjana Mathur, quoted in Tulasi Srinivas, "'As Mother Made It': The Cosmopolitan Indian Family, 'Authentic' Food, and the Construction of a Cultural Utopia," in *International Journal of Sociology of the Family* 32, no. 2, *Globalization and the Family* (Autumn 2006): 191–221, 206.

51. "Never Seconds," http://neverseconds.blogspot.com.

52. "What Indonesian School Kids Get for Lunch," http://www.wfp.org/photos/kupang-wfp-provides-nutritious-stew-children, accessed June 26, 2013.

53. "Taking America to Lunch," http://americanhistory.si.edu/lunchboxes/index.htm, accessed June 26, 2013.

54. Brobeck, *Lunch Box*, 7.

55. Brobeck, *Lunch Box*, 249.

56. Klinzman, *Lunch Box Cookbook*, 27.

57. Klinzman, *Lunch Box Cookbook*, 27–28.

58. Antoine Prost, "Public and Private Spheres," in *A History of Private Life*, vol. 5 of *Riddles of Identity in Modern Times*, ed. Philip Aries and Georges Duby (Cambridge, MA: Harvard University Press, 1991), 28.

59. Peter Mayle, *A Year in Provence* (New York: Vintage, 1989), 15.

60. Georgina Battiscombe, *English Picnics* (London: Harvill Press, 1949), 8.

61. Michel Jeanneret, "Ma Salade et Ma Muse," in *At the Table: Metaphorical and Material Cultures of Food in Medieval and Early Modern Europe*, ed. Timothy J. Tomasik and Juliann M. Vitullo, Arizona Studies in the Middle Ages and the Renaissance, vol. 18 (Turnhout: Brepols, 2007), 217.

62. Evelyn Rann, *The Automobile Lunch* (n.p.: The Buzza Company, 1925), 1.

63. Battiscombe, *English Picnics*, 1.

64. Osbert Sitwell, "Picnics and Pavilions," in *Sing High! Sing Low! A Collection of Essays* (New York: Macmillan, 1944), 143.

65. Battiscombe, *English Picnics*, 6, 3.

66. George Turbeville, *The Noble Art of Venerie*, quoted in Battiscombe, *English Picnics*, 36–37.

67. John Taylor, *The Pennyles Pilgrimmage*, quoted in Battiscombe, *English Picnics*, 43; Battiscombe, *English Picnics*, 56.

68. Battiscombe, *English Picnics*, 123.

69. Jennifer Brennan, *Curries and Bugles* (New York: Random House, 1990), 120.

70. Brennan, *Curries and Bugles*, 120.

71. Nelly Weeton, quoted in Battiscombe, *English Picnics*, 75, 102, 108.

72. Vicky Moon, *The Middleburg Mystique: A Peek Inside the Gates of Middleburg, Virginia* (Herndon: Capital Books, 2001), 145.

73. Donna C. Sheppard, *Favorite Meals from Williamsburg: A Menu Cookbook* (Williamsburg, VA: Colonial Williamsburg Foundation, 1982), 9.

74. Crosby Gaige, *Dining with My Friends* (New York: Crown, 1949), 47.

75. Lady Harriet St. Clair, *Dainty Dishes*, quoted in Battiscombe, *English Picnics*, 87–88.

76. St. Clair, *Dainty Dishes*, 87–88.

77. Anonymous author of an article in *Chambers Journal*, 1857, quoted in Battiscombe, *English Picnics*, 91.

78. Phineas Beck (Samuel Chamberlain), *Clementine in the Kitchen* (New York: Hastings House, 1943), 38–39.

79. Brobeck, *Lunch Box*, 251, 252.

80. Daisy Iny, *The Best of Baghdad Cooking* (New York: Saturday Review Press, 1976), 20.

81. Margaret Shaida, *The Legendary Cuisine of Persia* (Boston: Grub Street, 2000), 24.

82. Marty Klinzman, *The Lunch Box Cookbook* (London: New Holland, 1993), 7–16.

83. Josie Stow, *Recipes from the African Kitchen* (London: Conran Octopus, 1999), 52; 78–79.

84. Samuels, *My Japanese Table*, 149.

85. Jeffrey Pilcher, *Que Vivan Los Tamales!* (Albuquerque: University of New Mexico Press, 1998), 55.

86. Frank Dumont, *The Depot Lunch-Counter* (Philadelphia: Penn Publishing, 1916), 7.

87. N. S. Macintosh, *Profitable Cafeteria Management*, Little Gold Business Books series (Stamford, CT: J. O. Dahl, 1935), 5.

88. Macintosh, *Profitable Cafeteria Management*, 16.

89. Pierre Berard, *Pierre's 60 Profitable Sandwiches* (Stamford, CT: The Dahls, 1942).

90. Berard, *Pierre's 60 Profitable Sandwiches*, 9.

91. Berard, *Pierre's 60 Profitable Sandwiches*, 9.

92. Douglas Robert Brown, *The Restaurant Manager's Handbook* (Ocala, FL: Atlantic Publishing, 2003), C12–16.

CHAPTER 5

1. William S. Burroughs, *Naked Lunch* (New York: Grove Atlantic, 1959; 50th Anniversary edition, 2009), 199.

2. James Yood, *Feasting: A Celebration of Food in Art* (New York: Universe, 1992), 11, 14.

3. Donna Barnes and Peter G. Rose, *Matters of Taste: Food and Drink in Seventeenth-Century Dutch Art and Life* (Albany, NY: Albany Institute of History & Art/ Syracuse University Press, 2002), 19.

4. Barnes and Rose, *Matters of Taste*, 19, 12.

5. Pamela Todd, *Celebrating the Impressionist Table* (New York: Stewart, Tabori & Chang, 1997), 91.

6. Alexandra Leaf, *The Impressionists' Table* (New York: Rizzoli, 1994), 20.

7. Leaf, *Impressionists' Table*, 17, illustration.

8. Leaf, *Impressionists' Table*, 21.

9. Leaf, *Impressionists' Table*, 22.

10. Madeline Conway and Nancy Kirk, *The Museum of Modern Art Artists' Cookbook* (New York: Abrams, 1977), 58.

11. Conway and Kirk, *MOMA Artists' Cookbook*, 73.

12. Conway and Kirk, *MOMA Artists' Cookbook*, 77, 83.

13. Arthur C. Danto, *Unnatural Wonders: Essays from the Gap between Art and Life* (New York: Farrar, Strauss & Giroux, 2005), 138.

14. "A Casual Sunday Lunch," http://www.arazorashinyknife.com/a-casual-sunday-lunch.

15. Margaret Atwood, *The Canlit Foodbook* (Toronto: Totem Books, 1987), 3.

16. Atwood, *Canlit Foodbook*, 49.

17. Atwood, *Canlit Foodbook*, 53.

18. Atwood, *Canlit Foodbook*, 57.

19. Atwood, *Canlit Foodbook*, 181.

20. Maggie Lane, *Jane Austen and Food* (London: Hambledon, 1995), 37–38.

21. Anna Shapiro, *A Feast of Words: For Lovers of Food and Fiction* (New York: Norton, 1996), 27.

22. Charles Dickens, *David Copperfield* (Orchard Park, NY: Broadview Press, 2011), 303.

23. Charles Dickens, *The Pickwick Papers* (New York: W. A. Townsend and Company, 1861), 92.

24. Charles Dickens, *Little Dorrit* (New York: Books Inc., 1868), 225–226.

25. Dickens, *David Copperfield*, 131.

26. Charles Dickens, *Great Expectations*, Gutenberg.org, www.gutenberg.org/files/1400/1400-h/1400-h.htm.

27. Edith Wharton, "The Reckoning," in *The New York Stories of Edith Wharton* (New York: New York Review of Books, 2007), 186–87.

28. Norman Kiell, *Food and Drink in Literature* (Lanham, MD: Scarecrow, 1995), 10.

29. Alison Armstrong, *The Joyce of Cooking* (Barrytown, NY: Salton Hill Press, 1986), 216–17; James Joyce, *Ulysses*, 171, 764, 234.

30. Craig Boreth, *The Hemingway Cookbook* (Chicago: Chicago Review Press, 1998), 40–41.

31. Boreth, *The Hemingway Cookbook*, 62, 51.

32. Carol MacGregor, *The Storybook Cookbook* (Garden City, NY: Doubleday, 1967), 27–29.

33. MacGregor, *Storybook Cookbook*, 89–90.

34. Tove Jansson and Sami Malila, *Moomins Cook Book* (London: Self-Made Hero, 2010), 44.

35. Jansson and Malila, *Moomins Cook Book*, 68.

36. Jonathan Langford, "Sitting Down to the Sacramental Feast: Food and Cultural Diversity in *The Lord of the Rings*," in *Foods of the Gods*, ed. Gary Westfahl, George Slusser, and Eric S. Rabkin (Athens: University of Georgia Press, 1996), 123.

37. Thomas Haynes Bayly, *Songs and Ballads, Grave and Gay* (Philadelphia: Carey and Hart, 1844), 164–65.

38. Christian Isobel Johnstone, *The Cook and Housewife's Manual, by Margaret Dods* (Edinburgh: Oliver and Boyd, 1862), 64.

39. Louisa May Alcott, *Little Women*, part 2, chapter 26, "Artistic Attempts."

40. The Borden Company, *Food in Fiction* (New York: Borden, 1953), 17–18.

41. Samuel Clemens to Orion Clemens, September 29, 1860, quoted in Andrew Beahrs, *Twain's Feast* (New York: Penguin, 2010), 188.

42. Beahrs, *Twain's Feast*, 214.

43. Annette Wannamaker, "The Attack of the Inedible Hunk," in *Critical Approaches to Food in Children's Literature*, ed. Karla Keeling and Scott T. Pollard (New York: Routledge, 2009), 244.

44. Linda Matchan, "Honoring Lunch Ladies, Those Who Nourish Souls," *Boston Globe*, May 2, 2013.

45. Emile Zola, *The Belly of Paris* (New York: Oxford University Press, 2007), 171.

46. Frank O'Hara, *Lunch Poems* (San Francisco: City Lights, 1964), 18.

47. *Gone with the Wind Cook Book* (New York: Abbeville Press, 1991 facsimile), 3–4.

48. *Gone With the Wind Cook Book*, 7, 11.

49. Steve Zimmerman and Ken Weiss, *Food in the Movies* (Jefferson, NC: McFarland, 2009), 289.

50. Hank Moonjean, *Bring in the Peacocks* (Bloomington, IN: ArtHouse, 2004), 102.

51. Aljean Harmetz, "Exotic Hollywood Institution: Lunch," *New York Times*, November 27, 1986.

52. Larry Rohter, "Hollywood Memoir Tells All, and Many Don't Want to Hear," *New York Times*, March 14, 1991, http://www.nytimes.com/1991/03/14/movies/hollywood-memoir-tells-all-and-many-don-t-want-to-hear.html.

53. Monica Corcoran, "Let's Do Lunch, Now That There's Somewhere to Do It," *New York Times*, July 22, 2007.

54. Al Martinez, "'The horns gotta go. . . . And the red outfit. He'd wear nice pastel shades.': The Devil Is Making Me Do It," *The Los Angeles Times*, April 29, 1985, http://articles.latimes.com/1985-04-29/local/me-12951_1_little-devil, accessed July 2, 2013.

55. Gary Baum and Degen Pener, eds., "Hollywood's 25 Top Power Lunch Restaurants," *Hollywood Reporter*, January 23, 2013, http://www.hollywoodreporter.com/lists/hollywoods-25-top-power-lunch-414541, accessed July 2, 2013.

56. Aljean Harmetz, "Exotic Hollywood Institution: Lunch," *New York Times*, November 27, 1986.

57. Michael Pollack, "Bread, Cheese, and Talk," *New York Times*, May 29, 2005, www.nytimes.com/2005/05/29/nyregion/thecity/29fyi.html

58. Algonquin Hotel menu, http://menus.nypl.org/menu_pages/65003/explore; Franklin Pierce Adams and Laura Bonds, ed., *Bon Bons, Bourbon and Bon Mots: Stories from the Algonquin Round Table* (El Paso, TX: Traveling Press, 2012), 2.

59. Ruth Langland Holberg, *The Luncheon Cookbook* (New York: Thomas Y. Crowell, 1961), 11.

60. Holberg, *Luncheon Cookbook*, 67–68.

61. Nora Ephron, "Where Bookmen Meet to Eat," *New York Times*, June 22, 1969, BR8.

SELECTED
BIBLIOGRAPHY

Albala, Ken. *Eating Right in the Renaissance*. Berkeley: University of California Press, 2002.

Anderson, E. N. *The Food of China*. New Haven, CT: Yale University Press, 1990.

Banerji, Chitrita. *Eating India*. New York: Bloomsbury, 2007.

Barnes, Donna, and Peter G. Rose. *Matters of Taste: Food and Drink in Seventeenth-Century Dutch Art and Life*. Albany, NY: Albany Institute of History & Art/Syracuse University Press, 2002.

Belasco, Warren, and Philip Scranton. *Food Nations*. New York: Routledge, 2002.

Bower, Anne, ed. *African American Foodways*. Urbana and Chicago: University of Illinois Press, 2007.

Brubaker, Leslie, and Kallirroe Linardou, eds. *Eat, Drink and Be Merry: Food and Wine in Byzantium*. Aldershot: Ashgate, 2007.

Burnett, John. *England Eats Out: A Social History of Eating out in England from 1830 to the Present*. London: Pearson Longman, 2004.

Burton, David. *The Raj at Table: A Culinary History of the British in India*. London: Faber and Faber, 1993.

Chang, K. C. *Food in Chinese Culture*. New Haven, CT: Yale University Press, 1977.

Collingham, Lizzie. *Imperial Bodies*. Cambridge, UK: Polity Press, 2001.

Cox, Beverly, and Martin Jacobs. *Spirit of the Harvest*. New York: Stewart, Tabori & Chang, 1991.

Cwiertka, Katarzyna. *Modern Japanese Cuisine*. London: Reaktion Books, 2006.

Deutsch, Jonathan, and Anne Hauck-Lawson. *Gastropolis*. New York: Columbia University Press, 2009.

Diner, Hasia. *Hungering for America*. Cambridge, MA: Harvard University Press, 2001.

Duncan, Dorothy. *Canadians at Table*. Toronto: Dundurn Press, 2011.

Fernandez-Arnesto, Felipe. *Near a Thousand Tables*. New York: Free Press, 2002.

Gabaccia, Donna. *We Are What We Eat*. Cambridge, MA: Harvard University Press, 1998.

Gold, Carol. *Danish Cookbooks: Domesticity and National Identity, 1616–1901*. Seattle: University of Washington Press, 2007.

Gursoy, Deniz. *Turkish Cuisine in Historical Perspective*. Istanbul: Oglak Yayincilik ve Reklamcilik, 2006.

Harris, Jessica. *High on the Hog*. New York: Bloomsbury USA, 2011.

Horowitz, David. *Putting Meat on the American Table*. Baltimore: Johns Hopkins University Press, 2006.

Ishige, Naomichi. *The History and Culture of Japanese Food*. London: Kegan Paul, 2001.

Jakle, John A., and Keith A. Sculle. *Fast Food*. Baltimore: Johns Hopkins University Press, 1999.

Keeling, Karla, and Scott T. Pollard. *Critical Approaches to Food in Children's Literature*. New York: Routledge, 2009.

Leaf, Alexandra. *The Impressionists' Table*. New York: Rizzoli, 1994.

Levenstein, Harvey. *A Revolution at the Table*. Berkeley: University of California Press, 2003.

Levine, Susan. *School Lunch Politics*. Princeton: Princeton University Press, 2010.

Lewicka, Paulina. *Food and Foodways of Medieval Cairenes*. Leiden: Koninklijke Brill, 2011.

McCann, James. *Stirring the Pot*. Athens: Ohio University Press, 2009.

Neuhaus, Jessamyn. *Manly Meals and Mom's Home Cooking*. Baltimore: Johns Hopkins University Press, 2003.

Pilcher, Jeffrey. *Que Vivan Los Tamales!* Albuquerque: University of New Mexico Press, 1998.

Poppendiek, Janet. *Free for All: Fixing School Food in America*. Berkeley: University of California Press, 2011.

Rath, Eric C., and Stephanie Assmann. *Japanese Foodways, Past and Present*. Urbana: University of Illinois Press, 2010.

Ray, Krishnendu. *The Migrant's Table*. Philadelphia: Temple University Press, 2004.

Rich, Rachel. *Bourgeois Consumption*. Manchester, UK: Manchester University Press, 2011.

Root, Waverly, and Richard de Rochemont. *Eating in America*. New York: Ecco Press, 1981.

Schlosser, Eric. *Fast Food Nation*. New York: Houghton Mifflin, 2001.

Scully, Terence. *The Art of Cookery in the Middle Ages*. Woodbridge, UK: Boydell, 1995.

Shapiro, Anna. *A Feast of Words: For Lovers of Food and Fiction*. New York: Norton, 1996.

Smith, Woodruff. *Consumption and the Making of Respectability*. New York: Routledge, 2002.

Tannahill, Reay. *Food in History*. New York: Crown, 1989.

Todd, Pamela. *Celebrating the Impressionist Table*. New York: Stewart, Tabori & Chang, 1997.

Toussaint-Samat, Maguelonne. *A History of Food*. Cambridge, MA: Blackwell, 1993.

Wilkins, John, and Shaun Hill. *Food in the Ancient World*. Oxford: Blackwell, 2006.

Williams-Forson, Psyche. *Building Houses out of Chicken Legs*. Chapel Hill: University of North Carolina Press, 2006.

Wilson, C. Anne. *Luncheon, Nuncheon and Related Meals: Eating with the Victorians*. Dover, NH: Allan Sutton, 1994.

Yood, James. *Feasting: A Celebration of Food in Art*. New York: Universe, 1992.

Zimmerman, Steve, and Ken Weiss. *Food in the Movies*. Jefferson, NC: McFarland, 2005.

INDEX

ABOUT THE AUTHOR

Megan Elias is associate professor of history at Queensborough Community College, City University of New York. She is the author of *Stir it Up: Home Economics in American Culture* (2008) and *Food in the United States 1890–1945* (2009). She lives in Brooklyn but likes a ploughman's lunch best.